FIRST EDITION

GLOBAL POLITICS READER

THEMES, ACTORS, AND ISSUES

WRITTEN AND EDITED BY **ALI R. ABOOTALEBI**

University of Wisconsin, Eau Claire

cognella®
SAN DIEGO

D1226084

Bassim Hamadeh, CEO and Publisher
Angela Schultz, Senior Field Acquisitions Editor
Michelle Piehl, Senior Project Editor
Abbey Hastings, Associate Production Editor
Jess Estrella, Senior Graphic Designer
Stephanie Kohl, Licensing Associate
Natalie Piccotti, Director of Marketing
Kassie Graves, Vice President of Editorial
Jamie Giganti, Director of Academic Publishing

Copyright © 2020 by Cognella, Inc. All rights reserved. No part of this publication may be reprinted, reproduced, transmitted, or utilized in any form or by any electronic, mechanical, or other means, now known or hereafter invented, including photocopying, microfilming, and recording, or in any information retrieval system without the written permission of Cognella, Inc. For inquiries regarding permissions, translations, foreign rights, audio rights, and any other forms of reproduction, please contact the Cognella Licensing Department at rights@cognella.com.

Trademark Notice: Product or corporate names may be trademarks or registered trademarks and are used only for identification and explanation without intent to infringe.

Cover image copyright © 2014 Depositphotos/stori.

Printed in the United States of America.

cognella® | ACADEMIC PUBLISHING

3970 Sorrento Valley Blvd., Ste. 500, San Diego, CA 92121

CONTENTS

PREFACE

What you are about to read in this book is a compilation of selected articles meant to supplement primary texts used in the world politics introductory and upper-division undergraduate classes. We would like for students to get a deeper appreciation for what matters in world politics and how global affairs impact their lives in so many ways. I have been teaching global politics, including Introduction to World Politics, International Political Economy, and International Law and Organization for over 25 years in both public and private institutions of higher education, varying in class sizes between twenty to over one hundred students. The primary text I, like many of my colleagues, use in introductory classes are often comprehensive and dedicate hundreds of pages to present a comprehensive picture of global politics, along with many tables, charts, statistics, illustrations, and indexes. These books aim to inform and to convince mostly freshmen and sophomore students of the significance of the subject matter. There is also the additional challenge of keeping students interested in the subject matter since most students in introductory classes are freshmen without a declared major and are expected to take classes in General Education. Aside from the voluminous appearance of introductory books that can be intimidating to students, there are also concerns over the cost of such textbooks. There is also the very serious challenge of the changing nature of students' learning culture and attitudes toward learning and enlightenment.

The revolution in information technology and forces of globalization and transnationalism is rapidly changing "the state" and "the mechanisms" of teaching and learning. It is fair to say that the faculty-student relations and the teaching-learning environment along with it is experiencing unprecedented challenges because of technological changes. The arrival of the millennial generation is exciting the field of education and the educators at all levels. The millennials are inquisitive and are critical thinkers and seem impatient in systematically sequencing their academic learning priorities with their very busy social networking activities while worrying about their future career prospects. There is an increasing demand for group activity and class exercises and quick reading materials that can potentially jeopardize comprehensive learning and the absorption of the class lecture and discussion materials. The proliferation of information and data, blogosphere and social media sites, and even professional and academic and technical websites have created both opportunities and challenges to educators and students alike. The students' expectations by far supersede any ordinary lecture and discussion format based on routine lectures and presentations of factoids, assumptions, and theories. Most undergraduate students in my institution, for example, take different introductory classes as part of their liberal education requirement. The liberal education's emphasis is now, more than ever, on problem solving through collaborative learning and critical analysis. We, the educators, must deal with such challenges in ways we deem appropriate and based on our own field of expertise and individual experiences.

This global politics reader is meant to help educators teaching introductory and upper-division global politics to become more effective in engaging the student through discussion and analysis of central issues and areas pertinent to understanding global relations. The reader also is aimed to help students better appreciate the gap between, and the relevance of, the study and the practice of global politics. We understand the paradigmatic and theoretical limitations in explaining global relations and the gap between the theory and the practice of international relations. Yet, we believe that the thorough study of central issues and areas of concern to global relations can help to bridge this gap through the examination and rethinking of our theoretical assumptions. Furthermore, we do share the belief that while policymakers can benefit from the objective analysis of the academicians, the policy practitioner operates in the practical political world, where variables determining the final policy options are countless and are very difficult to contain in the intersection among different layers of interests entangled in the foreign-policy decision-making processes.

I have used in the past, for many years, the *Taking Sides* books series that posits a yes and a no argument to selected issues and areas pertinent to global relations: Will the rise of China lead to a conflict with the United States? Is Israel or the Palestinian authority at fault for the prolongation of the Arab-Israeli Conflict? Is the European Union doomed? or Can the United Nations be reformed? and the like. The *Taking Sides* series remains valuable for class use, but such book editions have been slow in their updates and their chosen articles often quickly become "old" and out of date. This has been at least based on my own personal experience. While this criticism can be a universal problem, our reader is better suited for its selection of articles and for quick revisions and updates since most of its articles are already pre-published and are copyrighted by Cognella Academic Publishing. We are better equipped to respond quickly to our readers' comments and demands to remain up to date and relevant. The reader also presents perennial theories, issues, and themes discussed thematically or as case studies and theoretical analyses, promising significance and relevance (e.g., ethnicity, power politics, national interest, conflict, and cooperation).

The selection of articles for this reader is the result of an extensive search in the vast archives of published articles available to Cognella Academic Publishing, in addition to the editors' four written and revised articles for the current edition. All the selected articles here represent either an issue or policy area of perennial concern to the global community. The great power politics, conflict over ethnicity, nationalism, authoritarian rule and power politics, the role of international organizations and law, democracy and good governance in the promotion of peace, and challenges facing the international political economy (e.g., trade, human security, the environment) are addressed. The reader's selected articles provide a crucial venue to the student to connect what is taught in the classroom through lectures and discussions with expert analyses of the complexities of actual issues and areas crucial to understanding global relations.

The reader is composed of articles organized into four areas: major power players and issues; sources of conflict; sources of peace; and, global challenges to peace and cooperation. Part I deals with the question of power and major players in global politics, including the rise of China, the Chinese-Russian relations, and what is in store for the United States and the West. Selected articles in part II cover some major sources of conflict in global politics, including ethnic and identity conflict, nationalism, and national interest and power politics. Part III includes four articles covering major sources promoting the cause of peace on the world stage, including the United Nations, the European Union and its trade policy, providing for and enhancing human security, and the place of international law in U.S. Middle Eastern policy. Part IV consists of four articles addressing some areas of challenge in global relations, namely, globalization and development, trade and development, the environment, and the place of democracy in good governance. We realize that these articles are not comprehensive and cannot possibly include all areas and issues to satisfy all educators and students. The omission of any issues here simply is a reflection of limitations of space and the final monetary price of the book. Our plan is to respond to our readers' comments on the subject matter and issues they wish to see included in the forthcoming editions of the reader.

The reader's 16 articles are comprehensive and cover issues and subject matters relevant in any introductory global politics class. These articles are shorter to keep students engaged and are yet comprehensive enough to provide a good foundation for in-class thorough discussion and analysis. We also truly believe that the selected articles in this volume are appropriate for upper undergraduate and graduate students interested in serious debates beyond any assigned world politics textbook. The educator can easily organize and direct the extent and the level of student engagement in class discussions of these articles' central concepts, issues, and theories in his or her own class lectures.

Lastly, we appreciate your decision to choose this reader for your class and look forward to hearing your comments and reflections in our preparation for future updates.

Ali R. Abootalebi, Editor

January 2019

ABOUT THE EDITOR

Ali R. Abootalebi is Professor of Middle Eastern and Global Politics in the Department of Political Science, the University of Wisconsin, UWEC. He is the author of *Islam and Democracy: State-Society Relations in Developing Countries, 1980–1994* (2000), he coauthored with Stephen Hill *Introduction to World Politics: Prospects and Challenges for the United States,* second edition (2018), and has written numerous articles on Iran, Arab politics, civil society and democracy, and U.S. foreign policy.

PART I

Major Power Players and Issues

The Future of Power

By Joseph Nye

....

For a concept that is so widely used, "power" is surprisingly elusive and difficult to measure. But such problems do not make a concept meaningless. Few of us deny the importance of love even if we cannot say, "I love you 3.6 times more than I love something else." Like love, we experience power in our everyday lives, and it has real effects despite our inability to measure it precisely. Sometimes, analysts have been tempted to discard the concept as hopelessly vague and imprecise, but it has proven hard to replace.[1]

The great British philosopher Bertrand Russell once compared the role of power in social science to the centrality of the concept of "energy" in physics, but the comparison is misleading. Physicists can measure relations of energy and force among inanimate objects quite precisely, whereas power refers to more ephemeral human relationships that change shape under different circumstances.[2] Others have argued that power is to politics as money is to economics. Again, the metaphor misleads us. Money is a liquid or fungible resource. It can be used to buy a wide variety of goods, but the resources that produce power in one relationship or context may not produce it in another. You can use money in a housing market, at a vegetable market, or in an Internet auction, whereas military capacity, one of the most important international power resources, may produce the outcomes you want in a tank battle, but not on the Internet.

Over the years, various analysts have tried to provide formulas that can quantify power in international affairs. For example, Ray Cline was a high-ranking official in the CIA whose job was to tell political leaders about the balance of American and Soviet power during the Cold War. His views affected political decisions that involved high risks and billions of dollars. In 1977, he published a distillation of the formula he used for estimating power:

$$\text{PERCEIVED POWER} = (\text{POPULATION} + \text{TERRITORY} + \text{ECONOMY} + \text{MILITARY}) \times (\text{STRATEGY} + \text{WILL})$$

Joseph S. Nye, Jr., "What is Power in Global Affairs?" *Future of Power*, pp. 3-24, 238-244. Copyright © 2011 by Perseus Books Group. Reprinted with permission.

After inserting numbers into his formula, he concluded that the Soviet Union was twice as powerful as the United States.[3] Of course, as we now know, this formula was not a very good predictor of outcomes. In a little more than a decade, the Soviet Union collapsed and pundits were proclaiming that the United States was the sole superpower in a unipolar world.

A more recent effort to create a power index included a country's resources (technology, enterprise, human, capital, physical) and national performance (external constraints, infrastructure, ideas) and how they determined military capability and combat proficiency.[4] This formulation tells us about relative military power, but not about all relevant types of power. Although effective military force remains one of the key power resources in international affairs, as we shall see in the next chapter, the world is no longer as unconstrained as in nineteenth-century Europe when historians could define a "great power" as one capable of prevailing in war.[5]

Military force and combat proficiency do not tell us much about outcomes, for example, in the world of finance or climate change. Nor do they tell us much about the power of nonstate actors. In military terms, Al Qaeda is a midget compared to the American giant, but the impact of terrorists relies less on the size of their forces than on the theatrical effects of their actions and narratives and the overreactions they can produce. In that sense, terrorism is like the sport of jujitsu in which the weak player uses the strength of the larger against himself. This dynamic is not caught by typical indices of military power.

In certain bargaining situations, as Thomas Schelling demonstrates, weakness and the threat that a partner will collapse can be a source of bargaining power.[6] A bankrupt debtor who owes $1,000 has little power, but if it owes $1 billion, that debtor may have considerable bargaining power—witness the fate of institutions judged "too big to fail" in the 2008 financial crisis. North Korea's Kim Jong-Il "is probably the only world leader who can make Beijing look powerless. … Diplomats say Mr. Kim brazenly plays on Chinese fears. If the Chinese do not pump aid into his crumbling economy, he argues, they will face refugees pouring across the border and possible unrest."[7]

Any attempt to develop a single index of power is doomed to fail because power depends upon human relationships that vary in different contexts.[8] Whereas money can be used to measure purchasing power across different markets, there is no standard of value that can summarize all relationships and contexts to produce an agreed overall power total.[9]

Defining Power

Like many basic ideas, power is a contested concept. No one definition is accepted by all who use the word, and people's choice of definition reflects their interests and values. Some define power as the ability to make or resist change. Others say it is the ability to get what we want.[10] This broad definition includes power over nature as well as over other people. For my interest in actions and policies, a commonsense place to start is the dictionary, which tells us that power is the capacity to

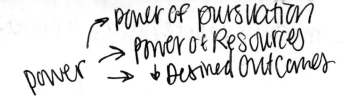

power → power of persuasion
power → power of resources
→ & desired outcomes

do things and in social situations to affect others to get the outcomes we want.[11] Some people call this influence, and distinguish power from influence, but that is confusing because the dictionary defines the two terms as interchangeable.

There are many factors that affect our ability to get what we want. We live in a web of inherited social forces, some of which are visible and others of which are indirect and sometimes called "structural." We tend to identify and focus on some of these constraints and forces rather than others depending on our interests. For example, in his work on civilizations, political scientist Peter Katzenstein argues that the power of civilizations is different from power in civilizations. Actors in civilizations command hard and soft power. Social power operates beneath the behavioral level by shaping underlying social structures, knowledge systems and general environment.[12] Even though such structural social forces are important, for policy purposes we also want to understand what actors or agents can do within given situations.[13] Civilizations and societies are not immutable, and effective leaders can try to shape larger social forces with varying degrees of success. As the famous German theorist Max Weber puts it, we want to know the probability that an actor in a social relationship can carry out his own will.[14]

Even when we focus primarily on particular agents or actors, we cannot say that an actor "has power" without specifying power "to do what."[15] We must specify *who* is involved in the power relationship (the scope of power) as well as *what* topics are involved (the domain of power). For example, the pope has power over some Christians, but not over others (such as Protestants). And even among Catholics, he may wish to have power over all their moral decisions, but some adherents may reject his power on some issues (such as birth control or marriage outside the church). Thus, to say that the pope has power requires us to specify the context (scope and domain) of the relationship between the pope and any individual.

A psychopath may have the power to kill and destroy random strangers, but not the power to persuade them. Some actions that affect others and obtain preferred outcomes can be purely destructive and not dependent on what the victim thinks. For example, Pol Pot killed millions of Cambodian citizens. Some say such use of force is not power because there was no two-way relationship involved, but that depends on context and motive. If the actor's motive is pure sadism or terror, the use of force fits within the definition of power as affecting others to get what the actor wants. Most power relationships, however, depend very much on what the victim thinks. A dictator who wishes to punish a dissident may be misled in thinking he exercised power if the dissident really sought martyrdom to advance her cause. But if the dictator simply wanted to destroy the dissident, her intentions did not matter to his power.

Actions often have powerful unintended consequences, but from a policy point of view we are interested in the ability to produce preferred outcomes. If a North Atlantic Treaty Organization (NATO) soldier in Afghanistan kills a child by a stray bullet, he had the power to destroy but not to achieve his preferred outcome. An air strike that kills one insurgent and many civilians demonstrates a general power to destroy, but it may prove counterproductive for a counterinsurgency policy. The

power over who & over what? A power over what.

different kinds of power. (next page)

power → relative
power → situational
→ issue related
→ dynamic

actions of a country with a large economy may have unintended effects that cause accidental harm (or wealth) in a small country.[16] Again, if the effects are unintended, then there is power to harm (or benefit), but it is not power to achieve preferred outcomes. Canadians often complain that living next to the United States is like sleeping with an elephant. From the Canadian point of view, intentions do not matter; it hurts if the beast rolls over. But from a policy-oriented perspective, intentions matter in terms of getting preferred outcomes.[17] A policy-oriented concept of power depends upon a specified context to tell us *who* gets *what, how, where,* and *when.*[18]

Practical politicians and ordinary people often find these questions of behavior and motivation too complicated and unpredictable. Behavioral definitions judge power by outcomes that are determined after the action (what economists call "ex post") rather than before the action ("ex ante"). But policymakers want predictions about the future to help guide their actions. Thus, they frequently define power simply in terms of the resources that can produce outcomes. By this second definition of power as resources, a country is powerful if it has a relatively large population, territory, natural resources, economic strength, military force, and social stability. The virtue of this second definition is that it makes power appear to be concrete, measurable, and predictable—a guide to action. Power in this sense is like holding the high cards in a card game. But this definition has major problems. When people define power as synonymous with the resources that (may) produce outcomes, they often encounter the paradox that those best endowed with power do not always get the outcomes they want.

This is not to deny the importance of power resources. Power is conveyed through resources, whether tangible or intangible. People notice resources. If you show the highest cards in a poker game, others may fold their hands rather than challenge you. But power resources that win in one game may not help at all in another. Holding a strong poker hand does not win if the game is bridge. Even if the game is poker, if you play your high hand poorly, or fall victim to bluff and deception, you can still lose. Power conversion—getting from resources to behavioral outcomes—is a crucial intervening variable. Having the resources of power does not guarantee that you will always get the outcome you want. For example, in terms of resources, the United States was far more powerful than Vietnam, yet lost the war. Converting resources into realized power in the sense of obtaining desired outcomes requires well-designed strategies and skillful leadership—what I call smart power. Yet strategies are often inadequate and leaders frequently misjudge.

Nonetheless, defining power in terms of resources is a shortcut that policymakers find useful. In general, a country that is well endowed with power resources is more likely to affect a weaker country and be less dependent upon an optimal strategy than vice versa. Smaller countries may sometimes obtain preferred outcomes because they pick smaller fights or focus selectively on a few issues. On average, and in direct conflicts, we would not expect Finland to prevail over Russia.[19]

As a first step in any game, it helps to start by figuring out who is holding the high cards and how many chips that player has. Equally important, however, is that policymakers have the contextual intelligence to understand what game they are playing. Which resources provide the best basis for power behavior in a particular context? Oil was not an impressive power resource before the industrial age, nor was uranium significant before the nuclear age. In traditional realist views of international affairs, war was the ultimate game in which the cards of international politics were played. When all the cards were on the table, estimates of relative power were proven and disproven. But over the centuries, as technologies evolved, the sources of strength for war often changed. Moreover, on an increasing number of issues in the twenty-first century, war is not the ultimate arbiter.

As a result, many analysts reject the "elements of national power" approach as misleading and inferior to the behavioral or relational approach that became dominant among social science analysis in the latter half of the twentieth century. Strictly speaking, the skeptics are correct. Power resources are simply the tangible and intangible raw materials or vehicles that underlie power relationships, and whether a given set of resources produces preferred outcomes or not depends upon behavior in context. The vehicle is not the power relationship.[20] Knowing the horsepower and mileage of a vehicle does not tell us whether it will get to the preferred destination.

In practice, discussions of power in global affairs involve both definitions.[21] Many of the terms that we use daily, such as "military power" and "economic power," are hybrids that combine both resources and behaviors. So long as that is the case, we must make clear whether we are speaking of behavioral- or resource-based definitions of power, and we must be aware of the imperfect relation between them. For example, when people speak of the rising power of China or India, they tend to point to the large populations and increased economic or military resources of those countries. But whether the capacity that those resources imply can actually be converted into preferred outcomes will depend upon the contexts and the country's skill in converting resources into strategies that will produce preferred outcomes. These different definitions are summarized in Figure 1.1. The figure also illustrates the more careful relational definition in which power is the ability to alter others' behavior to produce preferred outcomes.

This is what people are getting at when they say things like "Power doesn't necessarily lead to influence" (though for reasons already explained, that formulation is confusing).

Power of Resourse:
I have the $ so we are going to do what I want.

Resources → outcomes
Federal Gov. → State gov
I'll give you $ for interstate if you pass this law :) xo

(more on pg. 5 in an

Power Defined as Reso

context

Power = resources → conversion strategy

Power Defined as Behavior

Power = affect others → re: something → by means

(scope) (domain) (coercion,

FIGURE 1.1 Power as Resources and Power as Behavioral Outco

Relational Power: * commanding change
* controlling the agenda
* establishing preferences

In the end, because it is outcomes, not resources, that we care about, we must pay more attention to contexts and strategies. Power-conversion strategies turn out to be a critical variable that does not receive enough attention. Strategies relate means to ends, and those that combine hard and soft power resources successfully in different contexts are the key to smart power.

Three Aspects of Relational Power

In addition to the distinction between resource and relational definitions of power, it is useful to distinguish three different aspects of relational power: commanding change, controlling agendas, and establishing preferences. All too often these are conflated. For example, a recent book on foreign policy defines power as "getting people or groups to do something they don't want to do."[22] But such a narrow approach can lead to mistakes.

The ability to command others to change their behavior against their initial preferences is one important dimension of relational power, but not the only one. Another dimension is the ability to affect others' preferences so that they want what you want and you need not command them to change. Former president (and general) Dwight Eisenhower referred to this as getting people to do something "not only because you tell them to do so, but because they instinctively want to do it for you."[23] This co-optive power contrasts with and complements command power. It is a mistake to think that power consists of just ordering others to change. You can affect their behavior by shaping their preferences in ways that produce what you want rather than relying on carrots and sticks to change their behavior "when push comes to shove." Sometimes you can get the outcomes you want without pushing or shoving. Ignoring this dimension by using a too narrow definition of power can lead to a poorly shaped foreign policy.

The first aspect, or "face," of power was defined by Yale political scientist Robert Dahl in studies of New Haven in the 1950s, and it is widely used today even though it covers only part of power behavior.[24] This face of power focuses on the ability to get others to act in ways that are contrary to their initial preferences and strategies. To measure or judge power, you have to know how strong another person's or nation's initial preferences were and how much they were changed by your efforts. Coercion can be quite clear in a situation in which there appears to be some degree of choice. If a man holding a gun on you says, "Your money or your life," you have some choice, but it is small and not consistent with your initial preferences (unless they included suicide or martyrdom).[25] When Czechoslovakia succumbed to German and Soviet troops entering Prague in 1938 and again in 1968, it was not because that country wanted to.

Economic measures are somewhat more complex. Negative sanctions (taking away economic benefit) are clearly felt as coercive. Payment or economic inducement to do what you initially did not want to may seem more attractive to the subject, but any payment can easily be turned into a negative sanction by the implicit or explicit threat of its removal. A year-end bonus is a reward, but its removal is felt as a penalty. Moreover, in unequal bargaining relationships, say, between a millionaire landowner and a starving peasant, a paltry "take it or leave it" payment may give the peasant little sense of choice. The important point is that someone has the capacity to make others act against their initial preferences and strategies, and both sides feel that power.

In the 1960s, shortly after Dahl developed his widely accepted definition, political scientists Peter Bachrach and Morton Baratz pointed out that Dahl's definition missed what they called the "second face of power." Dahl ignored the dimension of framing and agenda-setting.[26] If ideas and institutions can be used to frame the agenda for action in a way that make others' preferences seem irrelevant or out of bounds, then it may never be necessary to push or shove them. In other words, it may be possible to shape others' preferences by affecting their expectations of what is legitimate or feasible. Agenda-framing focuses on the ability to keep issues off the table, or as Sherlock Holmes might put it, dogs that fail to bark.

Powerful actors can make sure that the less powerful are never invited to the table, or if they get there, the rules of the game have already been set by those who arrived first. International financial policy had this characteristic, at least before the crisis of 2008 opened things up somewhat when the Group of 8 (G-8) was supplemented by the Group of 20 (G-20). Those who are subject to this second face of power may or may not be aware of it. If they accept the legitimacy of the institutions or the social discourse that framed the agenda, they may not feel unduly constrained by the second face of power. But if the agenda of action is constrained by threats of coercion or promises of payments, then it is just an instance of the first face of power. The target's acquiescence in the legitimacy of the agenda is what makes this face of power co-optive and partly constitutive of soft power—the ability to get what you want by the co-optive means of framing the agenda, persuading, and eliciting positive attraction.

Still later, in the 1970s, sociologist Steven Lukes pointed out that ideas and beliefs also help shape others' *initial* preferences.[27] In Dahl's approach, I can exercise power over you by getting you to do what you would otherwise not want to do; in other words, by changing your situation, I can make you change your preferred strategy. But I can also exercise power over you by determining your very wants. I can shape your basic or initial preferences, not merely change the situation in a way that makes you change your strategy for achieving your preferences.

This dimension of power is missed by Dahl's definition. A teenage boy may carefully choose a fashionable shirt to wear to school to attract a girl, but the teenager may not be aware that the reason the shirt is so fashionable is that a national retailer recently launched a major advertising campaign. Both his preference and that of the other teenagers have been formed by an unseen actor who has shaped the structure of preferences. If you can get others to want the same outcomes that you want, it will not be necessary to override their initial desires. Lukes called this the "third face of power."[28]

There are critical questions of voluntarism in determining how freely people chose their preferences.[29] Not all soft power looks so soft to outside critics. In some extreme cases, it is difficult to ascertain what constitutes voluntary formation of preferences. For instance, in the "Stockholm

Table 1.1   Three Aspects of Relational Power

FIRST FACE: A uses threats or rewards to change B's behavior against B's initial preferences and strategies. B knows this and feels the effect of A's power.

SECOND FACE: A controls the agenda of actions in a way that limits B's choices of strategy. B may or may not know this and be aware of A's power.

THIRD FACE: A helps to create and shape B's basic beliefs, perceptions, and preferences. B is unlikely to be aware of this or to realize the effect of A's power.

syndrome," victims of kidnapping who suffered traumatic stress began to identify with their abductors. Captors sometimes try to "brainwash" their captives and sometimes try to win them over with kindnesses.[30] But in some situations, it is more difficult to be certain of others' interests. Are Afghan women oppressed when they choose to wear a burka? What about women who choose to wear a veil in democratic France?[31] Sometimes it is difficult to know the extent of voluntarism from mere outward appearances. Dictators such as Adolf Hitler and Stalin tried to create an aura of invincibility to attract followers, and some leaders in southeastern European countries succumbed to this effect. To the extent that force creates a sense of awe that attracts others, it can be an indirect source of co-optive power, but if the force is directly coercive, then it is simply an instance of the first face of power.

Some theorists have called these the public, hidden, and invisible faces of power, reflecting the degrees of difficulty that the target has in discovering the source of power.[32] The second and third faces embody aspects of structural power. A structure is simply an arrangement of all the parts of a whole. Humans are embedded in complex structures of culture, social relations, and power that affect and constrain them. A person's field of action is "delimited by actors with whom he has no interaction or communication, by actions distant in time and space, by actions of which he is, in no explicit sense the target."[33] Some exercises of power reflect the intentional decisions of particular actors, whereas others are the product of unintended consequences and larger social forces.

For example, why do large automobiles dominate our city streets? In part the answer reflects individual consumer choices, but these consumer preferences are themselves shaped by a social history of advertising, manufacturers' decisions, tax incentives, public transport policy, road-building subsidies, and urban planning.[34] Different choices on these issues by many visible as well as unseen past actors confront an urban resident today with a limited set of choices.

In 1993, Bill Clinton's political adviser James Carville is alleged to have joked that he wished he could be reborn as the bond market because then he would have real power.[35] When we speak of the power of markets, we are referring to a form of structural power. A wheat farmer who wants to earn more income to pay for his daughter's college tuition may decide to plant more wheat. But if other farmers plant more as well (and demand does not change), market forces may reduce his income and affect her educational prospects. In a perfect market, the agent has no pricing power. Millions of other unseen agents making independent choices create the supply and demand that determine the price. This is why poor countries that produce commodities are often subject to wide variations in their terms of trade. But if an agent can find a way to change the structure of a market by introducing an element of monopoly (a single seller) or monopsony (a single buyer), she can gain some power over price. She can do this by differentiating her product through advertising, creating brand loyalty, picking a special location, and so forth. Or in the case of oil-producing countries, agents can try to form a cartel like the Organization of Petroleum-Exporting Countries (OPEC).

Different analysts cut into the complex pattern of causation and draw the line between individual choice and larger structures at different places. For example, sociologists tend to focus less on specific actions and outcomes than political scientists do.[36] Analysts who focus only on individual agents, as the first face of power tends to do, are clearly failing to understand and describe power relationships fully. But those who focus only on broad social forces and longer historical perspective, as the second and third faces of power tend to do, pay too little attention to the individual choices and intentions that are crucial in policy. Some critics have called my approach too "agent centered," but it still allows some consideration of structural forces even if it does not include all aspects of structure.[37]

Some analysts regard these distinctions as useless abstractions that can all be collapsed into the first face of power.[38] If we succumb to this temptation, however, we are likely to limit what we see in terms of behavior, which tends to limit the strategies that policymakers design to achieve their goals. Command power (the first face) is very visible and readily grasped. It is the basis for hard power—the ability to get desired outcomes through coercion and payment. The co-optive power of faces two and three is more subtle and therefore less visible. It contributes to soft power, the ability to get preferred outcomes through the co-optive means of agenda-setting, persuasion, and attraction. All too often policymakers have focused solely on hard command power to compel others to act against their preferences and have ignored the soft power that comes from preference formation. But when co-opting is possible, policymakers can save on carrots and sticks.[39]

In global politics, some goals that states seek are more susceptible to the second and third than to the first face of power. Arnold Wolfers once distinguished between what he called possession goals—specific and often tangible objectives—and milieu goals, which are often structural and intangible.[40] For example, access to resources or basing rights or a trade agreement is a possession goal, whereas promoting an open trade system, free markets, democracy, or human rights is a milieu goal. In the terminology used previously, we can think of states having specific goals and general or structural goals. Focusing solely on command power and the first face of power may mislead us about how to promote such goals. For example, in the promotion of democracy, military means alone are less successful than military means combined with soft power approaches—as the United States discovered in Iraq. And the soft power of attraction and persuasion can have both agentic and structural dimensions. For example, a country can try to attract others through actions such as public diplomacy, but it may also attract others through the structural effects of its example or what can be called the "shining city on the hill" effect.

Another reason not to collapse all three faces of power into the first is that doing so diminishes attention to networks, which are an important type of structural power in the twenty-first century. Networks are becoming increasingly important in an information age, and positioning in social networks can be an important power resource. For example, in a hub-and-spokes network, power can derive from being the hub of communications. If you communicate with your other friends through me, that gives me power. If the points on the rim are not directly connected to each other, their dependence on communication through the hub can shape their agenda. For example, even after independence, many communications among former French African colonies ran through Paris, and that increased French power to shape their agenda.

In other more complex network arrangements, theorists point to the importance of structural holes that prevent direct communication between certain parts of the network.[41] Those who can bridge or exploit structural holes can use their position as a source of power by controlling communication between others. Another aspect of networks that is relevant to power is their extensiveness. Even weak extensive ties can be useful in acquiring and disseminating novel and innovative information. Weak ties provide the ability to link diverse groups together in a cooperative, successful manner.[42] This increases a country's ability to gain power with, rather than over, others. The ability to create networks of trust that enable groups to work together toward common goals is what economist Kenneth Boulding calls "integrative power."[43] According to psychologists, "Years of research suggest that empathy and social intelligence are vastly more important to acquiring and exercising power than are force, deception, or terror."[44]

Political theorist Hannah Arendt once said that "power springs up among men when they act together."[45] Similarly, a state can wield global power by engaging and acting together with other states, not merely acting against them. Princeton political scientist John Ikenberry argues that American power after World War II rested on a network of institutions that constrained the United States but were open to others and thus increased America's power to act with others.[46] This is an important point in assessing the power of nations in the current international system and an important dimension for assessing the future of American and Chinese power in the twenty-first century.[47] For example, if the United States is involved in more communication networks, it has a greater opportunity to shape preferences in terms of the third face of power.

For policy purposes, it can be useful to think of the three faces of power in a reverse sequence from the order in which they were invented by social scientists. A policymaker should consider preference formation and agenda-framing as means of shaping the environment before turning to the first, or command, face of power.[48] In short, those who insist on collapsing the second and third dimensions of power into the first will miss an increasingly important aspect of power in this century.

Realism and the Full Spectrum of Power Behavior

In the United States, the tendency to focus on the first face of power is partly a reflection of American political culture and institutions. No politician wants to appear "soft," and Congress finds it easier to boost the budget of the Pentagon than that of the State Department. That bias has been reinforced by prevailing theories of international politics. For centuries, the dominant classical approach to international affairs has been called "realism," and its lineage stretches back to such great thinkers as Thucydides and Niccolò Machiavelli. Realism assumes that in the anarchic conditions of world politics, where there is no higher international government authority above states, they must rely on their own devices to preserve their independence, and that when push comes to shove, the ultima ratio is the use of force. Realism portrays the world in terms of sovereign states aiming to preserve their security, with military force as their ultimate instrument. Thus, war has been a constant aspect of international affairs over the centuries. Realists come in many sizes and shapes, but all tend to argue that global politics is power politics. In this they are right, but some limit their understanding by conceiving of power too narrowly. A pragmatic or commonsense realist takes into account the full spectrum of power resources, including ideas, persuasion, and attraction. Many classical realists of the past understood the role of soft power better than some of their modern progeny.

Realism represents a good first cut at portraying some aspects of international relations. But as we have seen, states are no longer the only important actors in global affairs; security is not the only major outcome that they seek, and force is not the only or always the best instrument available to achieve those outcomes. Indeed, these conditions of complex interdependence are typical of relations among advanced postindustrial countries such as the United States, Canada, Europe, Australia, and Japan. Mutual democracy, liberal culture, and a deep network of transnational ties mean that anarchy has very different effects than realism predicts. In such conditions, a smart power strategy has a much higher mixture of the second and third faces of power.

It is not solely in relations among advanced countries, however, that soft power plays an important role. In an information age, communications strategies become more important, and outcomes are shaped not merely by whose army wins but also by whose story wins. In the fight against terrorism, for example, it is essential to have a narrative that appeals to the mainstream and prevents its recruitment by radicals. In the battle against insurgencies, kinetic military force must be accompanied by soft power instruments that help to win over the hearts and minds (shape the preferences) of the majority of the population.

Smart strategies must have an information and communications component. States struggle over the power to define norms, and framing of issues grows in importance. For instance, CNN and the BBC framed the issues of the First Gulf War in 1991, but by 2003 Al Jazeera was playing a large role in shaping the narrative in the Iraq War. Such framing is more than mere propaganda. In describing events in March 2003, we could say that American troops "entered Iraq" or that American troops "invaded Iraq." Both statements are true, but they have very different effects in terms of the power to shape preferences. Similarly, if we think of international institutions, it makes a difference if agendas are set in a Group of 8 with a few invited guests or in a Group of 20 equal invitees. These are just some examples of how the dimensions of the second and third faces of power are becoming more important in the global politics of an information age.

Soft Power Behavior and Resources

Some critics complain that the prevailing definition of soft power has become fuzzy through its expansion "to include both economic statecraft—used as both a carrot and as a stick—and even military power. ... Soft power now seems to mean everything."[49] But these critics are mistaken because they confuse the actions of a state seeking to achieve desired outcomes with the resources used to produce them. Many types of *resources* can contribute to soft power, but that does not mean that soft power is any type of *behavior*. The use of force, payment, and some agenda-setting based on them I call hard power. Agenda-setting that is regarded as legitimate by the target, positive attraction, and persuasion are the parts of the spectrum of behaviors I include in soft power. Hard power is push; soft power is pull. Fully defined, soft power is the ability to affect others through the co-optive means of framing the agenda, persuading, and eliciting positive attraction in order to obtain preferred outcomes.[50]

Here is a representation of a spectrum of power behaviors:[51]

H A R D	Command → Coerce Threaten Pay Sanction Frame Persuade Attract ← Co-opt	S O F T

In general, the types of resources associated with hard power include tangibles such as force and money. The types of resources associated with soft power often include intangible factors such as institutions, ideas, values, culture, and the perceived legitimacy of policies. But the relationship is not perfect. Intangible resources such as patriotism, morale, and legitimacy strongly affect the military capacity to fight and win. And threats to use force are intangible, even though they are a dimension of hard power.[52]

If we remember the distinction between power resources and power behavior, we realize that the resources often associated with hard power behavior can also produce soft power behavior depending on the context and how they are used. Command power can create resources that in turn can create soft power at a later phase—for example, institutions that will provide soft power resources in the future. Similarly, co-optive behavior can be used to generate hard power resources in the form of military alliance or economic aid. A tangible hard power resource such as a military unit can produce both command behavior (by winning a battle) and co-optive behavior (by attracting) depending on how it is used. And because attraction depends upon the mind of the perceiver, the subject's perceptions play a significant role in whether given resources produce hard or soft power behavior.

Hard power—millitary
Soft power—economy
Smart power—

For example, naval forces can be used to win battles (hard power) or win hearts and minds (soft power) depending on what the target and what the issue are. The U.S. Navy's help in providing relief to Indonesia after the 2004 East Asian tsunami had a strong effect on increasing Indonesians' attraction to the United States, and the U.S. Navy's 2007 Maritime Strategy referred not only to war-fighting but also to "maritime forces ... employed to build confidence and trust among nations."[53] Similarly, successful economic performance such as that of China can produce both the hard power of sanctions and restricted market access and the soft power of attraction and emulation of success.

Some analysts have misinterpreted soft power as a synonym for culture and then gone on to down-grade its importance. For example, the historian Niall Ferguson describes soft power as "nontraditional forces such as cultural and commercial goods" and then dismisses it on the grounds that "it's, well, soft."[54] Of course, eating at McDonald's or wearing a Michael Jackson shirt does not automatically indicate soft power. Militias can perpetrate atrocities or fight Americans while wearing Nikes and drinking Coca-Cola. But this criticism confuses the resources that may produce behavior with the behavior itself. Whether the possession of power resources actually produces favorable behavior depends upon the context and the skills of the agent in converting the resources into behavioral outcomes. Eating sushi, trading Pokemon cards, or hiring a Japanese pitcher (as the Boston Red Sox did) does not necessarily convey power to Japan. But this is not unique to soft power resources. Having a larger tank army may produce victory if a battle is fought in a desert, but not if it is fought in a swamp. Similarly, a nice smile can be a soft power resource, and you may be more inclined to do something for me if I smile whenever we meet, but if I smile at your mother's funeral, it may destroy soft power rather than create it.

Soft Power and Smart Power

As mentioned in the Preface, I developed the term "smart power" in 2004 to counter the misperception that soft power alone can produce effective foreign policy. I defined smart power as the ability to combine hard and soft power resources into effective strategies.[55] Unlike soft power, smart power is an evaluative as well as a descriptive concept. Soft power can be good or bad from a normative perspective, depending on how it is used. Smart power has the evaluation built into the definition. Critics who say "smart power—which can be dubbed Soft Power 2.0—has superseded Soft Power 1.0 in the U.S. foreign policy lexicon" are simply mistaken.[56] A more accurate criticism is that because the concept (unlike that of soft power) has a normative dimension, it often lends itself to slogans, though that need not be the case.

Smart power is available to all states (and nonstate actors), not just the United States. For example, as we will see in Chapter 7, small states have often developed smart power strategies. Norway, with 5 million people, has enhanced its attractiveness with legitimizing policies in peacemaking and development assistance, while also being an active and effective participant in NATO. And at the other extreme in terms of population size, China, a rising power in economic and military resources, has deliberately decided to invest in soft power resources so as to make its hard power look less threatening to its neighbors and thus develop a smart strategy.

Smart power goes to the heart of the problem of power conversion. As we saw earlier, some countries and actors may be endowed with greater power resources than others, yet not be very effective in converting the full range of their power resources into strategies that produce the outcomes they seek. Some argue that with an inefficient eighteenth-century government structure, the United States is weak in power conversion. Others respond that much of American strength is generated outside of government by the nation's open economy and civil society. And it may be that power conversion is easier when a country has a surplus of assets and can afford to absorb the costs of mistakes. But the first steps to smart power and effective power-conversion strategies are understanding the full range of power resources and recognizing the problems of combining them effectively in various contexts.

Hard and soft power sometimes reinforce and sometimes undercut each other, and good contextual intelligence is important in distinguishing how they interact in different situations. But it is a mistake to think of information campaigns in terms that misunderstand the essence of soft power. If we had to choose between having military or having soft power in world politics, we would opt for military power. But smart power suggests it is best to have both. "The military has to understand that soft power is more challenging to wield in terms of the application of military force—particularly if what that force is doing is not seen as attractive."[57] If the levers of soft power are not pulling in the same direction, then the military often cannot create favorable conditions on its own.

Early in 2006, Secretary of Defense Donald Rumsfeld said of the Bush administration's global war on terror, "In this war, some of the most critical battles may not be in the mountains of Afghanistan or the streets of Iraq but in newsrooms in New York, London, Cairo and elsewhere." As *The Economist* commented about Rumsfeld's speech, "Until recently he plainly regarded such a focus on 'soft power' as, well, soft—part of 'Old Europe's' appeasement of terrorism." Now he realized the importance of winning hearts and minds, but "a good part of his speech was focused on how with slicker PR America could win the propaganda war."[58] Unfortunately, Rumsfeld forgot the first rule of advertising: If you have a poor product, not even the best advertising will sell it. He also forgot that the administration's poor power-conversion strategy was wasting both hard and soft power assets. The first step toward developing more effective smart power strategies starts with a fuller understanding of the types and uses of power.

Notes

1. For a classic exploration of this problem, see James G. March, "The Power of Power," in David Easton, ed., *Varieties of Political Theory* (Englewood Cliffs, NJ: Prentice-Hall, 1966), 39–70. Other classic articles on power by Robert Dahl, John C. Harsanyi, Hebert Simon, and others are collected in Roderick Bell, David V. Edwards, and R. Harrison Wagner, eds., *Political Power: A Reader in Theory and Research* (New York: Free Press, 1969).

2. Bertrand Russell, *Power: A New Social Analysis* (London: Allen and Unwin, 1938), quoted in Dacher Keltner, Cameron Anderson, and Deborah Gruenfeld, "Power, Approach, and Inhibition," *Psychological Review* 110 (2003): 265.

3. Ray S. Cline, *World Power Assessment* (Boulder, CO: Westview Press, 1977). For a canonical approach, see Hans J. Morgenthau, *Politics Among Nations: The Struggle for Power and Peace* (New York: Knopf, 1948).

4. Ashley Tellis, Janice Bially, Christopher Layne, Melissa McPherson, and Jerry Solinger, *Measuring National Power in the Postindustrial Age: Analyst's Handbook* (Santa Monica, CA: RAND, 2000).

5. A. J. P Taylor, *The Struggle for Mastery in Europe, 1848–1918* (Oxford, UK: Oxford University Press, 1954), xxix.

6. "In bargaining, weakness may be strength." Thomas C. Schelling, *The Strategy of Conflict* (Oxford, UK: Oxford University Press, 1960), 62.

7. Christian Oliver and Geoff Dyer, "Kim Holds Ace as Visit Shows Limits of Chinese Influence," *Financial Times,* May 8, 2010.

8. Stefano Guzzini argues that the dependence of power on theory means that "there is no single concept of power applicable to every type of explanation." Stefano Guzzini, "Structural Power: The Limits of Neorealist Power Analysis," *International Organization* 47, no. 3 (Summer 1993): 446.

9. David A. Baldwin, "Power and International Relations," in Walter Carlsnaes, Thomas Risse, and Beth A. Simmons, eds., *Handbook of International Relations* (London: Sage, 2002), 179.

10. Kenneth E. Boulding uses both in *Three Faces of Power* (London: Sage, 1989), 15.

11. Power implies causation and is like the word "cause." When we speak of causation, we choose to pick out the relation between two items in a long and complex chain of events because we are interested in them more than the myriad other things that we might focus upon. We do not say in the abstract that "an event causes" without specifying what it causes.

12. Peter J. Katzenstein, ed., *Civilizations in World Politics: Plural and Pluralist Perspectives* (New York: Routledge, 2009).

13. As one economist put it, "One of the main purposes for which social scientists use the concept of A's power over B is for the description of the policy possibilities open to A." John Harsanyi, "The Dimension and Measurement of Social Power," reprinted in K. W. Rothschild, *Power in Economics* (Harmondsworth, UK: Penguin Books, 1971), 80.

14. Max Weber, *The Theory of Social and Economic Organization* (New York: Oxford University Press, 1947), 152.

15. Jack Nagel, *The Descriptive Analysis of Power* (New Haven, CT: Yale University Press, 1975), 14.

16. This general power is stressed by Susan Strange, *States and Markets* (New York: Blackwell, 1988).

17. On intentions and power, see Peter Morriss, *Power: A Philosophical Analysis*, 2nd ed. (Manchester, UK: Manchester University Press, 2002), 25–28. See also Baldwin, "Power and International Relations," 181. "There is no need for a fundamental reformulation of the concept of power in order to account for its unintended effects." For example, President Woodrow Wilson's ideas influenced rising anticolonial activism in Asia and the Middle East. This was unintended power in the broad sense of the capacity to make change, but not in the sense of achieving preferred outcomes because Wilson was not interested in freeing Asian nations. See Erez Manela, *The Wilsonian Moment: Self-Determination and the International Origins of Anticolonial Nationalism* (New York: Oxford University Press, 2007).

18. Harold Lasswell and Abraham Kaplan, *Power and Society: A Framework for Political Inquiry* (New Haven, CT: Yale University Press, 1950).

19. It is worth noting that after fighting Russia at the beginning of World War II, Finland was cautious not to challenge the Soviet Union during the Cold War and was able to preserve its independence. Outcomes are not always all or nothing.

20. Philosophers such as Antony Kenny and Peter Morriss argue that reducing power to resources constitutes the "vehicle fallacy," but Keith Dowding contends that "the vehicle fallacy is not a fallacy if resources are measured relationally, for example, the power of money is relative to its distribution. It follows that strategic considerations must enter into the very essence of the concept of power." Keith Dowding, "Power, Capability, and Ableness: The Fallacy of the Vehicle Fallacy," *Contemporary Political Theory* 7 (2008): 238–258.

21. Baldwin, "Power and International Relations," 185–186, contests my statement but does not offer compelling evidence that would make me change it. In my experience in government, policymakers do tend to focus on resources.

22. Leslie Gelb, *Power Rules: How Common Sense Can Rescue American Foreign Policy* (New York: HarperCollins, 2009), 28.

23. Alan Axelrod, *Eisenhower and Leadership: Ike's Enduring Lessons in Total Victory Management* (San Francisco: Jossey-Bass, 2006), 120, 283.

24. Robert A. Dahl, *Who Governs: Democracy and Power in an American City* (New Haven, CT: Yale University Press, 1961).

25. Preferences and strategies are closely related. Preferences rank outcomes in a given environment, and a strategy is an actor's effort to come as close as possible to preferred outcomes in that setting. From an analytical point of view, preferences in one setting may become strategies in another. See Jeffry A. Frieden, "Actors and Preferences in International Relations," in David A. Lake and Robert Powell, eds., *Strategic Choice and International Relations* (Princeton, NJ: Princeton University Press, 1999), 41. Thus, in the gunman example, in the original setting A's preferences include both life and money, and his strategy is to keep both. The gunman's threat changes the environment so that A must now rank his preferences and adopt a strategy of handing over his wallet. A's preferences do not change (life ranks over money), but when the gunman changes the environment, A has to change his strategy.

26. Peter Bachrach and Morton Baratz, "Decisions and Nondecisions: An Analytical Framework," *American Political Science Review* 57, no. 3 (September 1963): 632–642. William H. Riker has developed a somewhat similar concept that he calls "heresthetics," which "involves structuring the situation so that others accept it willingly." William H. Riker, "The Heresthetics of Constitution-Making: The Presidency in 1787, with Comments on Determinism and Rational Choice," *American Political Science Review* 78, no. 1 (March 1984): 8.

27. Steven Lukes, *Power: A Radical View,* 2nd ed. (London: Palgrave Macmillian, 2005).

28. As Lukes points out, my concept of soft power is similar but not identical to his third face of power. My concept includes voluntaristic dimensions of agenda-setting as well as preference-setting by attraction and persuasion. It is more concerned with the actions of agents and less concerned with the problematic concept of "false consciousness."

29. Lukes calls soft power "a cousin" of his concept of the third face of power. He is concerned, however, about distinguishing degrees of freedom or voluntarism. "Both the agent-centered, strategic view of Nye and the subject-centered structural view of Foucault lack this distinction. … We need to focus on both agents and subjects and ask the question: exactly how do agents succeed in winning the hearts and minds of those subject to their influence—by wielding power over them or by contributing to their empowerment?" Steven Lukes, "Power and the Battle for Hearts and Minds: On the Bluntness of Soft Power," in Felix Berenskoetter and M. J. Williams, eds., *Power in World Politics* (London: Routledge, 2007), 97.

30. "Humans are wired to form social bonds, and such scraps of kindness can deepen even a relationship built on manipulation and abuse. Some victims have profoundly ambivalent feelings toward abusive captors, psychologists say." Benedict Carey, "For Longtime Captive, a Complex Road Home," *New York Times,* September 1, 2009.

31. A French Muslim woman who objected to laws against veils complained, "Don't believe for a moment that I am submissive to my husband. I'm the one who takes care of the documents and the money." Steven Erlanger, "Burqa Furor Scrambles the Political Debate in France," *New York Times,* September 1, 2009.

32. John Gaventa, "Levels, Spaces, and Forms of Power," in Beren-skoetter and Williams, *Power in World Politics,* 206.

33. Clarissa Hayward, *De-facing Power* (Cambridge, UK: Cambridge University Press, 2000), 37.

34. Martin J. Smith, *Power and the State* (Basingstoke, UK: Palgrave Macmillan, 2009), 36.

35. Bob Woodward, *The Agenda: Inside the Clinton White House* (New York: Simon and Schuster, 1994), 139.

36. See Keith Dowding, "Agency and Structure: Interpreting Power Relationships," *Journal of Power Studies* 1, no. 1 (2008): 21–36.

37. The second and third faces of power incorporate structural causes such as institutions and culture but also leave room to focus on agents who make choices, albeit constrained by structural forces. Many power relations, like many markets, are imperfect in their structure and allow some voluntarism and choice for agents within the structures. Some writers have suggested a "fourth face" of power that would encompass primarily structural forces. For some purposes this can be fruitful, but it is less useful for understanding the policy options that leaders confront. Peter Digeser has used this term to refer to Michel Foucault's view that subjects and social practices are the effects of a power that one cannot escape, and knowledge presupposes power, but Digeser admits that "Foucault's use of power departs significantly from ordinary usage." Peter Digeser, "The Fourth Face of Power," *Journal of Politics* 54, no. 4 (November 1992): 990. See also Michael Barnett and Raymond Duvall, "Power in International Politics," *International Organization* 59, no. 1 (Winter 2005): 39–75, for an abstract fourfold typology that goes beyond the three faces of power categories. For my purposes, the insights that Foucault and other structuralists provide are purchased at too high a price in terms of conceptual complexity and clarity.

38. Baldwin, "Power and International Relations," 179.

39. In terms of the earlier example of the teenager choosing an attractive shirt, this can take the indirect form of shaping preferences (as in the advertisement example) or the direct form of using existing preferences to attract by wearing a stylish shirt.

40. Arnold Wolfers, *Discord and Collaboration: Essays on International Politics* (Baltimore, MD: Johns Hopkins University Press, 1962), 73–77.

41. Ronald Burt, *Structural Holes: The Social Structure of Competition* (Cambridge, MA: Harvard University Press, 1992), chap. 1.

42. Mark Granovetter, "The Myth of Social Network Analysis as a Special Method in the Social Sciences," *Connections* 13, no. 2 (1990): 13–16.

43. Boulding, *Three Faces of Power,* 109–110.

44. Dacher Keltner, "The Power Paradox," *Greater Good,* Winter 2007–2008, 15.

45. Hannah Arendt, *The Human Condition* (Chicago: University of Chicago Press, 1998), 200.

46. G. John Ikenberry, *Liberal Order and Imperial Ambition* (Cambridge, UK: Polity, 2006).

47. Anne Marie Slaughter, "America's Edge: Power in the Networked Century," *Foreign Affairs* 88, no. 1 (January–February 2009): 94–113.

48. I am indebted to Tyson Belanger for this point.

49. Leslie Gelb, *Power Rules,* 69.

50. At various times, in trying to explain soft power, I have shortened my formulation to statements such as "Soft power is attractive power," "Soft power is the ability to shape or reshape preferences without resort to force or payment," and "Soft power is the ability to get others to want what you want." These short forms are consistent with the longer, more formal definition of the concept.

51. The behaviors in the spectrum in Table 1.1 sometimes overlap, but they can be conceived in terms of the degree of voluntarism in B's behavior. In the middle of the spectrum, payment has a degree of voluntarism and agenda-setting can be affected by institutions and discourses that B may not fully accept. That aspect of agenda-setting is determined by hard power, but to the extent that hard power in one period can create in a later period institutions that limit the agenda but are widely regarded as legitimate, then agenda-setting is part of co-optive and soft power. The effect of World War II in changing power relations that set the framework for the postwar United Nations and Bretton Woods institutions is a case in point.

52. Baldwin and others have criticized my earlier discussion of tangibility. I should have made clearer that intangibility is not a *necessary* condition for soft power. I defined soft power in behavioral terms as the ability to affect others to obtain preferred outcomes by co-option and attraction rather than by coercion or payment, and I was careful to use language that suggested an imperfect relationship ("tend to be associated," "are usually associated") between soft power behavior and the intangibility of the resources that can produce it. But the criticism is justified, and that explains this restatement.

53. Admiral Gary Roughead, Chief of Naval Operations, General James T. Conway, Commandant of the Marine Corps, and Admiral Thad W. Allen, Commandant of the Coast Guard, *A Cooperative Strategy for 21st Century Seapower* (Washington, DC: U.S. Navy, October 2007), 3.

54. Niall Ferguson, "Think Again: Power," *Foreign Policy* 134 (January–February 2003): 18–22.

55. See Joseph S. Nye, *Soft Power: The Means to Success in World Politics* (New York: PublicAffairs, 2004), 32, 147. I am grateful to Fen Hampson for the term. Suzanne Nossel also deserves credit for using the term in "Smart Power," *Foreign Affairs* 83, no. 2 (March–April 2004): 131–142, but I was not aware of this until later.

56. Christopher Layne, "The Unbearable Lightness of Soft Power," in Inderjeet Parmer and Michael Cox, eds., *Soft Power and U.S. Foreign Policy* (London: Routledge, 2010), 67ff.

57. Angus Taverner, "The Military Use of Soft Power–Information Campaigns: The Challenge of Applications, Their Audiences, and Effects," in Parmar and Cox, *Soft Power and U.S. Foreign Policy*, 149.

58. "Why It Will Take So Long to Win," *The Economist*, February 23, 2006, www.economist.com/opinion/displaystory.cfm?story_id= E1_VV QRTTV.

DISCUSSION QUESTIONS

1. How would you summarize the main argument of the article in a sentence or two?

2. How does Joseph Nye conceive of possession versus the conversion of power?

3. According to social scientists, what are the three "faces" or aspects of power?

4. What is meant by power defined as resources versus power defined as behavioral outcomes?

5. What distinguishes soft power from hard power? What are some aspects of soft power?

6. What does Nye mean by "smart power"?

The Rise of China and the Future of the West: Can the Liberal System Survive?

By G. John Ikenberry

....

T he rise of China will undoubtedly be one of the great dramas of the twenty-first century. China's extraordinary economic growth and active diplomacy are already transforming East Asia, and future decades will see even greater increases in Chinese power and influence. But exactly how this drama will play out is an open question. Will China overthrow the existing order or become a part of it? And what, if anything, can the United States do to maintain its position as China rises?

Some observers believe that the American era is coming to an end, as the Western-oriented world order is replaced by one increasingly dominated by the East. The historian Niall Ferguson has written that the bloody twentieth century witnessed "the descent of the West" and "a reorientation of the world" toward the East. Realists go on to note that as China gets more powerful and the United States' position erodes, two things are likely to happen: China will try to use its growing influence to reshape the rules and institutions of the international system to better serve its interests, and other states in the system—especially the declining hegemon—will start to see China as a growing security threat. The result of these developments, they predict, will be tension, distrust, and conflict, the typical features of a power transition. In this view, the drama of China's rise will feature an increasingly powerful China and a declining United States locked in an epic battle over the rules and leadership of the international system. And as the world's largest country emerges not from within but outside the established post–World War II international order, it is a drama that will end with the grand ascendance of China and the onset of an Asian-centered world order.

That course, however, is not inevitable. The rise of China does not have to trigger a wrenching hegemonic transition. The U.S.-Chinese power transition can be very different from those of the past because China faces an international order that is fundamentally different from those that past rising states confronted. China does not just face the United States; it faces a Western-centered system that is open, integrated, and rule-based, with wide and deep political foundations. The nuclear revolution, meanwhile, has made war among great powers unlikely—eliminating the major tool that rising powers have used to overturn international systems defended by declining hegemonic states. Today's Western order, in short, is hard to overturn and easy to join.

G. John Ikenberry, "The Rise of China and the Future of the West," *Foreign Affairs*, vol. 87, no. 1, pp. 23-37. Copyright © 2008 by Council on Foreign Relations, Inc. Reprinted with permission.

This unusually durable and expansive order is itself the product of farsighted U.S. leadership. After World War II, the United States did not simply establish itself as the leading world power. It led in the creation of universal institutions that not only invited global membership but also brought democracies and market societies closer together. It built an order that facilitated the participation and integration of both established great powers and newly independent states. (It is often forgotten that this postwar order was designed in large part to reintegrate the defeated Axis states and the beleaguered Allied states into a unified international system.) Today, China can gain full access to and thrive within this system. And if it does, China will rise, but the Western order—if managed properly—will live on.

As it faces an ascendant China, the United States should remember that its leadership of the Western order allows it to shape the environment in which China will make critical strategic choices. If it wants to preserve this leadership, Washington must work to strengthen the rules and institutions that underpin that order—making it even easier to join and harder to overturn. U.S. grand strategy should be built around the motto "The road to the East runs through the West." It must sink the roots of this order as deeply as possible, giving China greater incentives for integration than for opposition and increasing the chances that the system will survive even after U.S. relative power has declined.

The United States' "unipolar moment" will inevitably end. If the defining struggle of the twenty-first century is between China and the United States, China will have the advantage. If the defining struggle is between China and a revived Western system, the West will triumph.

Transitional Anxieties

China is well on its way to becoming a formidable global power. The size of its economy has quadrupled since the launch of market reforms in the late 1970s and, by some estimates, will double again over the next decade. It has become one of the world's major manufacturing centers and consumes roughly a third of the global supply of iron, steel, and coal. It has accumulated massive foreign reserves, worth more than $1 trillion at the end of 2006. China's military spending has increased at an inflation-adjusted rate of over 18 percent a year, and its diplomacy has extended its reach not just in Asia but also in Africa, Latin America, and the Middle East. Indeed, whereas the Soviet Union rivaled the United States as a military competitor only, China is emerging as both a military and an economic rival—heralding a profound shift in the distribution of global power.

Power transitions are a recurring problem in international relations. As scholars such as Paul Kennedy and Robert Gilpin have described it, world politics has been marked by a succession of powerful states rising up to organize the international system. A powerful state can create and enforce the rules and institutions of a stable global order in which to pursue its interests and security. But nothing lasts forever: long-term changes in the distribution of power give rise to new challenger states, who set off a struggle over the terms of that international order. Rising states want to translate their newly acquired power into greater authority in the global system—to reshape the rules and institutions in accordance with their own interests. Declining states, in turn, fear their loss of control and worry about the security implications of their weakened position.

These moments are fraught with danger. When a state occupies a commanding position in the international system, neither it nor weaker states have an incentive to change the existing order. But when the power of a challenger state grows and the power of the leading state weakens, a strategic rivalry ensues, and conflict—perhaps leading to war—becomes likely. The danger of power transitions is captured most dramatically in the case of late-nineteenth-century Germany. In 1870, the United Kingdom had a three-to-one advantage in economic power over Germany and a significant military advantage as well; by 1903, Germany had pulled ahead in terms of both economic and military power. As Germany unified and grew, so, too, did its dissatisfactions and demands, and as it grew more powerful, it increasingly appeared as a threat to other great powers in Europe, and security competition began. In the strategic realignments that followed, France, Russia, and the United Kingdom, formerly enemies, banded together to confront an emerging Germany. The result was a European war. Many observers see this dynamic emerging in U.S.-Chinese relations. "If China continues its impressive economic growth over the next few decades," the realist scholar John Mearsheimer has written, "the United States and China are likely to engage in an intense security competition with considerable potential for war."

But not all power transitions generate war or overturn the old order. In the early decades of the twentieth century, the United Kingdom ceded authority to the United States without great conflict or even a rupture in relations. From the late 1940s to the early 1990s, Japan's economy grew from the equivalent of five percent of U.S. GDP to the equivalent of over 60 percent of U.S. GDP, and yet Japan never challenged the existing international order.

Clearly, there are different types of power transitions. Some states have seen their economic and geopolitical power grow dramatically and have still accommodated themselves to the existing order. Others have risen up and sought to change it. Some power transitions have led to the breakdown of the old order and the establishment of a new international hierarchy. Others have brought about only limited adjustments in the regional and global system.

A variety of factors determine the way in which power transitions unfold. The nature of the rising state's regime and the degree of its dissatisfaction with the old order are critical: at the end of the nineteenth century, the United States, a liberal country an ocean away from Europe, was better able to embrace the British-centered international order than Germany was. But even more decisive is the character of the international order itself—for it is the nature of the international order that shapes a rising state's choice between challenging that order and integrating into it.

Open Order

The postwar Western order is historically unique. Any international order dominated by a powerful state is based on a mix of coercion and consent, but the U.S.-led order is distinctive in that it has been more liberal than imperial—and so unusually accessible, legitimate, and durable. Its rules and institutions are rooted in, and thus reinforced by, the evolving global forces of democracy and capitalism. It is expansive, with a wide and widening array of participants and stakeholders. It is capable of generating tremendous economic growth and power while also signaling restraint—all of which make it hard to overturn and easy to join.

It was the explicit intention of the Western order's architects in the 1940s to make that order integrative and expansive. Before the Cold War split the world into competing camps, Franklin Roosevelt sought to create a one-world system managed by cooperative great powers that would rebuild war-ravaged Europe, integrate the defeated states, and establish mechanisms for security cooperation and expansive economic growth. In fact, it was Roosevelt who urged—over the opposition of Winston Churchill—that China be included as a permanent member of the UN Security Council. The then Australian ambassador to the United States wrote in his diary after his first meeting with Roosevelt during the war, "He said that he had numerous discussions with Winston about China and that he felt that Winston was 40 years behind the times on China and he continually referred to the Chinese as 'Chinks' and 'Chinamen' and he felt that this was very dangerous. He wanted to keep China as a friend because in 40 or 50 years' time China might easily become a very powerful military nation."

Over the next half century, the United States used the system of rules and institutions it had built to good effect. West Germany was bound to its democratic Western European neighbors through the European Coal and Steel Community (and, later, the European Community) and to the United States through the Atlantic security pact; Japan was bound to the United States through an alliance partnership and expanding economic ties. The Bretton Woods meeting in 1944 laid down the monetary and trade rules that facilitated the opening and subsequent flourishing of the world economy—an astonishing achievement given the ravages of war and the competing interests of the great powers. Additional agreements between the United States, Western Europe, and Japan solidified the open and multilateral character of the postwar world economy. After the onset of the Cold War, the Marshall Plan in Europe and the 1951 security pact between the United States and Japan further integrated the defeated Axis powers into the Western order.

In the final days of the Cold War, this system once again proved remarkably successful. As the Soviet Union declined, the Western order offered a set of rules and institutions that provided Soviet leaders with both reassurances and points of access—effectively encouraging them to become a part of the system. Moreover, the shared leadership of the order ensured accommodation of the Soviet Union. As the Reagan administration pursued a hard-line policy toward Moscow, the Europeans pursued détente and engagement. For every hard-line "push," there was a moderating "pull," allowing Mikhail Gorbachev to pursue high-risk reforms. On the eve of German unification, the fact that a united Germany would be embedded in European and Atlantic institutions—rather than becoming an independent great power—helped reassure Gorbachev that neither German nor Western intentions were hostile. After the Cold War, the Western order once again managed the integration of a new wave of countries, this time from the formerly communist world. Three particular features of the Western order have been critical to this success and longevity.

The Western order can turn the coming power shift into a peaceful change favorable to the United States.

First, unlike the imperial systems of the past, the Western order is built around rules and norms of nondiscrimination and market openness, creating conditions for rising states to advance their expanding economic and political goals within it. Across history, international orders have varied widely in terms of whether the material benefits that are generated accrue disproportionately to the leading state or are widely shared. In the Western system, the barriers to economic participation are low, and the potential benefits are high. China has already discovered the massive economic returns that are possible by operating within this open-market system.

Second is the coalition-based character of its leadership. Past orders have tended to be dominated by one state. The stakeholders of the current Western order include a coalition of powers arrayed around the United States—an important distinction. These leading states, most of them advanced liberal democracies, do not always agree, but they are engaged in a continuous process of give-and-take over economics, politics, and security. Power transitions are typically seen as being played out between two countries, a rising state and a declining hegemon, and the order falls as soon as the power balance shifts. But in the current order, the larger aggregation of democratic capitalist states—and the resulting accumulation of geopolitical power—shifts the balance in the order's favor.

Third, the postwar Western order has an unusually dense, encompassing, and broadly endorsed system of rules and institutions. Whatever its shortcomings, it is more open and rule-based than any previous order. State sovereignty and the rule of law are not just norms enshrined in the United Nations Charter. They are part of the deep operating logic of the order. To be sure, these norms are evolving, and the United States itself has historically been ambivalent about binding itself to international law and institutions—and at no time more so than today. But the overall system is dense with multilateral rules and institutions—global and regional, economic, political, and security-related. These represent one of the great breakthroughs of the postwar era. They have laid the basis for unprecedented levels of cooperation and shared authority over the global system.

The incentives these features create for China to integrate into the liberal international order are reinforced by the changed nature of the international economic environment—especially the new interdependence driven by technology. The most farsighted Chinese leaders understand that globalization has changed the game and that China accordingly needs strong, prosperous partners around the world. From the United States' perspective, a healthy Chinese economy is vital to the United States and the rest of the world. Technology and the global economic revolution have created a logic of economic relations that is different from the past—making the political and institutional logic of the current order all the more powerful.

Accommodating the Rise

The most important benefit of these features today is that they give the Western order a remarkable capacity to accommodate rising powers. New entrants into the system have ways of gaining status and authority and opportunities to play a role in governing the order. The fact that the United States, China, and other great powers have nuclear weapons also limits the ability of a rising power to overturn the existing order. In the age of nuclear deterrence, great-power war is, thankfully, no longer a mechanism of historical change. War-driven change has been abolished as a historical process.

The Western order's strong framework of rules and institutions is already starting to facilitate Chinese integration. At first, China embraced certain rules and institutions for defensive purposes: protecting its sovereignty and economic interests while seeking to reassure other states of its peaceful intentions by getting involved in regional and global groupings. But as the scholar Marc Lanteigne argues, "What separates China from other states, and indeed previous global powers, is that not only is it 'growing up' within a milieu of international institutions far more developed than ever before, but more importantly, it is doing so while making active use of these institutions to promote the country's development of global power status." China, in short, is increasingly working within, rather than outside of, the Western order.

China is already a permanent member of the UN Security Council, a legacy of Roosevelt's determination to build the universal body around diverse great-power leadership. This gives China the same authority and advantages of "great-power exceptionalism" as the other permanent members. The existing global trading system is also valuable to China, and increasingly so. Chinese economic interests are quite congruent with the current global economic system—a system that is open and loosely institutionalized and that China has enthusiastically embraced and thrived in. State power today is ultimately based on sustained economic growth, and China is well aware that no major state can modernize without integrating into the globalized capitalist system; if a country wants to be a world power, it has no choice but to join the World Trade Organization (WTO). The road to global power, in effect, runs through the Western order and its multilateral economic institutions.

China not only needs continued access to the global capitalist system; it also wants the protections that the system's rules and institutions provide. The WTO's multilateral trade principles and dispute-settlement mechanisms, for example, offer China tools to defend against the threats of discrimination and protectionism that rising economic powers often confront. The evolution of China's policy suggests that Chinese leaders recognize these advantages: as Beijing's growing commitment to economic liberalization has increased the foreign investment and trade China has enjoyed, so has Beijing increasingly embraced global trade rules. It is possible that as China comes to champion the WTO, the support of the more mature Western economies for the WTO will wane. But it is more likely that both the rising and the declining countries will find value in the quasi-legal mechanisms that allow conflicts to be settled or at least diffused.

The existing international economic institutions also offer opportunities for new powers to rise up through their hierarchies. In the International Monetary Fund and the World Bank, governance is based on economic shares, which growing countries can translate into greater institutional voice. To be sure, the process of adjustment has been slow. The United States and Europe still dominate the IMF. Washington has a 17 percent voting share (down from 30 percent)—a controlling amount, because 85 percent approval is needed for action—and the European Union has a major say in the appointment of ten of the 24 members of the board. But there are growing pressures, notably the need for resources and the need to maintain relevance, that will likely persuade the Western states to admit China into the inner circle of these economic governance institutions. The IMF's existing shareholders, for example, see a bigger role for rising developing countries as necessary to renew the institution and get it through its current crisis of mission. At the IMF's meeting in Singapore in September 2006, they agreed on reforms that will give China, Mexico, South Korea, and Turkey a greater voice.

As China sheds its status as a developing country (and therefore as a client of these institutions), it will increasingly be able to act as a patron and stakeholder instead. Leadership in these organizations is not simply a reflection of economic size (the United States has retained its voting share in the IMF even as its economic weight has declined); nonetheless, incremental advancement within them will create important opportunities for China.

Power Shift and Peaceful Change

Seen in this light, the rise of China need not lead to a volcanic struggle with the United States over global rules and leadership. The Western order has the potential to turn the coming power shift into a peaceful change on terms favorable to the United States. But that will only happen if the United States sets about strengthening the existing order. Today, with Washington preoccupied with terrorism and war in the Middle East, rebuilding Western rules and institutions might to some seem to be of only marginal relevance. Many Bush administration officials have been outright hostile to the multilateral, rule-based system that the United States has shaped and led. Such hostility is foolish and dangerous. China will become powerful: it is already on the rise, and the United States' most powerful strategic weapon is the ability to decide what sort of international order will be in place to receive it.

The United States must reinvest in the Western order, reinforcing the features of that order that encourage engagement, integration, and restraint. The more this order binds together capitalist democratic states in deeply rooted institutions; the more open, consensual, and rule-based it is; and the more widely spread its benefits, the more likely it will be that rising powers can and will secure their interests through integration and accommodation rather than through war. And if the Western system offers rules and institutions that benefit the full range of states—rising and falling, weak and strong, emerging and mature—its dominance as an international order is all but certain.

The first thing the United States must do is reestablish itself as the foremost supporter of the global system of governance that underpins the Western order. Doing so will first of all facilitate the kind of collective problem solving that makes all countries better off. At the same time, when other countries see the United States using its power to strengthen existing rules and institutions, that power is rendered more legitimate—and U.S. authority is strengthened. Countries within the West become more inclined to work with, rather than resist, U.S. power, which reinforces the centrality and dominance of the West itself.

Renewing Western rules and institutions will require, among other things, updating the old bargains that underpinned key postwar security pacts. The strategic understanding behind both NATO and Washington's East Asian alliances is that the United States will work with its allies to provide security and bring them in on decisions over the use of force, and U.S. allies, in return, will operate within the U.S.-led Western order. Security cooperation in the West remains extensive today, but with the main security threats less obvious than they were during the Cold War, the purposes and responsibilities of these alliances are under dispute. Accordingly, the United States needs to reaffirm the political value of these alliances—recognizing that they are part of a wider Western institutional architecture that allows states to do business with one another.

The United States should also renew its support for wide-ranging multilateral institutions. On the economic front, this would include building on the agreements and architecture of the WTO, including pursuing efforts to conclude the current Doha Round of trade talks, which seeks to extend market opportunities and trade liberalization to developing countries. The WTO is at a critical stage. The basic standard of nondiscrimination is at risk thanks to the proliferation of bilateral and regional trade agreements. Meanwhile, there are growing doubts over whether the WTO can in fact carry out trade liberalization, particularly in agriculture,that benefits developing countries. These issues may seem narrow, but the fundamental character of the liberal international order—its commitment to universal rules of openness that spread gains widely—is at stake. Similar doubts haunt a host of other multilateral agreements—on global warming and nuclear nonproliferation, among others—and they thus also demand renewed U.S. leadership.

The strategy here is not simply to ensure that the Western order is open and rule-based. It is also to make sure that the order does not fragment into an array of bilateral and "minilateral" arrangements, causing the United States to find itself tied to only a few key states in various regions. Under such a scenario, China would have an opportunity to build its own set of bilateral and "minilateral" pacts. As a result, the world would be broken into competing U.S. and Chinese spheres. The more security and economic relations are multilateral and all-encompassing, the more the global system retains its coherence.

In addition to maintaining the openness and durability of the order, the United States must redouble its efforts to integrate rising developing countries into key global institutions. Bringing emerging countries into the governance of the international order will give it new life. The United States and Europe must find room at the table not only for China but also for countries such as Brazil, India, and South Africa. A Goldman Sachs report on the so-called BRICS (Brazil, Russia, India, and China) noted that by 2050 these countries' economies could together be larger than those of the original G-6 countries (Germany, France, Italy, Japan, the United Kingdom, and the United States) combined. Each international institution presents its own challenges. The un Security Council is perhaps the hardest to deal with, but its reform would also bring the greatest returns. Less formal bodies—the so-called G-20 and various other intergovernmental networks—can provide alternative avenues for voice and representation.

The Triumph of the Liberal Order

THE KEY thing for U.S. leaders to remember is that it may be possible for China to overtake the United States alone, but it is much less likely that China will ever manage to overtake the Western

Projections of GDP, 2005–30

at Purchasing Power Parity in U.S. Dollars (trillions)

	China	U.S.	OECD
2005	9	12	34
2010	14	17	44
2015	21	22	55
2020	30	28	73
2025	44	37	88
2030	63	49	105

sources: OECD, Economist Intelligence Unit.

order. In terms of economic weight, for example, China will surpass the United States as the largest state in the global system sometime around 2020. (Because of its population, China needs a level of productivity only one-fifth that of the United States to become the world's biggest economy.) But when the economic capacity of the Western system as a whole is considered, China's economic advances look much less significant; the Chinese economy will be much smaller than the combined economies of the Organization for Economic Cooperation and Development far into the future. This is even truer of military might: China cannot hope to come anywhere close to total OECD military expenditures anytime soon. The capitalist democratic world is a powerful constituency for the preservation—and, indeed, extension—of the existing international order. If China intends to rise up and challenge the existing order, it has a much more daunting task than simply confronting the United States.

The "unipolar moment" will eventually pass. U.S. dominance will eventually end. U.S. grand strategy, accordingly, should be driven by one key question: What kind of international order would the United States like to see in place when it is less powerful?

This might be called the neo-Rawlsian question of the current era. The political philosopher John Rawls argued that political institutions should be conceived behind a "veil of ignorance"—that is, the architects should design institutions as if they do not know precisely where they will be within a socioeconomic system. The result would be a system that safeguards a person's interests regardless of whether he is rich or poor, weak or strong. The United States needs to take that approach to its leadership of the international order today. It must put in place institutions and fortify rules that will safeguard its interests regardless of where exactly in the hierarchy it is or how exactly power is distributed in 10, 50, or 100 years.

Projections of Defense Expenditures, 2003–30

in U.S. Dollars (billions)*

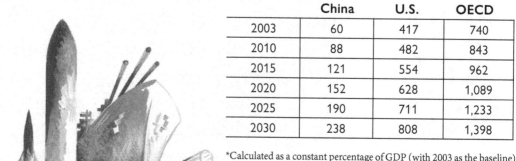

	China	U.S.	OECD
2003	60	417	740
2010	88	482	843
2015	121	554	962
2020	152	628	1,089
2025	190	711	1,233
2030	238	808	1,398

*Calculated as a constant percentage of GDP (with 2003 as the baseline), using OECD and Economist Intelligence Unit GDP projections.

Fortunately, such an order is in place already. The task now is to make it so expansive and so institutionalized that China has no choice but to become a full-fledged member of it. The United States cannot thwart China's rise, but it can help ensure that China's power is exercised within the rules and institutions that the United States and its partners have crafted over the last century, rules and institutions that can protect the interests of all states in the more crowded world of the future. The United States' global position may be weakening, but the international system the United States leads can remain the dominant order of the twenty-first century.

DISCUSSION QUESTIONS

1. How would you summarize the main argument of the article in a sentence or two?

2. How was the United States' behavior as the major rising power in post WWII different from such historical episodes?

3. What does the motto "The road to the West runs through the West" mean?

4. According to Ikenberry, what are the important factors to watch during international power transition?

5. Given the rise of China's power, what does John Ikenberry advise for the United States?

6. Why do some political scientists like John Mearsheimer think that the United States and China are likely to engage in an intense security competition with considerable potential for war?

China's Belt and Road Initiative

A Strategy to Sustain its Global Dominance?

By Shwetha Kumari

··

Case Study

"I think it's two things. First, it's more evidence of China's rising role in the global economy so China has launched these various big initiatives. One's the Asia Infrastructure Investment Bank, and now we have One Belt, One Road. But it's really about connectivity." "... it's about connecting or reinvigorating all of these old trade routes that have existed for quite a long time and let's be honest the Chinese have demonstrated they're very good infrastructure so building out various rail lines, freight lines, ports, dry ports, et cetera—this is something where you know China could naturally take the lead in this part of the world."[1]

—Paul Gruenwald, S&P Global Chief Economist —Asia Pacific

The 'Belt and Road Initiative' (BRI), launched by China's President Xi Jinping (Jinping) in September 2013, aimed to expand and advance China with the rest of Asia, the Middle East, Africa and Europe. The initiative envisaged the creation of multiple economic corridors under the Silk Road Economic Belt and the 21st Century Maritime Silk Road, which were the two main division of BRI initiative. Nearly 65 countries that accounted for 62% of the world's population and 30% of its economic output, agreed to cooperate in the BRI projects. It aimed to foster industrial development not only in the developing nations of Asia and Africa, but also developed countries.

"... The Initiative is an ambitious economic vision of the opening-up of and cooperation among the countries along the Belt and Road. Countries should work in concert and move toward the objectives of mutual benefit and common security. To be specific, they need to improve the region's infrastructure, and put in place a secure and efficient network of land, sea and air passages, lifting their connectivity to a higher level; further enhance trade and investment facilitation, establish a network of free trade areas that meet high standards, maintain closer economic ties, and deepen political trust; enhance cultural exchanges; encourage different civilizations to learn from each other and flourish together; and promote mutual understanding, peace and friendship among people of all countries", noted the State Council of China, who further added, "The Belt and Road Initiative is a

Shwetha Kumari, "China's Belt and Road Initiative: A Strategy to Sustain its Global Dominance?" pp. 1-16. Copyright © 2017 by Amity Research Centers. Reprinted with permission by The Case Centre.

way for win-win cooperation that promotes common development and prosperity and a road toward peace and friendship by enhancing mutual understanding and trust, and strengthening all-around exchanges. The Chinese government advocates peace and cooperation, openness and inclusiveness, mutual learning and mutual benefit. It promotes practical cooperation in all fields, and works to build a community of shared interests, destiny and responsibility featuring mutual political trust, economic integration and cultural inclusiveness."[2]

On speaking about China's benefit from the BRI, Benjamin Habib (Habib) and Viktor Faulknor (Faulknor) from La Trobe University stated in their article, "BRI projects are likely to increase China's economic and political leverage as a creditor." "The BRI has been viewed as a way for China to productively use its enormous, $3 trillion capital reserves, internationalise the renminbi, and deal with structural issues as its economy navigates the so-called 'new normal" of lower growth", added Habib and Faulknor.[3]

"At first glance, given the massive scope of the B&R initiative, there appears to be an abundance of opportunities across several sectors for foreign companies to bring their worldclass expertise. These are attractive projects not only because they have significant Chinese financing but also because they are being driven by Chinese SOEs, which enjoy strong political support, helping address potential political and financial risks. Furthermore, the B&R's association with global funding entities such as the World Bank and the Asian Development Bank (ADB) further demonstrates its much-emphasised commercial focus. Some foreign companies are already reaping benefits from involvement in the B&R initiative, such as General Electric, whose orders from Chinese EPC companies increased threefold last year", noted PWC report while talking about opportunities for foreign multinational companies from BRI project.[4]

On the flipside, many countries had always been suspicious of China's intentions through BRI project. They don't consider the project as a boon. One of them was India. "... The Indian government has expressed reservations over the BRI's China-Pakistan Economic Corridor and China's Indian Ocean ambitions," opined Habib and Faulknor.[5] China expert Tom Miller alleged 'parts of it could be described as a "giant bribe" in which China promises investment in exchange for political concessions'.[6]

Clyde Prestowitz, President of the Economic Strategy Institute, a Washington-based think tank, stated, "On one hand it will be a way of handling China's excess capacity and continue to create jobs with investment in China. Secondly, it creates a kind of a zone of influence for China." As of 2017, the country had vowed to invest more than $100 billion in BRI, which included 'the $46 billion China-Pakistan corridor and a high-speed railway connecting China and Singapore'. "But, there are risks that come with China extending such huge credit lines", opined Bianca Mascarenhas.[7]

Various economists from Oxford Economics opined, "The initiative can also increase China's international influence by providing a platform for it to enhance its role in global financial governance, and eventually help the internationalisation of the yuan."[8] The PWC report affirmed that, "... This is an exciting time of development not only for China and all those countries along the Belt and Road, but for the world."[9] Amidst this backdrop, it remained to be seen whether China be able to reinforce its economic and political influence globally through BRI initiative.

Belt and Road Initiative: Connecting the World with China

China's Global Dominance

The People's Republic of China (China), the second largest economy, robust growth genesis began in 1950 during the agrarian reform, which offered infrastructure, land, credits and technical support to hundreds of millions of landless and poor farmers, and landless rural workers. Subsequently, during this period, roads, airfields, bridges, canals, railroads and also the basic industries were built by the government. Consequently, this became the backbone of the modern Chinese economy.[10] Another reason which engendered China's excellent prosperity was its decision to open up to the international market and move out of the Soviet province of influence. This concreted the way for the country to the Western world and other parts of the world. China, finally, revised its system of political economy to a precise unique system of private enterprise market economy. This strategy was politically and economically successful for China and other part of world in trade, commerce and international peace.[11]

Phoenix Weekly[12] asserted, "As China's global impact increases, its influence in the developing world is also growing, particularly in Africa and Latin America." "The overall comparison of China's ties to Latin America and Africa is interesting for a number of reasons. First, both of these regions fit into China's formal diplomatic framework as 'developing country' regions and as such are a high priority for Chinese diplomats and foreign policy thinkers. This is because China has revived an old interest from Mao-era diplomacy in being a leader of the 'Third World.' Today this is most clearly expressed in China's efforts to promote South-South relations, in particular with both Africa and Latin America," noted Matt Ferchen (Ferchen), Non-resident Scholar at Carnegie-Tsinghua Center for Global Policy.[13]

Isaac Stone Fish (Isaac), Senior Fellow at Asia Society's Center on U.S. —China Relations, averred that, "China, over the last decade or so, has been prioritizing bilateral and multilateral relations, rather than alliances." Further, Isaac mentioned, "Beijing is not only accepting warmer greetings from nations that feel spurned by the United States; it is actively trying to coerce America's allies to distance themselves from China to assert its power." Ely Ratner, ex-deputy National Security Advisor at the Council on Foreign Relations, opined, "In Asia, we're seeing a region that's equally afraid of being subject to Chinese retaliation as a region fleeing from Donald Trump. I wouldn't underestimate the former." Further, Isaac stated, "In a June 2012 conversation, a high-ranking Chinese diplomat told me Beijing doesn't believe in alliances. Rather, it sees relationships, including with the United States, in bilateral terms. The diplomat said two countries are like neighbors. As Beijing's plants keeps growing —China now has legitimate political and economic interests and entanglements in almost every country in the world —Washington should recognize that new reality and gracefully yield, the diplomat told me.

"Beijing is providing frameworks for all these nations to plug into a Chinese world order. The most prominent is 'One Belt, One Road,' Chinese President Xi Jinping's signature trade initiative, which seeks to recreate the old Silk Road trading routes, with China once again at the center of the world's economy," Isaac added.[14] In 2013, Chinese President Xi Jinping (Jinping) announced its most ambitious economic project called Belt and Road Initiative (BRI).[15]

China's Belt and Road Initiative

The BRI project was formally unveiled by Jinping in September 2013 during his speech at a university in Kazakhstan. He used the platform to call for the formation of a 'Silk Road Economic Belt'.[16] The Ministry of Foreign Affairs of China website mentioned, "Xi Jinping expressed that more than 2100 years ago, during China's Western Han Dynasty (206 BC-AD 24), imperial envoy Zhang Qian was sent to Central Asia twice to open the door to friendly contacts between China and Central Asian countries as well as the transcontinental Silk Road linking East and West, Asia and Europe. Kazakhstan, as a major stop along the ancient Silk Road, has made important contributions to the exchanges and cooperation between different nationalities and cultures. People in regional countries created the history of friendship along the ancient Silk Road through the ages." Further, the website noted, "Xi Jinping proposed that in order to make the economic ties closer, mutual cooperation deeper and space of development broader between the Eurasian countries, we can innovate the mode of cooperation and jointly build the 'Silk Road Economic Belt' step by step to gradually form overall regional cooperation."[17]

The BRI, a most ambitious foreign and economic project, was Jinping's pet project. The aim of the project was to reinforce China's economic leadership through a wide number of programs of infrastructure building throughout its neighbouring regions.[18]

"China's Belt and Road Initiative (BRI) is a multifaceted economic, diplomatic and geopolitical undertaking that has morphed through various iterations, from the 'New Silk Road' to 'One Belt One Road'. ... First proposed in September 2013, it is the signature foreign policy initiative of Chinese President Xi Jinping. It is a project of unprecedented geographical and financial scope", said Habib and Faulknor.[19] The BRI project of China was open to all the countries, but it had identified 65 nations along the Belt and Road that would participate in BRI project. Together these 64 countries plus China accounted for 62% of the world's population and 30% of its economic output.[20]

The BRI project constituted two components, namely, the Silk Road Economic Belt above land and the 21st Century Maritime Silk Road, which was a chain of ports and railways. Together, the initiative encompasses over 60 countries and 4.4 billion people, passing through Asia, Europe, Africa and the Middle East, covering up approximately 40% of global GDP.[21] (Figure 1.2). By the BRI project, China envisioned building trade routes between China and the countries in Central Asia, Southeast Asia

FIGURE 1.2 Belt and Road Initiative

Source: Mascarenhas Bianca, "Here's why China's 'Belt and Road' initiative is risky—think tanker", https://www.cnbc.com/2017/07/18/heres-why-chinas-belt-and-road-initiative-is-risky-think-tanker-says.html, July 18th 2017

and through Europe.[22] Further, through the BRI initiative, China aimed to build the world's biggest platform for economic collaboration and assistantships, including trade and financing collaboration, policy coordination, and social and cultural cooperation.[23]

At the Peripheral Diplomacy Work Conference, Jinping stated that, "China's neighbors had extremely significant strategic value", due to which he wanted "to improve relations between China and its neighbours, strengthening economic ties and deepening security cooperation." "Maintaining stability in China's neighbourhood is the key objective of peripheral diplomacy. We must encourage and participate in the process of regional economic integration, speed up the process of building up infrastructure and connectivity. We must build the Silk Road Economic Belt and 21st Century Maritime Silk Road, creating a new regional economic order," mentioned Jinping.[24]

Michal Meidan (Meidan), Founder and Director of consultancy China Matters and an Associate Fellow at London-based think tank Chatham House, alleged, "The drivers for OBOR are multiple." "Firstly, China needs to export its overcapacity in heavy industry. Secondly, investing in infrastructure links in Asia and Eurasia potentially offers better returns on China's large foreign exchange reserves than T-bills from the United States. Thirdly, OBOR acts as a counter to the U.S.-led Trans-Pacific Partnership, placing China at the heart of Asian and Eurasian economic integration," noted Meidan.[25]

China had considerable objectives to promote its BRI project. Simeon Djankov (Simeon), Non-resident Senior Fellow at the Peterson Institute for International Economics, noted in his paper titled, 'The Rationale Behind China's Belt and Road Initiative', that, "As the world's biggest trading nation, China's main interest is to reduce the costs of transporting goods. Projects that are already funded under the initiative all report statistics on how much travel time and cost will be reduced as a result of their completion. Because such improvements will affect all cargo using these transport routes, they will benefit world trade. The success of the Belt and Road Initiative is thus of interest to countries beyond the designated Silk Road routes, as their exporters will also use the upgraded infrastructure." In addition to decreasing trade costs, there were four other rationales behind the initiative. First, China was trying to reduce its economic dependence on its national infrastructure investment and the related growth that came with such investment. It meant that Chinese construction companies, equipment makers, and other businesses that had been ripping the benefit of the country's building boom had to look outside China for opportunities. Main objective was to find opportunities for these firms abroad. China expected that its own firm would plan, construct and supply the projects the BRI. Second, focus on infrastructure could help China in its pursuit of superior international stature for its currency—the renminbi, to ultimately accomplish the status of a global reserve currency. Third goal for the BRI was to secure its energy supply via new pipelines in Central Asia, Russia, and Southeast Asia's deepwater ports, as energy sufficiency had been persistent worry for Chinese companies. Fourth goal was infrastructure development in nations along the Belt and Road routes that could increase growth in their economies and consequently contribute to an increasing demand for China's goods and services. Simeon emphasised that "In March 2015, China's President Xi Jinping stated that annual trade with the countries along the Belt and Road Initiative would surpass $2.5 trillion by 2025. In smaller countries such as Georgia, projects funded by the initiative may increase annual economic growth by 1.5 percent for the next decade, a considerable boost. Data are not yet sufficient to suggest the extent of this growth effect in other countries, but the initiative clearly represents an interest in finding work for Chinese construction and equipment companies and their engineers."[26] (Figure 1.3).

The Economist noted in its article, "Behind this broad strategic imperative lie a plethora of secondary motivations —and it is the number and variety of these that prompts scepticism about the coherence and practicality of the project. By investing in infrastructure, Mr Xi hopes to find a more profitable home for China's vast foreign-exchange reserves, most of which are in low-interest-bearing American government securities. He also hopes to create new markets for Chinese companies, such as high-speed rail firms, and to export some of his country's vast excess capacity in cement, steel and other metals. By investing in volatile countries in central Asia, he reckons he can create a more stable neighbourhood for China's own restive western provinces of Xinjiang and Tibet. And by encouraging more Chinese projects around the South China Sea, the initiative could bolster China's claims in that area (the "road" in "belt and road" refers to sea lanes)."[27]

Primary Goals	Additional Strategic Goals
❖ **Increase exports and facilitate trade** • Trade between China and Belt & Road countries have exceeded US$916bn in 2016, which is 25.9% of China's total foreign trade volume • Chinese companies have since established over 70 overseas economic and trade cooperation zones	❖ **Establish global infrastructure capability** • Jakarta–Bandung high speed railway, the Hungarian–Serbian Railway, the hydropower extension project and construction of a national motorway in Pakistan, and the Carmel Tunnel project in Israel • Chinese SOEs are taking up main contractor roles in Belt and Road projects
❖ **Address surplus in industrial capacity** • China has surplus industrial output which can be beneficially utilised along the B&R • The Asian Development Bank (ADB) forecasts 580mn tonnes of cement is needed yearly for infrastructure projects in Asia alone, which is a quarter of China's output • Construction of railways, pipelines and other projects along the B&R trade route may create demand for 272mn tonnes of steel	❖ **Internationalise currency and diversify currency risks** • In line with China's 'Go Out' outbound investment policy, and massive funding of B&R projects by China • China has conducted Renminbi (RMB) bilateral swap agreements with nations that stretch new Silk Routes • Expands circulation of RMB and internationalises its currencies
❖ **Enhance geopolitical relations** • Over 100 countries and international bodies are already participating in B&R, 50 co-operation agreements have been signed between governments, as of March 2017, >20 nations are co-operating on industrial projects • For bigger countries, B&R enhances relationships • For smaller developing countries, B&R is a 'defining feature of bilateral ties with China' and a 'crucial trigger for trade and investment'	❖ **A part of China's economic reform** • Aligns with China's overall development policies to 'set up development-oriented financial institutions so as to form a new pattern of all round opening' • Transition away from traditional manufacturing capacity • Form a community of mutual interests

FIGURE 1.3 China's Rationale for the Belt and Road Initiative

Source: "Repaving the ancient Silk Routes", https://www.pwc.com/sg/en/publications/assets/gmc-repaving-the-ancient-silk-routes-2017.pdf, June 2017

The initiative was backed by substantial financial investments in infrastructure such as rail, airports, roads, ports, pipelines, and communications. The country had committed itself to allocate $1.4 trillion to the initiative that would leverage varieties of private finance to base the bill for building and servicing the infrastructure.[28]

During 2014, China formed the $40 billion Silk Road fund to finance these projects. However, these projects were only the beginning as BRI entered a new stage of lucid and comprehensive development. This initiative led to the development of six largest economic corridors, including the New Eurasian Land Bridge, China-Mongolia-Russia, China-Central Asia-Western Asia, Indo-China Peninsula, China-Pakistan, and Bangladesh-China-India-Myanmar. These economic corridors could be sites of energy and industrial clusters and formed through the use of rail, roads, waterways, air, pipelines, and information highways. Tian Jinchen, the Director of the Western Development Department of China's National Development and Reform Commission noted, "By both connecting and enhancing the productivity of countries along the new Silk Road, China hopes the benefits of cooperation can be shared and that the circle of friendship will be strengthened and expanded."[29]

Moreover, China also promised an additional funding by three different sources. These funding sources included the state-owned Silk Road Fund, which had invested about $40 billion of initial capital in 2015. Also, two Chinese policy banks—the China Development Bank and the Export and Import Bank of China, provided fund for various BRI projects. Further, two Chinese-based multilateral organisations, namely, Asian Infrastructure Investment Bank (AIIB), and the Shanghai-based New Development Bank, financed BRI project. In 2016 alone, AIIB sanctioned $1.7 billion in loans to nine development projects along the Belt and Road. The country's lenders were also in full support of financing the new Silk Road plan. Zhou Xiaochuan (Xiaochuan), Governor of the Chinese central bank, assured to help national banks fund more BRI projects in future. Xiaochuan added that, "China is also seeking financial cooperation with other OBOR nations, as its own resources are limited."[30]

However, despite China's substantial investments, the scale of the BRI initiative and the related financing requirements surpassed the required level of funding. Subsequently, BRI project leaders had been promoting BRI project and pursing foreign investors to invest. Rashid Gaissin, Head of Eurasian Legal Practice Partner at PwC Kazakhstan, alleged, "Given the scale of Belt and Road and projected massive spending that will potentially dominate global infrastructure spending, it is increasingly unlikely for foreign companies to remain uninvolved." Besides funding, the Chinese leaders had sought overseas partnerships to access new technologies and equipment, expertise, management and operational experience in managing likewise large scale, complex infrastructure projects.[31]

The PwC report averted that 'the value of newly announced projects has been flattening, going up just 2.1% in 2016 from the earlier year to about $400 billion. And M&A deals in 2016 fell 49%

in dollar value from the previous year, citing stricter capital controls amid a weakening yuan.'[32] (Figure 1.4).

Nevertheless, as contemplated, the BRI initiative had made various hands on achievements. China signed a bilateral cooperation pact related to BRI projects with Hungary, Tajikistan, Mongolia, Turkey and Russia. A series of projects were also under way, such as a train connection from eastern China to Iran that could be further expanded to Europe. Further there were new railway links as well with Laos and Thailand and high-speed railway initiatives in Indonesia. Also, Ningbo Shipping Exchange of China partnered 'with the Baltic Exchange on a container index of rates between China and the Middle East, the Mediterranean, and Europe'. As expected, over 200 enterprises singed cooperation pacts for BRI projects along BRI routes.[33]

The Guardian news report stated in its article, "Beijing has championed a number of achievements, foremost among them the $62 billion China-Pakistan economic corridor (CPEC), a sprawling web of motorways, power plants, wind farms, factories and railways, that supporters say will spark an 'economic revolution' and create up to one million jobs in Pakistan. Other high-profile schemes include a $1.1 billion port project in Sri Lanka, a high-speed rail link in Indonesia and an industrial park in Cambodia."[34]

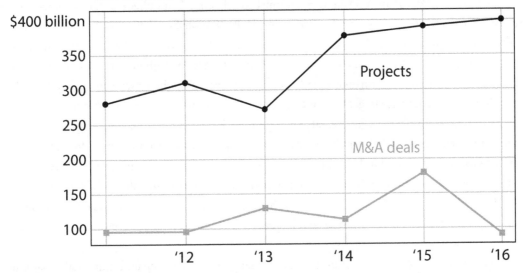

FIGURE 1.4 Infrastructure Investment in Belt and Road Initiatives Countries

Source: Huang Zheping, "ONE BELT, ONE ROAD –Your guide to understanding OBOR, China's new Silk Road plan", https://qz.com/983460/obor-an-extremely-simple-guide-to-understanding-chinas-one-belt-one-road-forum-for-its-new-silk-road/, May 15th 2015

Is BRI an Over-Ambitious Project for China?

Opportunities

"The Belt and Road initiative is in China's interest, and also in the interest of the rest of the world," said Daniel Rosen (Rosen), Founding Partner of US consulting firm Rhodium Group. Rosen further added, "... initiative could not only benefit countries that lag behind China in the development process, but also advanced economies as well. For the advanced economies, China has strategically decided to deploy its resources in this manner ... not fighting over an existing pie, but rather adding to the size of the pie by putting a lot of money to work around the world."[35]

Frank Lyn, Markets Leader, PwC China and Hong Kong, stated, "In many ways, the initiative serves as a blueprint for how China wants to further connect itself into the global economy and strengthen its influence in the region. The initiative has added fresh impetus to China and the rest of the world to promote regional cooperation and presented numerous opportunities for foreign and Chinese companies to be involved. It is a driver for long term growth and expansion as well as corporate profitability. Therefore, strategically, companies need to be involved at an early stage to reap the long term benefits." "China's One Belt, One Road initiative is one of the government's top priorities and a plan identified closely with President Xi Jinping. It is an ambitious vision coupled with generous government funding and should create business opportunities for foreign companies who can support the plan's objectives. Our members are paying close attention," stated Kenneth Jarrett, President at The American Chamber of Commerce in Shanghai.[36]

Nick Marro (Marro), an Analyst at Economist Intelligence Unit, alleged, "China is looking to use OBOR as a way to ship its own domestic overproduction offshore." Further Jin-Yong Cai (Cai), ex-head of the International Finance Corporation, stated, "The project will also open new markets for Chinese goods, shoring up the country's economy against any potential slowdown in demand from Europe or the US." Cai further added, "(China is) leveraging their own capital to get involved in helping (other) countries to get wealthier so they can become customers of Chinese products."

Apart from economic benefits, BRI also had political benefits for China. Christopher Balding, a Professor of Economics at Peking University, alleged, "The project is more like a diplomatic effort for China to win friends and influence people, rather than a strictly economic program." As per Tom Miller (Miller), the author of 'China's Asian Dream: Empire Building along the New Silk Road', "OBOR is part of a plan by China focused on 'restoring its historical status as Asia's dominant power'. China's new 'empire' will be an informal and largely economic one, posited on cash and held together by hard infrastructure."[37]

However, besides reinforcing China's economy, geopolitical standing and industrial capabilities, the BRI project was vital for infrastructure development in various least developed countries in the world and at the same time, driving economic growth through encouraging trade and creating domestic jobs. The BRI project's infrastructure investments could affect minimum two-thirds of the world's population, as the 65 nations along its main routes had approximately total population of 4.4 billion. As these developing countries had young working populations, the BRI project had great potential for creating a huge number of jobs. Further, the BRI project could also resolve the problem of financing by providing a tool to mitigate the considerable financing needs in developing and least developed nations in the world along its routes.[38]

"The global response to OBOR has been guardedly positive. With more than 50 countries joining the AIIB, one of the main financial platforms for facilitating OBOR, there is much enthusiasm among Western and non-Western countries for the initiative and the opportunities it may create," wrote The East West Bank.[39]

Numerous nations who were part of BRI projects had several grim necessities. According to ADB, the emerging Asian nations were in need of $1.7 trillion every year in infrastructure to retain growth, tackle poverty and combat climate change. In Kenya, China stepped up to upgrade a railway from the port of Mombasa to Nairobi, which could make it easier to bring Chinese products into the nation The Kenyan administration had failed to convince others to help them in bettering their infrastructure, while China had been 'transforming crumbling infrastructure in Africa for more than a decade'.[40]

"China's Belt and Road initiative has the potential to accelerate economic growth and development in neighbouring countries. The ten nations of the Association of Southeast Asian Nations (ASEAN), for example, will see their collective urban population expand by 20,000 people every day for the next ten years, creating significant demands for new infrastructure. The Belt & Road initiative is well placed to support that process," said Justin Wood Head of Asia Pacific Member of the Executive Committee, World Economic Forum. The PWC report found out that, "According to World Bank estimates, Africa requires US$38bn for infrastructure financing annually, and a further US$37bn annually in operations and maintenance, which is about 12% of its GDP. Currently, the funding gap remains substantial at US$35bn, and therefore Africa has welcomed China's investments to partially fill this gap. China's significant funding and its willingness to venture into the risky and volatile market environments of developing countries have been welcomed by most countries in need. In Southeast Asia, China has begun work on a planned US$23bn investment in railways in order to connect Kunming with Singapore."[41] (Figure 1.5).

In May 2017 at the Belt and Road Forum (BRF), Jinping declared in his keynote speech that, "China will endeavor to build a win-win business partnership with other countries participating in the Belt and Road Initiative, enhance trade and investment facilitation with them, and build a Belt and Road free trade network. These efforts are designed to promote growth both in our respective regions and globally. During this forum, China will sign business and trade cooperation agreements with over 30 countries and enter into consultation on free trade agreements with related countries. China will host the China International Import Expo starting from 2018. China will enhance cooperation on innovation with other countries. We will launch the Belt and Road Science, Technology and Innovation Cooperation Action Plan, which consists of the Science and Technology People-to-People

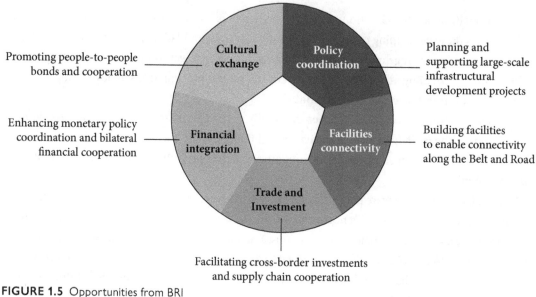

FIGURE 1.5 Opportunities from BRI

Source: "Belt and Road Basics", https://beltandroad.hktdc.com/en/belt-and-road-basics

Exchange Initiative, the Joint Laboratory Initiative, the Science Park Cooperation Initiative and the Technology Transfer Initiative. In the coming five years, we will offer 2,500 short-term research visits to China for young foreign scientists, train 5,000 foreign scientists, engineers and managers, and set up 50 joint laboratories. We will set up a big data service platform on ecological and environmental protection. We propose the establishment of an international coalition for green development on the Belt and Road, and we will provide support to related countries in adapting to climate change."

"In the coming three years, China will provide assistance worth RMB 60 billion to developing countries and international organizations participating in the Belt and Road Initiative to launch more projects to improve people's well-being. We will provide emergency food aid worth RMB 2 billion to developing countries along the Belt and Road and make an additional contribution of US$1 billion to the Assistance Fund for South-South Cooperation. China will launch 100 "happy home" projects, 100 poverty alleviation projects and 100 health care and rehabilitation projects in countries along the Belt and Road. China will provide relevant international organizations with US$1 billion to implement cooperation projects that will benefit the countries along the Belt and Road," added Jinping at the BRF.[42]

Miller alleged, "China's Belt and Road initiative is starting to deliver useful infrastructure, bringing new trade routes and better connectivity to Asia and Europe. But Xi will struggle to persuade skeptical countries that the initiative is not a smokescreen for strategic control."[43]

Underlying Issues and Challenges

"Despite these attractions, the complexity of these transcontinental B&R projects, which are planned to last many years and involve multiple stakeholders from several countries, brings a number of challenges which heighten the risks of delays or even the cancellation of projects. These projects are more complex than any other developing market's infrastructure project. For example, work on the Jakarta-Bandung railway has stalled temporarily halfway due to some paperwork that remains to be completed and some issues that needed to be resolved," reported PwC.[44]

"A major issue for the scaling-up of financing for infrastructure as well as for industrial projects in the framework of the Belt and Road initiative are the limits to debt financing, particularly financing in foreign currencies, be it US$, Euro or Renminbi. A number of countries eligible for Belt and Road investments have reached limits to indebtedness. The high indebtedness of regions in China, due to their rapid scaling up of infrastructure investments—albeit mainly in local currency—is a warning signal. Private investments will probably not flow into countries which face the danger of debt crises. The limits to debt finance can be a binding constraint for Belt and Road investments ...," mentioned Peter Wolff (Wolff) from German Development Institute in 2016 annual meeting of the Asian development bank report.

Another critical issue was the massive development costs for BRI projects. "The large number of additional shovel ready projects in the regions of the Belt and Road to be financed in the short to medium-term does simply not exist. Sources for financing project development, to be financed either through public grants or through equity, are rather scarce ...," noted Wolff.[45]

"A transnational B&R project is exposed to uneven economic development across B&R countries, with varying degrees of 'trade openness', different political environments, regulations, operating standards and cultural differences. Security threats as a result of strife, conflicts and terrorism compound matters. Furthermore, given the length of each project, it is likely that different governments will be in power during its lifespan, which may have differing policies towards foreign investments, resulting in delays due to renegotiations midproject," mentioned PwC report.[46]

Further, although opportunities for foreign firms in BRI projects were copious, overseas firms was at the risk, especially from a geopolitical, funding and operational viewpoint. David Wijeratne (David), Growth Markets Centre Leader at PwC, noted in his The World Economic Forum article that, "Geopolitical risk takes on an additional facet in B&R projects that often span across many territories, due to the exposure to changes in political regimes and bilateral relations. Furthermore, companies should be cognizant of the funding risk in B&R projects. Aside to financing sources from China, companies also need to be aware of the other sources of funding available. This takes into consideration that many growth markets along the B&R routes have a varied ability to pay back the loans they need. In addition to geopolitical and financing considerations, interested companies ought to remain vigilant in operational planning, even as State Owned Enterprises (SOEs) from both China and the host countries are starting to gain international experience. Operational risks include gaps

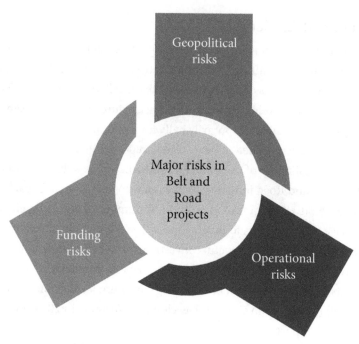

FIGURE 1.6 Challenges in BRI Initiatives

Source: Wijeratne David, "How can we realize the opportunities of China's Belt and Road strategy?", https://www.weforum.org/agenda/2017/05/repaving-the-ancient-silk-routes-realising-opportunities-along-the-belt-and-road/, May 11th 2017

in experience of stakeholders and the increased complexity of B&R transnational projects which result in delays or costs overruns. It is true that the B&R initiative holds rich promise, but the risks are sometimes accentuated and unique."[47] (Figure 1.6).

Further, BRI project was criticised due to its massive ambitions and for being unattainable. Moreover, it was also censured on the ground that impact of BRI projects could be enjoyed by other countries that were not part of BRI officially. Furthermore, "For some countries, including BRICS stalwarts like India, the project challenges the current global order, replacing it with a Sino-centric one. Others believe the initiative presents an alternative approach to globalisation in an era where powers like the US seem intent on increasing protectionism and retreating from their global leadership role," mentioned various scholars and analysts on The Conversation article.[48]

Many countries were apprehensive about the BRI project impact. "Others, however, feared that by becoming indebted to Beijing they would become 'economic vassals'. Some countries, such as India, suspect the project is simply a smokescreen China is using to seize strategic control of the Indian Ocean. India's Prime Minister, Narendra Modi, has accused Beijing of trying to 'undermine the sovereignty of other nations' and will shun this week's summit. Many in the west are also wary. Beijing has said 28 heads of state and government leaders will attend Xi's forum but German chancellor Angela Merkel has turned down an invitation and US president Donald Trump is not expected to attend. Only one G7 leader, Italian Prime Minister Paolo Gentiloni, has confirmed," alleged Tom Philips.[49,50]

SOAS China Institute expert Yuka Kobayashi (Yuka) alleged, "While Chinese President Xi Jinping's 2013 speech on the plan has seen it hyped as a 'new strategy', it's actually a 'continuation' of an old idea to assert Chinese political and economic power." Yuka further added, "The initiative is a complex one. It encompasses areas of security and economics and is also China's challenge to US hegemony. It's part and parcel of China trying to assert itself as a rising power and having this influence in power politics commensurate with their status." "The focus on economic is also part of China 'trying to present itself in a palatable way' to others. It's presented as a win-win initiative, with fuzzy Confucian ideals so that is not perceived as threatening for these border regions," noted Yuka.[51]

"It's about making China the dominant country in the region," said Miller. Peter Cai (Peter)[52] stated, it was unquestionable that BRI would have geopolitical repercussion, giving Beijing bigger clout over its neighbours. "It will give China more influence," added Peter.[53]

Jörg Wuttke of the EU Chamber of Commerce in China, cautioned that "the initiative has increasingly been hijacked by Chinese companies, which have used it as an excuse to evade capital controls, smuggling money out of the country by disguising it as international investments and partnerships." Marro noted, "Chinese overseas investment, and the way it is run, is maturing but expressed concerns that the OBOR project is so large, exercising effective supervision over the varying elements may prove difficult."[54]

"The fear that Obor is a vehicle for Beijing to increase its political influence abroad could also create a backlash," opined Tom Hancock[55], who further added, "Australia declined an opportunity to embrace the initiative formally last month—following its ally the US, which has also kept a clear distance. (New Zealand, however, did not have such objections.)" "There is increasing buy-in from other parties but [Beijing] has got to overcome the political minefields," stated David Kelly, Head of Research at China Policy, a Beijing consultancy.[56]

However, David opined, "The B&R initiative is a vast and ambitious undertaking, which foreign companies ought to not ignore as a purely Asian affair, but instead embrace. It is possibly the largest transcontinental infrastructure programme the world has ever known. And it is only just beginning."[57]

Notes

1. "China's One Belt, One Road Initiative: Overview And Implications", https://www.platts.com/podcasts-detail/policy/2017/may/china-belt-road-obor-051617, May 16th 2017 "© 2017, Amity Research Centers HQ, Bangalore. All rights reserved."

2. "Full text: Action plan on the Belt and Road Initiative", http://english.gov.cn/archive/publications/2015/03/30/content_281475080249035.htm, March 30th 2015

3. Habib Benjamin and Faulknor Viktor, "The Belt and Road Initiative: China's vision for globalisation, Beijing-style", https://theconversation.com/the-belt-and-road-initiative-chinas-vision-for-globalisation-beijing-style-77705, May 17th 2017

4. "Repaving the ancient Silk Routes", https://www.pwc.com/sg/en/publications/assets/gmc-repaving-the-ancient-silk-routes-2017.pdf, June 2017

5. "The Belt and Road Initiative: China's vision for globalisation, Beijing-style", op.cit.

6. Craw Victoria, "China's Belt and Road Initiative could redraw the map on global trade", http://www.news.com.au/finance/economy/world-economy/chinas-belt-and-road-initiative-could-redraw-the-map-on-global-trade/news-story/eb752b6332e24ea219e36d0f16742463, July 23rd 2017

7. Mascarenhas Bianca, "Here's why China's 'Belt and Road' initiative is risky—think tanker", https://www.cnbc.com/2017/07/18/heres-why-chinas-belt-and-road-initiative-is-risky-think-tanker-says.html, July 18th 2017

8. Tianjie He and Kuijs Louis, "Initiative backs growth along Belt and Road", http://www.telegraph.co.uk/news/world/china-watch/business/economic-growth-along-belt-and-road/, May 24th 2017

9. "Repaving the ancient Silk Routes", op.cit.

10. Petras James, "China: Rise, Fall and Re-Emergence as a Global Power", http://www.globalresearch.ca/china-rise-fall-and-re-emergence-as-a-global-power/29644, May 17th 2017

11. Kamrany Nake M. and Jiang Frank, "China's Rise to Global Economic Superpower", http://www.huffingtonpost.com/nake-m-kamrany/chinas-rise-to-global-eco_b_6544924.html

12. This magazine covers current affairs and cultural issues and is affiliated with the Phoenix television network founded by mainland-born media tycoon Liu Changle.

13. Ferchen Matt, "Chinese Diplomacy in Latin America and Africa: Not Two Sides of the Same Coin", http://carnegietsinghua.org/2015/03/27/chinese-diplomacy-in-latin-america-and-africa-not-two-sides-of-same-coin-pub-60045, March 27th 2015

14. Fish Isaac Stone, "Is China Becoming the World's Most Likeable Superpower?", https://www.theatlantic.com/international/archive/2017/06/china-jinping-trump-america-first-keqiang/529014/, June 2nd 2017

15. "CPEC: A Corridor of Opportunities", http://www.opf.org.pk/media/1507/cpec-a-corridor-of-opportunities.pdf

16. Phillips Tom, "The $900bn question: What is the Belt and Road initiative?", https://www.theguardian.com/world/2017/may/12/the-900bn-question-what-is-the-belt-and-road-initiative, May 12th 2017

17. "President Xi Jinping Delivers Important Speech and Proposes to Build a Silk Road Economic Belt with Central Asian Countries", http://www.fmprc.gov.cn/mfa_eng/topics_665678/xjpfwzysiesgjtfhshzzfh_665686/t1076334.shtml, September 9th 2013

18. Cai Peter, "Understanding China's Belt And Road Initiative", https://www.lowyinstitute.org/publications/understanding-belt-and-road-initiative, March 22nd 2017

19. "The Belt and Road Initiative: China's vision for globalisation, Beijing-style", op.cit.

20. Huang Zheping, "ONE BELT, ONE ROAD –Your guide to understanding OBOR, China's new Silk Road plan", https://qz.com/983460/obor-an-extremely-simple-guide-to-understanding-chinas-one-belt-one-road-forum-for-its-new-silk-road/, May 15th 2017

21. "China's Belt and Road Initiative could redraw the map on global trade", op.cit.

22. Meltzer Joshua P., "China's One Belt One Road initiative: A view from the United States", https://www.brookings.edu/research/chinas-one-belt-one-road-initiative-a-view-from-the-united-states/, June 19th 2017

23. Jinchen Tian, "'One Belt and One Road': Connecting China and the world", http://www.mckinsey.com/industries/capital-projects-and-infrastructure/our-insights/one-belt-and-one-road-connecting-china-and-the-world, July 2016

24. "Understanding China's Belt And Road Initiative", op.cit.

25. Allen Daniel, "New Opportunities in China's 'One Belt One Road' Initiative", https://www.eastwestbank.com/ReachFurther/News/Article/New-Opportunities-In-Chinas-One-Belt-One-Road-Initiative

26. Djankov Simeon, "The Rationale Behind China's Belt and Road Initiative", http://cdf2000-2016.cdrf.org.cn/uploads/soft/PDF/20160325/17%20The%20Rationale%20Behind%20China%E2%80%99s%20Belt%20and%20Road%20Initiative.pdf

27. J.P., "What is China's belt and road initiative?", https://www.economist.com/blogs/economist-explains/2017/05/economist-explains-11, May 15th 2017

28. Meltzer Joshua P., "A View from the United States", http://www.theasanforum.org/a-view-from-the-united-states-2/#1, June 19th 2017

29. "'One Belt and One Road': Connecting China and the world", op.cit.

30. "ONE BELT, ONE ROAD—Your guide to understanding OBOR, China's new Silk Road plan", op.cit.

31. "Repaving the ancient Silk Routes", op.cit.

32. "ONE BELT, ONE ROAD—Your guide to understanding OBOR, China's new Silk Road plan", op.cit.

33. "'One Belt and One Road': Connecting China and the world", op.cit

34. "The $900bn question: What is the Belt and Road initiative?", op.cit.

35. "China's Belt and Road Initiative benefits world: experts", http://english.gov.cn/news/top_news/2015/10/15/content_281475212268936.htm, October 15th 2015

36. "Repaving the ancient Silk Routes", op.cit.

37. Griffiths James, "Just what is this One Belt, One Road thing anyway?", http://edition.cnn.com/2017/05/11/asia/china-one-belt-one-road-explainer/index.html, May 12th 2017

38. "Repaving the ancient Silk Routes", op.cit.

39. "New Opportunities in China's 'One Belt One Road' Initiative", op.cit.

40. Perlez Jane and Huang Yufan, "Behind China's $1 Trillion Plan to Shake Up the Economic Order", https://www.nytimes.com/2017/05/13/business/china-railway-one-belt-one-road-1-trillion-plan.html?mcubz=0, May 13th 2017

41. "Repaving the ancient Silk Routes", op.cit.

42. Yamei, "Full text of President Xi's speech at opening of Belt and Road forum", http://news.xinhuanet.com/english/2017-05/14/c_136282982.htm, May 14th 2017

43. "Behind China's $1 Trillion Plan to Shake Up the Economic Order", op.cit.

44. "Repaving the ancient Silk Routes", op.cit.

45. Wolff Peter, "China's 'Belt and Road' Initiative –Challenges and Opportunities", https://www.die-gdi.de/uploads/media/Belt_and_Road_V1.pdf, 2016

46. "Repaving the ancient Silk Routes", op.cit.

47. Wijeratne David, "How can we realize the opportunities of China's Belt and Road strategy?", https://www.weforum.org/agenda/2017/05/repaving-the-ancient-silk-routes-realising-opportunities-along-the-belt-and-road/, May 11th 2017

48. Wu Yu-Shan, et al., "Where Africa fits into China's massive Belt and Road Initiative", https://theconversation.com/where-africa-fits-into-chinas-massive-belt-and-road-initiative-78016, May 28th 2017

49. Tom Phillips is the Beijing correspondent for the Guardian.

50. "The $900bn question: What is the Belt and Road initiative?", op.cit.

51. "China's Belt and Road Initiative could redraw the map on global trade", op.cit.

52. A Non-resident Fellow at the Lowy Institute.

53. "The $900bn question: What is the Belt and Road initiative?", op.cit.

54. "Just what is this One Belt, One Road thing anyway?", op.cit.

55. Financial Times China Consumer and Leisure Industries Correspondent.

56. Hancock Tom, "China encircles the world with One Belt, One Road strategy", https://www.ft.com/content/0714074a-0334-11e7-aa5b-6bb07f5c8e12, May 4th 2017

57. "How can we realize the opportunities of China's Belt and Road strategy?", op.cit.

DISCUSSION QUESTIONS

1. How would you summarize the main argument of the article in a sentence or two?

2. What are the security threats facing the Belt and Road Initiative (BRI)?

3. What are the geographical risk challenges facing the Belt and Road Initiative (BRI)?

4. What are the economic cost challenges facing the Belt and Road Initiative (BRI)?

5. Why do some think that the BRI project is a power grab for China?

6. How should the United States respond to China's BRI initiative? Hint: Have in mind what John Ikenberry discussed in the previous article.

China-Russia Relations: Politics of "Reluctant Allies"

By Yu Bin

The China-Russia relationship was both extraordinary and ordinary. On one hand, both sides were visibly, albeit reluctantly, moving toward more security-strategic coordination to offset growing pressure from the US and its allies. On the other hand, they continued to interact with a mix of cooperation, competition, and compromise for interests and influence in a range of areas including trade, investment, and regional development. None of these trends was definitive, given the complex dynamics between the two, as well as their respective relations with others, which are beyond the full control of either Moscow or Beijing. The asymmetry between "high" and "low" politics in their bilateral ties may be normal, if not necessarily desirable. Nevertheless, the scope, speed, and sustainability of the emerging Sino-Russian strategic alignment, deserves careful scrutiny.

Growing Ties?

Both sides used the term "unprecedentedly high level of trust" and "best ever" to describe the bilateral relationship. Nevertheless, neither side would define the steadily warming ties as an alliance. In an interview with Chinese media on June 17, President Putin offered his own interpretation of Russia's relationship with China: "As we had never reached this level of relations before, our experts have had trouble defining today's general state of our common affairs. It turns out that to say we have strategic cooperation is not enough anymore. This is why we have started talking about a comprehensive partnership and strategic collaboration." "'Comprehensive' means that we work virtually on all major avenues; 'strategic' means that we attach enormous inter-governmental importance to this work."

Regardless of the wording of their growing ties, the substance of the China-Russia relationship appeared to deepen and broaden over the summer. From May 26–28 the two militaries held their first ever joint command/headquarters missile defense exercise, named *Aerospace Security 2016,* in Moscow at the Aerospace Defense Forces Central Scientific Research Institute. The goal was to practice interoperability for joint operations between Russian and Chinese air defense and missile

Yu Bin, "China-Russia Relations: Politics of "Reluctant Allies," *Comparative Connections*, vol. 18, no. 2, pp. 129-143, 172. Copyright © 2016 by Center for Strategic and International Studies. Reprinted with permission. Provided by ProQuest LLC. All rights reserved.

defense groups for territorial defense against accidental and provocative ballistic and cruise missile strikes. Ten days later (June 9), Russian and Chinese warships entered the waters "in a contiguous zone" near the Diaoyu/Senkaku Islands, to the surprise of the Japanese. During the second four months of 2016, Russia consistently sided with China over the South China Sea (SCS) issue, and opposed outside interference in the SCS disputes. The two sides were also actively preparing for a joint naval exercise in the South China Sea planned for September, the first of this kind between the two navies.

Putin: "Speedboat to China"

Just one day after the Shanghai Cooperation Organization Summit in Tashkent (June 22–23), the Russian and Chinese presidents met again, this time in Beijing. However, President Vladimir Putin spent less than 24 hours in China for his 15th visit to China as Russian president. Russian media described it as a "speedboat to China," while Chinese media described it as a "hurricane visit." Putin spent more than five hours with President Xi. He also met separately with Premier Li Keqiang and Chairman of China's Legislature Zhang Dejiang, as well as three vice premiers and two vice chairmen of the Chinese legislative body.

Despite its format and duration, Putin's visit marked a significant movement toward some kind of de facto alliance, or "strategic alignment," the favored term by Chinese and Russian pundits seeking to avoid more sensitive term "alliance." The visit was viewed through a more political-strategic lens than an economic focus, particularly for Beijing. In the Great Hall of the People, the two presidents held "very intensive and productive talks" (Putin's words) and "exchanged in-depth views on international and regional hotspot issues of common concern." They agreed to the spirit of strategic coordination and everlasting friendship, increased mutual support, enhanced mutual political and strategic trust, and unswerving commitment to deepening their comprehensive strategic partnership of coordination. After the talks, the two presidents signed three joint statements: a China-Russia governmental statement, on strengthening global strategic stability, and on promoting the development of information and cyber space.

The joint governmental statement was perhaps the longest document (over 8,000 Chinese characters) ever issued by the two governments. It summarized the outcomes of the bilateral relationship since the signing of the China-Russia Good-Neighborly Treaty of Friendship and Cooperation (Friendship Treaty), 15 years earlier. The statement claimed that the spirit and framework of the Friendship Treaty allowed the two sides to resolve the border disputes, which paved the way for turning the China-Russia border into of a line of peace, cooperation, and exchanges. The treaty therefore served the fundamental interests of the two countries and will guide future trajectory of the bilateral interactions. During his brief stay in Beijing, Putin also joined Xi for a ceremony for the 15th anniversary of the signing of the Friendship Treaty.

The joint statement on global strategic stability was the first of the kind issued by the two governments and voiced concern over increasing "negative factors" affecting global strategic stability.

Without naming any specific countries, the statement said that "Some countries and military-political alliances seek decisive advantage in military and relevant technology, so as to serve their own interests through the use or threat of use of force in international affairs. Such policy resulted in an out-of-control growth of military power and shook the global strategic stability system." Particularly, the statement expressed concern over the unilateral deployment of anti-missile systems all over the world—the Aegis Ashore ballistic missile defense system in Europe and the possible deployment of the Terminal High Altitude Area Defense (THAAD) in Northeast Asia), which severely infringe upon the strategic security interests of countries in the region. Aside from missile defense, the statement expressed concern about the looming arms race regarding long distance precision attack weapons, such as the global system for instant attack, as well as the rising danger of chemical and biological weapons falling into the hands of nonstate entities for the conducting of terrorist and violent extremist activities.

Until recently, the concept of "strategic stability" has been used largely for issues of nuclear arms control between the US and Russia/Soviet Union. The China-Russia joint statement addresses the concept from a wider angle, covering both military-technical and political-strategic areas. The latter means that all countries and groups of countries should abide by the principle on use of force and coercive measures stipulated by the UN Charter and international law, respect the legitimate rights and interests of all countries and peoples while handling international and regional issues, and oppose interference in other countries' political affairs.

The statement on promoting the development of information and cyberspace spelled out the "increasing security challenges" in this area, including the abuse of information technology. Countries should conduct dialogues and cooperate on how to guarantee the security of cyberspace and promote the development of information networks. The two sides therefore called for respect for countries' Internet sovereignty and voiced opposition to actions that infringe on that sovereignty. They also agreed to strengthen network governance and crack down on terrorism and other crimes conducted through the Internet. Regular meetings on cyberspace cooperation will be held between Russia and China, according to the document.

Aside from these three general documents, the two foreign ministers also signed a Joint Declaration on Promotion and Principles of International Law, which was designed to target the South China Sea dispute. Again, the joint statement was unprecedented, reflecting both the growing challenge China faces over the South China Sea issue and the more active mutual support between Russia and China of the other's vital interests.

President Putin's hurricane-style visit to Beijing was also for promoting business. Putin brought with him more than 200 people, including almost all of the top officials from large state-run energy firms. The two sides signed more than 30 major contracts covering a wide range of items such as trade, energy, aerospace (*RD-180* rocket engines), nuclear energy, high-speed trains, cross-border E-commerce, joint development of wide-body passenger airplanes, heavy helicopters, etc. The two sides also signed a memorandum on the possibility of concluding an agreement between the Eurasian

Economic Union and China. In the cultural arena, the two sides signed a document detailing planned Russian assistance for training Chinese hockey players and creating hockey clubs and training centers for teens.

SCO's Tashkent Summit

Like China-Russia bilateral relations, the Shanghai Cooperation Organization (SCO) also underwent some significant changes and developments over the summer. The Tashkent summit was held at the time of the 15th anniversary of the security group and it represented a major step forward for at least two areas: beginning the expansion process (India and Pakistan accession to full membership of the SCO presumably will occur in 2017), and starting talks on linking China's Road and Belt Initiative and the Russia-led Eurasian Economic Union (EEU) for the creation of a Eurasian economic network. The summit also addressed the joint fight against terrorism, separatism and extremism, drug and weapon smuggling, dissemination of weapons of mass destruction, the development of economic and cultural-humanitarian cooperation among member states, and the situation in Afghanistan.

As in the past, the summit opened with an "exclusive meeting" of the heads of state of the six SCO members before inviting other non-core members (observers, dialogue partners, representatives of other international organizations, etc.) for an expanded session. At the SCO's 15th anniversary, leaders believed that the Shanghai Spirit–mutual trust, mutual benefit, equality, consultation, respect for diverse civilizations and pursuit of common development–served the needs and interests of the SCO member states and therefore should be upheld and continued. These sessions were described as reaching broad consensus on issues regarding SCO's development, and those of regional and global importance. SCO leaders then signed the Tashkent declaration on the 15th anniversary of the establishment of the SCO, several resolutions to approve an action plan for the SCO's development in the next five years (2016–2020), and the working reports of the SCO secretary general and the organization's anti-terrorism institution. They also witnessed the signing of the memorandums of obligations for India and Pakistan to join the SCO, which is a key step for the two countries to obtain formal membership in the organization in 2017.

As a regional security group created by China and with the post-Soviet nations including Russia, the SCO had come a long way in its coordination against various separatist, extremist, and criminal activities. In its first few years of existence, The SCO's Regional Anti-terrorist Structure (RATS) was unable to come up with even a common definition of terrorism given the diverse social and cultural background of the member states. Its performance improved after 2007 with a three-year program of cooperation in the fight against terrorism, separatism and extremism approved by the SCO Council of Heads of State. In the second three-year phase, RATS became more efficient and facilitated SCO law enforcement authorities halt preparations for more than 500 terrorist and religious extremism crimes, liquidate over 440 terrorist training bases, end the criminal activity of more than 1,050 members of international terrorist organizations, and seize 654 improvised explosive devices, over 5,000 firearms, 46 tons of explosives, and over 500,000 rounds of ammunition.

Presidents Xi and Putin met briefly in Tashkent ahead of the formal SCO sessions. One of the main issues discussed was the link-up of China's Belt and Road [the Silk Road Economic Belt and the 21st Century Maritime Silk Road] Initiative and the Russia-led Eurasian Economic Union (EAEU). The two also touched on cooperation in the economic and security areas within the SCO framework. Xi urged drawing up the Convention on Combating Extremism at the earliest possible time. Putin agreed on synergizing the EAEU and the Belt and Road Initiative within the SCO framework.

The SCO Summit also witnessed the third tripartite meeting of Chinese President Xi Jinping, Russian President Putin and Mongolian President Tsakhia Elbegdorj, which took place on the sidelines of the summit. The three leaders inked a development plan to build an economic corridor linking the three neighbors, pledging to boost transportation connectivity and economic cooperation in border regions. Much of this was an extension from the "road map" (consisting of 32 investment projects) for tripartite cooperation signed on the sideline of the SCO's Ufa summit in 2015. Largely initiated by Moscow, the project aims to benefit from China's Belt and Road Initiative through Mongolia, which has been in the Russian/Soviet shadow since the early 20th century. After the meeting, the three heads of state also witnessed the signing of a trilateral agreement on the mutual recognition of the customs supervision results on certain commodities. Xi presided over the meeting and was quoted as saying that China was satisfied with the momentum of the tripartite cooperation, which linked up the China's Silk Road Economic Belt, Russia's Trans-Eurasian Corridor, and Mongolia's Steppe Road.

South China Sea

For China, the SCO Summit provided a timely opportunity to gain support for its contestation over the South China Sea. Prior to the arbitration initiated by the Philippines, China had searched for diplomatic support for its stance calling for bilateral negotiations on the South China Sea disputes without outside interferences. The Tashkent Declaration issued immediately after the SCO summit states:

> Member States reaffirm their commitment to maintaining law and order at sea on the basis of the principles of international law, in particular, those set out in the United Nations Convention on the Law of the Sea. All relevant disputes should be resolved peacefully through friendly negotiations and agreements between the parties concerned without their internationalization and external interference. In this context, Member States have called for the full respect of the provisions of the aforementioned Convention, as well as the Declaration on the Conduct of Parties in the South China Sea (DOC) and the Guiding principles for its implementation.

All of the SCO member states except Russia are inland states with little direct interests in the issue of the law of sea in general and in the freedom of navigation in particular. The support from those Central Asian states in the form of the SCO's collective decision was both timely and significant for Beijing in its disputes with both South China Sea regional players (the Philippines, Vietnam, and Malaysia,) and their external supporters (the US, Japan and Australia).

Prior to the SCO Summit, China also obtained support for its South China Sea position from Russia. The SCO Foreign Ministers Meeting in Tashkent on May 24 issued a joint statement supporting China's position. Shortly after this, the Russian Foreign Ministry reiterated its support for China's stance, saying disputes should be resolved through negotiations. "All relevant disputes should be resolved peacefully through friendly negotiations and agreements between the parties concerned, without internationalization or external interference," the ministry said in an online press note. On June 10, Russian Foreign Ministry official Maria Zakharova said in a briefing that Russia does not side with any of the parties to these disputes on principle, continuing, "We are firmly convinced that third parties' involvement in these disputes will only increase tensions in this region." The day of the SCO Summit, Russian Ambassador to China Andrei Denisov attributed the tense situation in the South China Sea region to the interference from outside countries. In response, the Chinese Foreign Ministry spokesperson applauded the remark, calling it a just voice from the international community.

For much of July and August, China and Russia were actively planning a joint naval exercise in the South China Sea area. The two navies have exercised together before, but never in the South China Sea. The drills will "consolidate and develop" their comprehensive strategic partnership as well as "enhance the capabilities of the two navies to jointly deal with maritime security threats," said a Chinese spokesman in late July. On June 9, one Chinese and three Russian warships entered the waters "in a contiguous zone" near the Diaoyu/Senkaku Islands. Russia said that it was a normal operation in keeping with international vessel navigation and that Russia was surprised by Japan's reaction. Chinese media in Hong Kong described it as "joint operation of Chinese and Russian naval forces."

SCO Growing Pains?

Uzbekistan President Islam Karimov, the chair of the Tashkent summit, expressed concern that the first step toward SCO expansion with the acceptance of India and Pakistan as full members, no matter how significant for the future of the regional security group, may well be a source of its possible stagnation, unmanageability and even decline, given the "difficult and complicated" process. In their speeches at the summit, the Russian and Chinese presidents had considerable overlap regarding the current operation and future orientations of the SCO, particularly in the security areas. There was, however, a growing difference in Moscow and Beijing's views regarding SCO expansion. While Moscow sees SCO expansion as leading to more influence and legitimacy for the regional group, Beijing perceives a more complex and perhaps less efficient decision-making mechanism with added members to an organization already plagued by internal and external contradictions and constraints.

With its growing influence, the SCO has received several membership applications. The regional group, however, has not been eager to expand its ranks from its inception. Part of the reason has been the belief, particularly by China, that the SCO still needs to improve its institution building and solidify the basis for cooperation, making hasty expansion is ill-advised. Expansion risks are internal conflicts, increasing decision-making costs and dampening the unity of the organization, argued Sun Zhuangzhi, secretary general of the SCO Research Center, Chinese Academy of Social Sciences in Beijing. Although the formal decision was made to accept India and Pakistan as full members of the SCO at the 2015 Ufa summit, China is still concerned about the mutual hostility between the two South Asian nations over Kashmir, Afghanistan, and other regional affairs. The intense rivalry between the two is unlikely to be dispelled any time soon. Together with their complicated relations with China and Russia, many Chinese analysts believe their admission may have negative effects on the SCO, bringing more internal conflicts and lowering the level of mutual political trust and the efficiency of multilateral cooperation.

President Putin attaches more importance to the expansion of the SCO in order to "strengthen its role in international and regional affairs." Noting that its current "triple-6" construct (the six founding members, six observer states, and six dialogue partners) accounts for more than 16 percent of gross global product; their share in the world's population, however, stands at 45 percent, remarked Putin in the expanded session of SCO's Council of Heads of State in Bishkek. Reminding the audience that the decision to begin the India and Pakistan's accession procedure was made last year in Ufa, Putin urged that "We hope that our partners will complete these steps as soon as possible." Meanwhile, Putin called for "directly integrating India and Pakistan into the SCO's regular cooperation mechanisms such as the Council of Heads of State and the regular meetings of member states' foreign ministers."

Iran was Putin's next focus for SCO expansion. Pointing to the fact that Iran had been a longstanding and active observer state in the SCO since 2005, he believed that there should be no obstacles in the way of a positive assessment of Tehran's membership application after the Iranian nuclear issue had been settled and the UN sanctions lifted. For Russia, Iran's SCO membership should have been granted in the "first wave" of the SCO expansion, along with those of India and Pakistan. "There is a position of Russia, with which the partners agree. We all understand that there will be India and Pakistan, and it would be logical to also include in this list Iran, which filed a request back in 2008 and has worked as an observer since 2005," said Russian presidential envoy on SCO affairs Bakhtiyer Khakimov in Tashkent.

President Xi Jinping of China made five points in his speech and SCO expansion came at the last point. He did mention India and Pakistan, but not Iran, for the SCO's current expansion. The goal for an open and encompassing SCO, according to Xi, was to perfect its organizational construct, broadening and deepening its areas of cooperation. The goal should also be its healthy operation, and its organizational expansion constitutes one of the means for that goal. For that purpose, Xi put the "Shanghai Spirit" on the top of his talking points: mutual trust, mutual benefit, equality, consultation, respect for diverse civilizations and pursuit of common development. In keeping with and promoting the Shanghai Spirit, Xi prioritized security (including Afghanistan) as the foundation for the SCO's development; trade, investment and infrastructure construction including China's Belt and Road Initiative as a means for "practical cooperation"; and people-to-people exchanges in health, environmental protection, youth exchange, etc. as "bridges" for future development. SCO expansion came as the last item in Xi's priority list.

China's reluctance to move ahead with Iran's SCO membership may well be technical, particularly the timing of Iran's accession. For Beijing, granting the two South Asian countries SCO membership is already a huge complicating factor, despite the added visibility of the SCO in world geopolitics as a result of the two new members. Another possible factor behind China's lack of interest in Iran's accession to full membership was perhaps Tehran's continuing rocky relationship with the West. Despite the fact that Western economic sanctions had been lifted following the nuclear deal in July 2015, the Islamic state continues to be viewed by the West as a problem as Tehran is involved in military activities in Syria, Iraq, and Lebanon. China may not want to turn the SCO into a regional group with more visibly anti-Western orientation with the inclusion of Iran as its "core" member states.

Russia, however, did not seem to be bothered by the perceived negative impact of Iran's accession to the SCO full membership. For several months, Russian diplomats had pushed the envelope for Iran's SCO acceptance. Foreign Minister Sergei Lavrov publicly raised the issue during the SCO Foreign Ministers Meeting in late May. "The Russian position is clear in its support of initiating the SCO admission process (for Iran) without delays, if possible," presidential envoy Khakimov told reporters. He did not name the objecting parties, but acknowledged that Russia's initiative for Iranian membership failed as the joint statement by the SCO heads of state did not mention Iran's accession to full membership status. Russia, however, would continue to press for Iran's inclusion, according to Khakimov.

Beyond the Iranian case, the idea of revising the SCO structure and procedure has also been tossed around, including the concept of a narrower format of permanent members of the SCO, exclusively reserved for its six founding members. This UN Security Council type of format, however, runs counter to the "Shanghai spirit" of equality and mutual respect. SCO's customary decision-making model is by consensus but not by vote. There is debate as to what extent future members may be allowed to obtain this status. Alternatively, the SCO may have to slow down its accession process, allowing more time to digest the upcoming accession of India and Pakistan.

China's experience in the SCO development is a mix of both fruitful outcomes and frustration over many issues within a multilateral environment. The diverse interests and policies of each member state, plus the consensus building decision-making style, made cooperation more difficult and less efficient, noted Yan Jin, an associate research fellow of the Institute of Russian, Eastern European, Central Asian Studies at the Chinese Academy of Social Sciences. China had proposed a SCO development bank in 2010. Russia, however, suggests building the SCO development bank on the basis of

Eurasian Development Bank (EDB) or by expanding the functions of the SCO Interbank Consortium. Uzbekistan, which is not an EDB member, opposes Russia's proposals. Kazakhstan favors China's idea of the SCO free trade zone, which is also supported by Kyrgyzstan and Tajikistan. However, it is opposed by Russia and Uzbekistan. For Russia, energy cooperation, particularly within the framework of Russia's traditional domination of the Central Asia's pipelines, should be one of the key goals of the SCO. Instead, most energy projects between the SCO members have been bilateral, such as the China-Central Asia gas and oil pipelines. And all of those mega financial institutions China has been creating in the past few years are outside the SCO framework.

These divergences are caused by diversifying diplomatic strategies and interests. Beyond these intra-SCO diversities and constraints, the global financial crisis, the sluggish prices of commodities and Russia's economic deterioration have exerted negative effects as well. Outside powers have also deeply intervened in regional affairs, upsetting SCO members' joint interests. The future growth of the SCO would only complicate, not simplify, the existing situation.

China's more cautious approach to Iran's accession to full SCO status apparently prevailed in both the foreign ministers meeting in late May and in the summit in late June. In the Tashkent Declaration of the 15th Anniversary of the SCO and the Joint Statement of the SCO Heads of State, as well as the Joint Statement issued at the end of the SCO Foreign Ministers Meeting, Iran's accession was not discussed, to the disappointment of Moscow. India and Pakistan, however, have one foot inside the SCO. The coming of the "elephant" (India) into the SCO community is seen as favoring Moscow more at the expense of China's influence within the SCO, given Russia's more pivotal posture within the Russia-India-China triangle.

Tales of Two Eurasian Integrations: "Belt and Road" and EAEU

If there is anything that defines China's foreign policy under President Xi, it is the Belt and Road Initiative. The Silk Road Economic Belt and the 21st-Century Maritime Silk Road run through Asia, Europe and Africa, connecting the vibrant Asian economic circle at one end and developed Europe and the vast African continent at the other. Indeed, the SCO Summit appeared to be a major step forward for China's Eurasian integration effort through the old Silk Road.

In September 2013, Xi kicked off his "Silk Road Economic Belt" concept during his visit to Kazakhstan. In October, Xi proposed a "21st Century Maritime Silk Road" design for the China-ASEAN relationship. Combined, they form the "Belt and Road" project to broaden and deepen China's economic interaction with the entire Eurasian continent. Call it the Xi Jinping Doctrine, which has both foreign and domestic implications. In geopolitical terms, it would help China avoid frontal confrontation with the US rebalancing to Asia-Pacific. It will also provide new outlets for China's excessive industrial capacities. Ultimately, a more integrated Eurasian continent would create a stable and sustainable environment for China's future development.

Russia's immediate reaction to China's Belt and Road initiative was quite negative, if not hostile (See Yu Bin, "Putin's Glory and Xi's Dream"). Xi's strategy was seen as competing with Moscow's traditional sphere of interests (Central Asia) and Russia's own integration efforts such as the Commonwealth of Independent States (CIS), Collective Security Treaty Organization (CSTO), and the then Eurasian Economic Space.

Despite Moscow's reservations, China continued to pursue its Belt and Road Initiative. In November 2014, China announced that it would contribute $40 billion to set up a Silk Road Fund to finance projects. Meanwhile, China was also creating several other large-scale financial institutions, such as the Asian Infrastructure Investment Bank (AIIB) with $100 billion initial capital, the $100 billion BRICS Contingency Fund, and the BRICS Development Bank (or the New Development Bank) of $100 billion. In early 2015, China released an action plan on the principles, a framework, and cooperation priorities and mechanisms of the initiative.

Finally in May 2015, when Xi visited Moscow for the 70th anniversary of Russia's V-D parade, the two leaders reached a "broad consensus on jointly building the 'Silk Road' Economic Belt and cooperating on Eurasian economic integration." The two sides then signed the Joint Declaration of the Ministry of Commerce of the People's Republic of China and the Eurasian Economic Commission Regarding Launching an Economic Partnership Agreement between China and the Eurasian Economic Union, which represented a major departure from Russia's guarded posture regarding China's Silk Road policy. Nothing really happened in the following year after many brainstorming sessions at the expert and academic levels. The two sides were simply unable to find any mechanism to link the Chinese and Russian visions for Eurasian integration. In March 2016, the Valdai Discussion Club published a report titled "Toward the Great Ocean 4: Turn to the East," which articulated a "Greater Eurasian Partnership" as a linkage between China's Belt and Road initiative and Russia's the EAEU.

Some Chinese experts do not see how Russia's Greater Eurasian Partnership tallies with China's interests for at least two reasons. One is that Russia certainly does not want to see China unilaterally engage with Central Asian countries to advance its Belt and Road Initiative. Second, Russia's new Greater Eurasian Partnership design means that the discussion about integration of the Silk Road Economic Belt and the EEU would be held at a multilateral platform.

In early 2016, China and Russia started preparation work for the trade agreement between the EAEU and China. Meanwhile, President Putin started to entertain the idea of creating a broader economic partnership between the EAEU, the SCO, and ASEAN, according to Foreign Minister Lavrov. The idea of a trilateral economic union was officially articulated on May 17 by Russian Deputy Foreign Minister Igor Morgulov. "The idea of combining the integration process, a kind of integration of integrations, is completely logical. ... An interesting initiative has been put forth by Russia—an initiative to form a broad economic partnership of the EEU, the SCO and ASEAN," Morgulov told a press briefing in Sochi. In his speech at the Saint Petersburg Economic Forum on June 18, Putin's vision for an extensive Eurasian partnership continued to evolve to include CIS countries, South

Asian countries, and even the EU. In almost all of these blueprints for future Eurasian integration, China's Belt and Road Initiative would be embedded in this grand design of the Russians for almost the entire Eurasian continent.

While Putin was stretching his imagination for creating a huge economic space with Russia at the center of a web of commercial deals, his Chinese counterpart was busy reaching out to countries along the old Silk Road. In January 2016, President Xi traveled to Saudi Arabia, Egypt and Iran. All agreed to expand cooperation in the Belt and Road Initiative. Prior to the SCO Summit in June 2016, Xi paid official visits to Serbia, Poland, and Uzbekistan to enhance Belt and Road cooperation. In all of these places, dozens of large trade and investment deals were inked. By the time of the summit, more than 70 countries and international organizations were participating in the construction of Belt and Road projects. Chinese enterprises have invested a total of $14 billion in countries along the route and created about 60,000 local jobs.

Given the huge difference between China's more tangible Belt and Road projects and Russia's grand and still-emerging design, it is not a surprise to see that both the Tashkent declaration and the Joint Statement of the SCO Heads of State this time explicitly embraced China's Belt and Road Initiative. None of them, however, mentioned Moscow's Greater Eurasian Partnership.

China-Russian Alliance: To Be or Not to Be?

Many in the West believe that Russia and China are trying to create a new world order to replace the US as a global leader. Chinese and Russian pundits, however, seem to care far less about the format of bilateral relations than the complex chemistry between the two. In a broad sense, they tend to see that Russia and China are trying to adjust themselves to the new emerging geopolitical configuration, namely, NATO expansion into the post-Soviet space and the US pivot to the Asia-Pacific. From China's perspective, which is increasingly shared by the Russia, the US-led Trans-Pacific Partnership (TPP) is aimed at deterring and undermining growing Chinese power and influence in the region. "The only way to break through this geopolitical encirclement for China is to move closer to Russia and the EEU. The successful advancement of the 'Belt and Road' may reduce the dependence on routes through the South China Sea and the Strait of Malacca. So it may ease tensions between China and the US. The realization of the project will give independence and geopolitical and geo-economic leverage to Russia and China," observed Oleg Ivanov, vice rector of research at the Moscow-based Diplomatic Academy, in late June.

Shi Yinhong, professor at the School of International Studies at China's Renmin University, echoed this sentiment, arguing that the US has negatively affected global stability and "severely infringed upon the strategic security interests" of countries like China and Russia with its "unilateral deployment of anti-missile systems all over the world." As both countries were "ostracized" by the US, it was "not difficult" to understand their current move toward closer ties.

In August, Moscow and Beijing apparently stepped up their coordination in dealing with the perceived threat from the THAAD deployment in South Korea, as talks of joint counter measures to offset it were proliferating in both the public and official space in the two countries. On Aug. 11, Russian Ambassador Denisov was quoted as saying that the two countries were coordinating efforts to prevent further escalation of tension in Korea.

The current strategic partnership relationship between Moscow and Beijing is "still not" an alliance, and "these are Beijing and Moscow's real thoughts," said an editorial of Beijing's *Global Times* after President Putin's China trip in late June. The factors behind their "reluctance" in moving toward an alliance are that:

- A China-Russia alliance would impact the world situation in a game-changing way, and neither country hopes for that. Instead, they want each of them to develop comprehensive diplomacy and maintain relations with the West.

- However, the United States' strategic squeezing of the China and Russia has intensified, and this has increasingly shaped the necessity for China and Russia to support each other on core issues. The China-Russia joint statements mentioned the word "support" 18 times, and it has to be said that the US factor "contributed" to this …

- There is still a lot of strategic space for China and Russia to support each other further, and the more pressure the United States puts on them, then the more intensified such mutual support will be.

The editorial was the brainchild of Hu Xijin (胡锡进), editor in chief of *Global Times*. The opinion of this Russian-speaking journalist veteran may not represent the entire spectrum of the China's Russian studies and decision making community. His view, however, draws heavily from the elite and popular opinions about Russia and China-Russia relations. It should be noted that like Russia, there has been a growing public space in China about Russia and Russian-China relations, thanks for the proliferation of social media of various kinds. Hu Xijin's editorials and op-ed pieces (with the pen name of Shan Renping, 单仁平) would at best compete with multiple opinions in the Chinese society. This emergent public space in China also features more and more foreign inputs from various sources, including some from Russia.

Regarding the frequent disagreements and even contractions between the Eurasian giants, the editorial argued that the West cannot understand the open nature of China-Russia relations and Westerners tend to miss the point about the nature of China-Russia relations in that temporary inability to conclude talks on specific cooperation or difficulty in implementing something will not shake the overall bilateral relationship. For those who think bilateral relations are like they are today because of Putin, this is at best a fallacy. China-Russia relations began during the Yeltsin era, but Yeltsin was once one of the "most disliked" Russian leaders by Chinese society, so China and Russia getting closer was a product of the times, said the editorial.

Russian scholars tend to see that the Russian-Chinese relations are already the relations of allies in many aspects, all that is lacking is the official label – something that could be changed relatively swiftly if (and when) it is expedient. In their assessment of relations, Vasiliy Kashin and Anastasiya Pyatachkova noted "The abundance of coordination mechanisms and this scale of military cooperation obviously go beyond the framework of ordinary good-neighborliness."

Even in the Chinese scholarly community, opinions are diverse. Shen Dingli, deputy dean of the Institute of International Studies at Fudan University, argued that Russia's heart is always with the West. Its biggest hope is to earn the respect from the West and integrate into the West. Russia's own "turn to the East" strategy, its current Greater Eurasian partnership, and its collaboration with China is therefore more a matter of expediency instead of a "strategy," wrote Shen in an opinion piece in Global Times. Shen further pointed out that Russia is also on guard against China, particularly over China's growing influence in its peripheral countries via the "Belt and Road" Initiative. As a leading foreign policy specialist, Shen is known for his realist mindset and is also a well-respected expert on the US and China-US relations. His strong questioning of the current state of Beijing-Moscow relationship, though rooted in historical and theoretical bases, may well be a sign of the division among both policy and academia groups regarding the degree, scope, and even limits of China's tilt toward Russia.

Realists in China's policy and academic community, however, also produced entirely opposite policy prescriptions from those of Shen. Yan Xuetong, dean of the Qinghau University's School of International Affairs in Beijing, has been a leading advocate for China to abandon its non-alliance foreign policy. Instead, he argues that China should actively pursue a balance of power foreign policy by seeking, building, and maintaining a viable alliance network.

Both Shen and Yan are "American watchers." But even some engaged in the Russia studies questioned the wisdom of embracing Russia's "greater Eurasian partnership" without fully understanding the nature of the Moscow-led EAEU and the purpose of Putin's emerging greater Eurasian partnership plan. Han Kedi, an associate research fellow of the Institute of Russian, Eastern European and Central Asian Studies at the Chinese Academy of Social Sciences, pointed to the very low yield from those numerous deals inked by the two sides in the past. Indeed, it was the implementation, not the cheers for signing the contracts that mattered. The real obstacle was Russia's unsatisfactory domestic investment environment. Yet, it has not showed a sign of willingness to compromise in negotiations with foreign companies. Indeed, China should learn from Russia about how to safeguard its own interests, argued Han. Specifically, Han questioned the wisdom of China providing large payment in advance before the project is carried out, which leaves China with little space for any debt default or breach of contract. At the higher level of strategic interactions between the US and Russia, Han saw both Washington and Moscow trying to maintain dominance in the Asia Pacific (for US) and Eurasia (for Russia). "Uniting with one side to oppose the other does not serve China's national interests. China must ponder how to keep its diplomatic independence," insisted Han.

Han's unusually critical views of Russia and Russia's China policy drew strong reactions from both China's domestic sources and from the Russians. In late July, *Global Times* carried a sharp rebuttal by Georgy Zinoviev, charge d'affaires ad interim of the Russian Federation in China, who categorically repudiated almost every point Han made. Aside from its obviously official tone, Zinoviev's argument was far more persuasive than Han's in his more comprehensive grasp of the nature and trajectory of the bilateral relationship. To counter Han's harsh critique of Russia's position on the South China Sea, Zinoviev wrote:

> The 'proof' of the South China Sea issue is that Russia emphasized the importance of protecting freedom of navigation there—same as the US and Japan, as Mr Han points out. Well, not only them, but also China and actually everyone else supports freedom of navigation and no one opposes it. Russia's position is clearly stated in many cases, including bilateral and multilateral documents and can easily be analyzed and compared with positions of other states. No one willing to do so objectively would reach same conclusions as Mr Han.

Han's view has a lot of appeal even beyond the Russian studies community in China. His urge to think before jumping into Moscow's still-developing concept makes a lot of sense. In early July, Chinese pundits engaged in serious discourse about the goals and likely impacts of Russia's greater Eurasia partnership. Xing Guangcheng, director of the Institute of Chinese Borderland Studies under the Chinese Academy of Social Sciences, went so far as to argue that it was actually in China's own interests to see Russian success in creating and running both EAEU and the greater Eurasian partnership projects. Russia's success would provide China with more opportunities. At a minimum, it would reduce China's workload in negotiating trade deals by working with a group of nations, instead of making deals with each individual state. Wu Dahui, a prominent Russia specialist at Qinghua University, believed that the timing of Putin's proposal for a greater Eurasian partnership was a strategic calculation. It was put forward on the eve of UK's referendum regarding its EU membership, which may lead to greater disintegration of EU. The US effort to create separate trading blocs (TTP for Asia-Pacific and TTIP for Europe) has been seriously challenged by anti-globalization populism across the West. Putin's greater Eurasian partnership, therefore, engages multiple parties: China's Belt and Road, Russia-led EAEU, India, Pakistan, ASEAN and EU (this writer would even add Japan onto Putin's matrix), at a time when West-led regional and trade blocs are facing growing challenges. If this is what Putin has in mind, his reaching out to China in late June was by no means be a tactical move based on short-term expediency.

Chronology of China-Russia Relations
May – August 2016

May 4–6, 2016: Speaker of the Russian State Duma Sergei Naryshkin leads a group of Russian lawmakers for a visit to China to attend the second meeting of Sino-Russian Parliamentary Cooperation Committee. They meet Zhang Dejiang, chairman of the Standing Committee of the Chinese National People's Congress and President Xi Jinping.

May 20–22, 2016: Shanghai Cooperation Organization (SCO) Foreign Ministers Meetings is held in Tashkent. Russian Foreign Minister Sergei Lavrov meets Chinese Foreign Minister Wang Yi on the sidelines.

May 24, 2016: The 18th round of strategic consultation between Chinese and Russian militaries is held in Beijing, co-chaired by Adm. Sun Jianguo, deputy chief of Joint Staff Department of China's Central Military Commission, and Lt. Gen. Sergey Rudskoy, deputy chief of General Staff of the Russian Armed Forces.

May 26–28, 2016: Russia and China hold their first joint computer command-headquarters missile defense exercise, *Aerospace Security 2016,* in Moscow.

June 3, 2016: Russian Deputy Defense Minister Anatoly Antonov and Deputy Chief of the Joint Staff of the Chinese Central Military Council Adm. Sun meet at the Shangri-La Dialogue.

June 6, 2016: Third Sino-Russia Northeast Asia Security Talks are held in Beijing. Chinese Assistant Foreign Minister Kong Xuanyou and Russian Deputy Foreign Minister Igor Morgulov jointly chair the talks.

June 8, 2016: SCO defense ministers meet in Astana. They agree to improve security coordinating mechanisms and to develop cooperation and information exchanges to counter military threats in direct vicinity of the borders of the SCO countries.

June 9, 2016: One Chinese and three Russian warships enter the waters "in a contiguous zone" near the Diaoyu/Senkaku Islands.

June 19–20, 2016: Chinese Vice Premier Wang Yang and Russian Deputy Prime Minster Dmitry Rogozin meet in Huangshan, China to coordinate President Putin's visit to China.

June 22–23, 2016: Military officials from SCO member countries meet to prepare for the *Peace Mission 2016* military exercises to be held in Kyrgyzstan in 2016.

June 23, 2016: The China-Russia-Mongolia Trilateral Meeting is held on the sidelines of the SCO Summit in Tashkent.

June 23–24, 2016: SCO Summit is held in Tashkent.

June 3–6, 2016: Chinese Vice Premier Liu Yandong visits Russia to co-chair the seventh session of the China-Russia Committee on Humanities Cooperation with Russian Deputy Prime Minister Olga Golodets.

June 25, 2016: President Putin visits and meets President Xi Jinping and other senior leaders.

July 3-16, 2016: The Russian National Guard's Special Forces conduct joint training exercise *Cooperation 2016* with China's People's Armed Police Force (APF).

July 12-14, 2016: Chinese Vice Premier Wang Yang visits Russia to attend the third China-Russia Exposition and the chairmen's meeting of the Joint Commission for Regular Meetings between the Chinese and Russian Prime Ministers in Yekaterinburg.

July 15, 2016: Russian Prime Minister Dmitry Medvedev and Chinese Prime Minister Li Keqiang meet on the sidelines of the Asia-Europe Meeting (ASEM) Summit in Ulaanbaatar.

July 18-20, 2016: Chinese State Councilor Yang Jiechi visits Ulyanovsk, to co-chair the first meeting of the Sino-Russian Regional Cooperation Council with Mikhail Babich, Russia's presidential envoy to the Volga Federal District meeting.

July 22, 2016: Russian Deputy Defense Minister Anatoly Antonov and the Chinese Defense Ministry's head of international military cooperation, Maj. Gen. Xi Gowei, meet in Moscow to discuss bilateral military and military-technical cooperation.

July 25, 2016: Foreign Minister Lavrov meets Chinese Foreign Minister Wang Yi on the sidelines of the ASEAN-related events in Laos.

July 28, 2016: Fourth meeting on Northeast Asia security is held in Moscow, co-chaired by Chinese Assistant Minister of Foreign Affairs Kong Xuanyou and Russian Deputy Foreign Minister Igor Morgulov. They voice serious concern over THAAD deployment in South Korea.

August 25, 2016: Russian and Chinese officials hold talks in Moscow related to missile defense and regional security.

DISCUSSION QUESTIONS

1. How would you summarize the main argument of the article in a sentence or two?

2. Yu Bin calls China-Russia relations "politics of reluctant allies." What does he mean by this?

3. What is the United States' policy of "Pivot to Asia," and what are some of the military and security outcomes of this policy?

4. What is the Shanghai Cooperation Organization (SCO) and who are its founding members? Should the United States be concerned about it?

5. Some see potential for synergy among the Shanghai Cooperation Organization (SCO), the Eurasian Economic Union (EAEU), and the Belt and Road Initiative (BRI). Should the United States be worried about such a possibility? Hint: Consider the previous three articles you have already read.

6. Why would the U.S. deployment of the THADD anti-missile systems in Northeast Asia and the expansion of NATO worry both China and the Russian Federation?

PART II

Sources of Conflict

"Ethnic Warfare on the Wane," Council on Foreign Relations

By Ted R. Gurr

....

A New Way to Manage Nationalist Passions

In November 1999, Indonesia's new president, Abdurrahman Wahid, promised in both Jakarta and Washington to hold a referendum on autonomy in the secessionist province of Aceh. His government reportedly started negotiating with representatives of the Free Aceh movement—something flatly unthinkable under Wahid's autocratic predecessor, Suharto.

Wahid's actions are hardly isolated. Indeed, they bespeak a new global strategy to contain ethnic conflict. Its essential principles are that threats to divide a country should be managed by the devolution of state power and that communal fighting about access to the state's power and resources should be restrained by recognizing group rights and sharing power. The conventional wisdom, of course, is that tribal and nationalist fighting is still rising frighteningly. But in fact, the rash of ethnic warfare peaked in the early 1990s—countered, in most regions, by the application of these principles.

The brutality of the conflicts in Kosovo, East Timor, and Rwanda—and the messiness of the international responses to them—obscures the larger shift from confrontation toward accommodation. But the trends are there: a sharp decline in new ethnic wars, the settlement of many old ones, and proactive efforts by states and international organizations to recognize group rights and channel ethnic disputes into conventional politics. In Kosovo and East Timor, intervention was chosen only after other means failed. The fact that the United States, NATO, the United Nations, and Australia intervened was itself a testament to the underlying premise that managing ethnic conflict has become an international responsibility.

Evidence about the shift toward accommodation comes from tracking some 300 politically active ethnic and religious groups over half a century.[1] The eruption of ethnic warfare in the early 1990s was the culmination of a long-term general trend that began in the 1950s and peaked shortly after the end of the Cold War. The breakup of the Soviet Union and Yugoslavia opened the door to new ethnic and national claims, and about a dozen new ethnic wars erupted in the erstwhile Soviet

Ted Robert Gurr, "Ethnic Warfare on the Wane," *Foreign Affairs*, vol. 79, no. 3, pp. 52-64. Copyright © 2000 by Council on Foreign Relations, Inc. Reprinted with permission.

empire between 1988 and 1992. In the southern hemisphere, more than two dozen ethnic wars began or resumed in roughly the same period, most of them not directly related to the end of the Cold War.

By mid-decade, a strategic shift was under way. Over the course of the 1990s, the number of ethnic groups using violent tactics fell modestly (from 115 to 95). But a more important indicator was the balance between escalation and de-escalation: of the 59 armed ethnic conflicts under way in early 1999, 23 were de-escalating, 29 had no short-term trend, and only 7 were escalating—including Kosovo. By the late 1990s, the most common strategy among ethnic groups was not armed conflict but prosaic politics.

Another way of tracking the trends is by timing when new episodes of ethnic and political conflict start. Two-thirds of all new campaigns of protest and rebellion since 1985 began between 1989 and 1993; few have started since. The decline in new protest movements foreshadows a continued decline in armed conflict. Recent history shows that ten years of nonviolent political action generally precede the start of a new ethnic rebellion. Since the number of new ethnically based protest campaigns has declined—from a global average of ten per year in the late 1980s to four per year since 1995—the pool of potential future rebellions is shrinking.

A third perspective on the overall trends comes from examining wars of self-determination, such as those in Aceh, Sri Lanka, southern Sudan, and Nagorno-Karabakh. Their protagonists claim the right to their own communally based zones or demand unification with their ethnic kindred across state borders. These wars are among the most deadly and protracted of all ethnic conflicts, and their spillovers have posed the greatest regional security threats of the post–Cold War decade. But they also are being contained. Between 1993 and the beginning of 2000, the number of wars of self-determination has been halved. During the 1990s, 16 separatist wars were settled by negotiated peace agreements, and 10 others were checked by cease-fires and ongoing negotiations. Fewer separatist wars are being fought today—18 by my count—than at any time since the early 1970s. This steep decline puts the Kosovo rebellion in perspective. The bombings and ambushes by the Kosovo Liberation Army in late 1997 started the only new ethnic war in Europe since 1994.

Conflicts in 1999

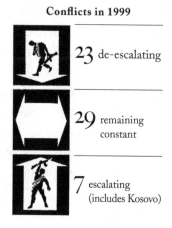

23 de-escalating

29 remaining constant

7 escalating (includes Kosovo)

Less visible than the shift toward settling separatist wars is a parallel trend toward accommodating ethnic demands that have not yet escalated into armed conflict. Leaders of ethnic movements appeal to minorities' resentment about rights denied—political participation, autonomy, and cultural recognition. In the 1990s, separatists almost always justified such claims by invoking international norms. But minority groups are doing better these days, so such appeals now sometimes fall on deaf ears. Discrimination eased for more than a third of the groups monitored by the Minorities at Risk Project between 1990 and 1998, mainly because governments formally recognized and guaranteed their political and cultural rights. The new democracies of Europe, Asia, and Latin America were especially likely to protect and promote minority rights. Even authoritarian governments were not immune to this trend, especially in Asia. Vietnam and Indonesia both lifted some restrictions on their Chinese minorities, although for reasons that had more to do with improving relations with mainland China and maintaining access to Chinese capital than any newfound fealty to group rights. Still, the overall trend is unmistakable: ethnic conflict is on the wane.

The New New Thing

No "INVISIBLE HAND" guided the global decline in serious ethnic conflict during the 1990s. Rather, it was the result of concerted efforts by a great many people and organizations, including domestic and international peacemakers and some of the antagonists themselves. Relations between ethnic groups and governments changed in the 1990s in ways that suggest that a new regime governing minority-majority relations is being built—a widely held set of principles about how to handle intergroup relations in heterogeneous states, a common repertoire of strategies for handling crises, and an emerging domestic and international consensus on how to respond to ethnic repression and violence.

The first and most basic principle of this emerging regime is recognizing and actively protecting minority peoples' rights. This means freedom from discrimination based on race, national origin, language, or religion; it also entails institutional remedies that organized ethnic groups can use to protect and promote their collective cultural and political interests. A corollary is the right of national peoples to exercise some autonomy within existing states. After all, it follows that if minorities who make up a majority of one region of a multiethnic democracy have the right to protect and promote their collective interests, they should have the right to local or regional self-governance.

Western democracies have taken the lead here. After World War II, the Atlantic democracies emphasized the protection of individuals, but during the early 1990s, Western advocates shifted their emphasis from individual rights to the collective rights of national minorities. The Organization for Security and Cooperation in Europe (OSCE) and the Council of Europe adopted standards in 1990–95 that prohibit forced assimilation and population transfers, endorse autonomy for minorities within existing states, and acknowledge that minority claims are legitimate subjects of international discussion at both UN and European regional organizations.

Virtually all European democracies have implemented these principles. In the first stage of democratization in postcommunist Europe, some ethnic leaders manipulated democracy to stoke nationalist passions at the expense of minorities like the Russians in the Baltics, the Hungarians in Slovakia and Romania, and the Serbs in Croatia. In most of these countries, a combination of diplomatic engagement by European institutions and elections checked the new wave of discrimination. The status of Hungarians in Slovakia and Romania improved markedly in the late 1990s, when old-line communists-turned-nationalists were ousted by coalitions that included ethnic parties. European diplomatic initiatives and OSCE missions helped persuade Baltic nationalists to moderate their treatment of Russians. Croatia's new, more moderate government today promises to respect the minorities that suffered from former President Franjo Tudjman's ultranationalism. That leaves Serbia as the last holdout, and once Slobodan Milošević's successor takes office, the Serbian government, too, will probably give more than lip service to minority rights.

For several reasons, however, creating autonomy within the state for minorities is harder than simply banning discrimination. Most governing elites want to hold on to central authority. Many also fear that autonomy will lead to outright secession. Finally, negotiating arrangements that satisfy all parties and address each situation's unique quirks is not easy.

The second fear—autonomy as a slippery slope—is not supported by the facts on the ground. In very few contemporary instances did negotiated autonomy lead to independence. Sometimes an autonomous regional government pushes hard for greater authority, as the Basques have done in Spain. But the ethnic statelets that won de facto independence in the 1990s—Somaliland, Abkhazia, the Trans-Dniester Republic, and Iraqi Kurdistan—did so in the absence of negotiations, not because of them. Those truly looking to reduce ethnic bloodshed should embrace autonomy, not fear it.

There are now many models of autonomy agreements to draw on. The best-known such pacts were reached through negotiated settlements of wars of self-determination, like the Oslo accords between Israel and the Palestine Liberation Organization and Northern Ireland's Good Friday agreement. Less has been written about the conflict-containing agreements that established a federal state for India's Mizo people in 1986, an autonomous republic for the Gaguaz minority in Moldova in 1994, and regional autonomy for the Chakma tribal group in Bangladesh's Chittagong Hills in 1997.

Some authoritarian leaders have also recognized that negotiations can end protracted conflicts. In the mid-1990s the junta that rules Burma concluded cease-fire agreements and offered concessions that checked protracted separatist rebellions by the Kachin and Mon peoples of northern Burma, although similar efforts failed to end resistance by the more numerous Shans and Karens who live in the south and east of the country.

> Most recent ethnic wars began with demands for complete independence and
> ended with autonomy.

In most recent wars of self-determination, fighting usually began with demands for complete independence and ended with negotiated or de facto autonomy within the state. There are many reasons why most ethnic nationalist leaders are willing to settle for 50 cents (or less) on the dollar, but it usually comes down to being strategically and politically overmatched. Nationalists willing to continue fighting for total independence, like the rebel leaders in Chechnya and East Timor, are rare. Central governments, on the other hand, tend increasingly to conclude that it is cheaper to negotiate regional and cultural autonomy and redistribute some funds than it is to fight endless insurgencies—especially when other states and international organizations are encouraging them to negotiate. The Turkish government's obdurate resistance to organized Kurdish political participation has become an anachronism; even Saddam Hussein is more open to cooperation with (some) Kurdish groups than Turkish nationalists are.

If the parties in separatist wars recognize that the costs of accommodation are probably less than the costs of prolonged conflict, it is only a short step to mutual decisions to settle after an initial show of forceful resolve rather than after prolonged warfare. Gagauz and Moldovan nationalists came to such a conclusion in 1992, as did Tuareg rebels and the governments of Mali and Niger in the mid-1990s. Nationalist Serbia became the pariah state and the bombing range of Europe in 1999 precisely because it refused to negotiate with the Kosovars throughout the 1990s and (most immediately) blatantly violated principles about group rights accepted elsewhere in the region.

Protecting collective rights is one of the three elements of the new preferred strategy for managing ethnic heterogeneity. Democracy is another; it provides the institutional means whereby minorities in most societies secure their rights and pursue their collective interests. Of course, other institutional mechanisms can protect groups' interests—take, for example, the communal power-sharing arrangements found in many nondemocratic African states. Nonetheless, European-style democracy is widely held to be the most reliable guarantee of minority rights. It is, after all, inherent in the logic of democratic politics that all peoples in heterogeneous societies should have equal civil and political rights, and democracy also implies resolving civil conflicts by peaceful means.

Accommodating Behavior

A third element of this new regime is the principle that disputes over self-determination are best settled by negotiation and mutual accommodation. One of democratic Russia's most important but least-noticed achievements has been its negotiation of power-sharing agreements with Tatarstan, Bashkiria, and some 40 other regions in the Russian Federation, only some of which have non-Russian nationalities. The agreement between Russia proper and Tatarstan went the greatest symbolic distance: strikingly, it actually treated the parties as equals. (This pact could and should have been a model for settling the dispute between Moscow and Chechnya, but Chechen leaders were interested only in total independence.)

The principle that serious ethnic disputes should be settled by negotiation is backed up actively by most major powers, the UN and some regional organizations, especially in Europe and Africa. These entities mix diplomacy, mediation, sweeteners, and threats to encourage accommodation. Preventive diplomacy is widely popular—not only because early engagement can be cheaper than belated crisis management but because it is the preferred instrument of the new regime. Coercive intervention, as in Kosovo, is the international system's response of last resort to gross violations of human rights and to ethnic wars that threaten regional security.

Four regional and global forces reinforce the trend toward accommodation in mixed societies. First is the active promotion of democratic institutions and practices by the Atlantic democracies. Modern democracies fight one another rarely and temper their repression against internal opponents. Before-and-after comparisons of national and minority peoples in new democracies show that their status usually improves substantially during democratic transitions.

A second buttressing factor is engagement by the UN regional bodies, and interested nongovernmental organizations on behalf of minority rights. International entities such as the OSCE, the Council of Europe, the Organization for African Unity, and the Organization of the Islamic Conference have often used diplomacy and mediation to soften their members' policies toward minorities and move ongoing conflicts toward agreement. The Organization of the Islamic Conference, not usually considered a peacemaker, was for two decades the key international player supporting a negotiated settlement to the Muslim Moros' separatist war in the Philippines.

Third is the virtually universal consensus among the international political class—the global foreign policy elite—in favor of reestablishing and maintaining global and regional order. Empire-building is out of fashion. Interstate rivalries in the 1990s focused mainly on economic productivity and competition for markets, and wars of any stripe threaten regional order and prosperity. Hence the UN the United States, regional powers, and the regional organizations of Europe, Latin America, and Africa have sought to contain local conflicts by preventive measures where possible and by mediation and peacekeeping where necessary.

Finally, the costs of ethnic conflict have become evident to both governing elites and rebel leaders. The material and social costs of civil war have been bitterly acknowledged in countries where postwar settlements are taking hold—in Bosnia, the Philippines, Mozambique, and elsewhere. The lesson drawn by outside observers of the mid-1990s war in Chechnya was that the Russian military could not defeat highly motivated guerrillas—remember Afghanistan. But the lesson the protagonists in Chechnya should have learned was that the war was not worth fighting; neither side gained much that could not have been won through negotiations before the Russian tanks rolled. Caution about the likely costs of war and the unlikely chances of victory on either side probably helped check ethnic rebellions elsewhere on Russia's periphery and in most Soviet successor states. Nato's spring 1999 campaign against Serbia conveyed a similar message to other states whose leaders have refused to compromise with ethnic nationalists. The lesson has reached as far as Beijing, where the Kosovo crisis reportedly prompted Communist Party officials to begin drafting alternative policies for dealing with restless Tibetans and Uigurs.

Not So Easy

Of course, conventional wisdom sees things somewhat differently. Most Western policymakers and foreign affairs analysts view ethnic conflict as getting worse, not becoming more manageable. What about communal warfare and genocide in central Africa, ethnic cleansing in Kosovo, Muslim and Hindu fundamentalism, or regional rebellions in Indonesia? The answer is a paradox. Objectively, there are substantially fewer such conflicts now than in the early 1990s. But they now get more public attention—precisely because they challenge the emerging norms that favor group rights and the peaceful accommodation of ethnic conflicts. Bloody crises also rivet Western publics because they threaten the comforting assumption that the "international community" can guarantee local and regional security.

Why, then, was Kosovo wracked by massacres and ethnic cleansing despite international doctrines of minority rights, past examples of ethnic conflicts that were successfully settled, and a world willing to get engaged? For starters, in no sense was ethnic war in Kosovo unprecedented. Indeed, Kosovo was the most dreaded flash point in post-Bosnia Europe. Empirically, a decade of political activism and protest typically precedes ethnic wars. Kosovo fit the pattern neatly: its ethnic Albanians resisted the dissolution of the province's regional government in 1989 by forming a parallel government, but the first Kosovar terrorist attacks did not begin until 1997. Large-scale armed conflict began a year later. Milošević's ultranationalist policies and intransigence fundamentally contradicted European and international principles about minority rights, but international attempts to prevent calamity faltered. True, the Bush administration warned the Yugoslav government in December 1992 not to repress the Kosovars, but the issue was not addressed in the 1995 Dayton Accord that the Clinton administration negotiated to end the war in Bosnia, and the Serbs' October 1998 preparations for another round of ethnic cleansing elicited little international response. The failure, then, was not so much due to international spinelessness as to sheer disbelief that the Serbs would try it again.

The world system emerging from the settlement of ethnic and regional conflicts is more complex than its Cold War predecessor. So containing ethnic conflict requires more foresight and better-coordinated international responses, as demonstrated in Kosovo and East Timor. The new liberal wisdom holds that sovereignty can be trumped by humanitarianism and that the international cavalry will ride to the rescue of minorities who face genocide. Chechen and Tibetan nationalists remain unconvinced.

The liberal vision is still too neat. Better to think of the system as multilayered, with three inter-dependent sets of political actors: states; ethnic movements, some within an existing country and some straddling several of them; and the regional and international organizations that are increasingly responsible for managing relations between the other two. States remain the paramount actors, and the powerful among them can still get away with the sort of thing that the Russians are doing in Chechnya and the Chinese are doing in Tibet. But most states, even major powers, are held back by a growing network of mutual obligations regarding minorities, regional organizations, multinationals, and world bodies. Countries that ignore those obligations risk their future world status, prosperity, and amicable foreign relations.

The new regime is not fully developed, and a depressingly long list of states and ethnic movements that reject its principles will challenge it violently. Few states in the Muslim world, for example, are prepared to grant full political and cultural rights to religious minorities. Some protracted ethnic conflicts are almost immune to regional and international influence. The struggles in places such as Afghanistan and Sudan probably will remain intractable unless and until one side wins decisively. The odds are against durable settlements for the longstanding conflicts between Kurdish nationalists and Iraq and Turkey or the containment of communal strife between Hutu and Tutsi in Rwanda. Some ethnic wars are being held in check by cease-fires and contested agreements that could easily come apart—consider Georgia, Azerbaijan, Iraqi Kurdistan, Bougainville, or Northern Ireland. South Asia alone is home to a dozen thorny ethnic and political conflicts. Since the 1950s, India has faced a series of separatist challenges, especially in the northeast; no sooner has one movement been accommodated than another emerges. Some conflicts that have been "settled" in the traditional way—by overwhelming force—could flare up again; think of what Burma did in the Karen and Shan states, or of Indonesia's crackdown in the provinces of Aceh and Irian Jaya, or China in Tibet. Repression without accommodation regularly leads to renewed resistance and rebellion, as it did in Indonesia after Jakarta began its democratic transition. So international efforts should focus on helping rulers negotiate with rebellious groups, providing both sides with incentives for choosing autonomy rather than secession.

The world simply did not believe that the Serbs would try ethnic cleansing again.

The greatest challenges to the new international way of containing ethnic conflicts are in Africa. In a vast conflict zone from Sudan and Ethiopia through the Great Lakes region to Angola's highlands and the Congo, rivalries between states and communities form an extraordinarily complex web. The UN hopes to send 500 observers and 5,000 peacekeepers to the region to help implement the Lusaka accords and thereby stop the fighting, but this plan ignores the blunt political reality that many of the armed bands do not want their conflicts managed. If the Lusaka accords and the peacekeeping mission were to fail, the credibility of future international attempts to ease the area's misery would be undercut. Instead, the world should concentrate on trying to negotiate settlements on the conflict zone's periphery, notably in Sudan and Angola.

Other challenges lie in West Africa. Revolutionary and ethnic wars have been doused in Niger, Mali, and Liberia but sporadically flare up in Sierra Leone and Chad. The greatest risk here has been that of civil war in Nigeria, which is divided between Muslims in the north and Christians in the south and has many of the factors that elsewhere predict ethnic warfare—a legacy of repressive rule, the emergence of militant ethnic nationalist groups, and a lack of international engagement. The prospects of ethnic war in Nigeria depend on how well its transition to democracy goes. The highest priority for preventive engagement in West Africa should therefore be supporting Nigeria's democratization, in the course of which the Ijaw, Ogoni, and Yoruba peoples' grievances against the northern-dominated regime should be addressed.

This survey highlights the highest-priority ethnic conflicts, which urgently need remedies and preventive action. But by whom and how? The answers depend on which actors have the will, the political leverage, and the resources to act. Kosovo, East Timor, and Chechnya illustrate that the reach of the new strategy for managing ethnic conflict depends equally on whether that doctrine is accepted by the combatants and on the will and ability of regional and international organizations to implement it. International and regional bodies are most likely to effectively prevent conflict in areas where the Western powers have vital interests, which means Europe, Latin America, and the Middle East. African and Asian conflicts are more remote and therefore more resistant to outside influence. The strategy there should be to encourage and assist regional organizations, especially the Organization of African Unity and the Association of Southeast Asian Nations (which, if quietly encouraged, may expand beyond its usual agenda of regional economics). When prevention fails or is not pursued in the first place, the international challenges are different: providing humanitarian aid and keeping the fighting from spreading throughout the region.

After Ethnicity

The evolution of good international practices for managing ethnic conflict is one of the signal accomplishments of the first post–Cold War decade. It also has had some unintended consequences. The most obvious is that accommodation of ethnic claims encourages new groups and political entrepreneurs to make similar demands in the hope of gaining concessions and power. Some latecomers are the Cornish in Britain, the Reang tribe in India, and the Mongols in China—each of which is now represented by organizations calling for autonomy and more public resources. But the pool of potential ethnic contenders is not infinite, and we have already heard from most of them. Ethnic identity and interest per se do not risk unforeseen ethnic wars; rather, the danger is hegemonic elites who use the state to promote their own people's interests at the expense of others. The "push" of state corruption and minority repression probably will be a more important source of future ethnic wars than the "pull" of opportunity.

A less obvious threat is the potential emergence of alternative forms of popular opposition. During the last several decades, the entrepreneurs behind ethnic political movements tapped into a reservoir of resentment about material inequality, political exclusion, and government predation and channeled it to their purposes. They drew on some of the same grievances that once fueled revolutionary movements. In fact, some conflicts are hybrids: ethnic wars when seen through one set of analytic lenses and revolutionary wars when seen through another. Leftists in Guatemala recruited indigenous Mayans to fill the ranks of a revolutionary movement, Jonas Savimbi built his rebel movement through the support of Angola's Mbundu people, and Laurent Kabila led a revolutionary army to Kinshasa made up of Tutsi, Luba, and other disaffected tribal peoples in the eastern Congo.

The larger point is that popular support for mass movements is to some degree fungible. All but a few of the Cold War's socialist movements failed, discrediting revolutionary rhetoric and action for most of their target audience, the urban and rural poor. Ethnic-national movements have met greater political success, but their appeal is limited to groups with some prior sense of cultural identity. And since ethnic conflicts tend to end in compromise, disillusionment is inevitable. So the field is open for other forms of mass opposition that may supplant ethnic movements, just as ethnic nationalism in its time preempted most revolutionary movements. Faith, in the form of militant Islam, Christianity, or Buddhism, can also motivate mass movements: consider the Falun Gong, a personal and spiritual movement whose persecution by the Chinese government virtually ensures its politicization. Today, class, ethnicity, and faith are the three main alternative sources of mass movements, and class-based and religious movements may well drain away some of the popular support that now energizes ethnic political movements. With a little bit of luck and a great deal of international engagement, ethnic conflict's heyday will belong to the last century.

Note

1. All evidence herein comes from the Minorities at Risk Project. The data and interpretations are reported in greater detail in the author's forthcoming book, *Peoples Versus States: Minorities at Risk in the New Century*, forthcoming from the United States Institute of Peace Press. Coded data, chronologies, and assessments for all groups are available from the project's Web site at www.bsos.umd.edu/cidcm/mar.

DISCUSSION QUESTIONS

1. How would you summarize the main argument of the article in a sentence or two?

2. What is the author's preferred strategy for managing ethnic heterogeneity?

3. When discussing ethnic wars, what are the "push" and "pull" factors?

4. Other than ethnicity, what are other sources contributing to mass movements and ethnic conflict?

5. What are wars of "self-determination" and why are they the deadliest forms of all ethnic conflicts? Provide some examples of such wars.

6. According to the article, what are the four regional and global forces that can help with the settlement of ethnic conflict through reinforcing trend toward accommodation?

The Trump Administration and Prospects for a Palestinian-Israeli Peace

By Ali R. Abootalebi

President Trump recently told the Palestinian National Authority (PNA), Mahmoud Abbas, that "[he's] always heard that perhaps the toughest deal to make is the deal between the Israelis and the Palestinians. Let's see if we can prove them wrong," insisting that "[w]e will get it done." This is while vice president Mike Pence said some days prior that President Trump was still "giving serious consideration to moving the American embassy in Tel Aviv to Jerusalem."[1] Interestingly enough, the administration's "front men" in negotiations between Palestinians and the Israelis are none other than Jared Kushner, the president's son-in-law, and Thomas Friedman, a lawyer with a long history of ties with Israel, both men having strong ideological and business ties with Israel. Then, Armin Rosen in an article in *Foreign Policy* argues that President Trump's front-man negotiator in the Israel-Palestine conflict, Jason Greenblatt, is "perfectly unqualified" and that "might be exactly why he pulls off a peace deal."[2] This is because he is not part of the Washington establishment and entrenched interests. Although there is merit in this observation, the reasons behind the failure of a Palestinian-Arab-Israeli peace agreement is a great deal more complex. The U.S. relocation of its Embassy to Jerusalem on May 14, 2018, may be pleasing to President Trump's pro-Israeli religious right constituencies, but it dedicates nothing to the cause of permanent peace between Israel and the Palestinians. No, Mr. President, the resolution to the conflict is far more difficult.

This is purely a simplification of the situation and a concocted fantasy. Whether deliberately stated to gain a political score or to naively believe that a quick-fix is within reach, beyond such declarations remains the hard reality of the state of the conflict and what has prevented its resolution throughout decades: the imbalance in power of the opposing negotiating sides. First, Arab governments have been too inept and corrupt[3] to effectively negotiate on behalf of their own peoples and in the interest of the Palestinians. Second, successive Israeli governments have had the upper hand in "power parameters" and in negotiations, with the intention to dictate the terms of a Palestinian surrender while neutralizing Arab States' security threats. Finally, the United States has been far from a neutral

Adapted from Ali R. Abootalebi, "Trump and the Israeli/Palestine: Art of the Deal or End of 2-States?" *Informed Comment*, 2017.

third-party mediator, using its hard and soft power in the service of a peace settlement or a conflict resolution and not reaching for a true "positive peace."[4]

It is well known that the mother of all conflicts is the Arab (Palestinian)-Israeli conflict that has engaged major actors in global politics before and since the creation of the state of Israel. After decades of conflict and repeated wars since 1948,[5] the result for the Arab States has been military defeat and loss of territories and national pride. Years of negotiations and attempts at safeguarding peace has resulted in a cold peace between Israel and some Arab States—Egypt in 1979 and Jordan in 1994—and a long arduous negotiation process resulting in the 1993 Declaration of Principles and the Palestinian self-rule in parts of the occupied territories. That Oslo process, as imperfect as it was, finally saw its demise after the assassination of Prime Minister Yitzhak Rabin in 1995 and the rise of the political right in Israel in the ensuing years. The failure of Camp David II in 2000 witnessed President Clinton blaming the late Yasser Arafat for his refusal to accept the terms of a peace deal while praising the Israeli Prime Minister Ehud Barak for his steadfast commitment to a peace deal. In reality, the Camp David II Accord would have created a discontinuous and parceled "swiss cheese" State of Palestine with no sovereign control over its borders and the city of Jerusalem, and minimum say about the Israeli settlements throughout the West Bank and Gaza, the "right of return" of millions of Palestinian refugees, and full sovereignty over Eastern part of the city of Jerusalem. The presumed Palestinian State would have also remained at the mercy of Israel for its access to wider water resources. That is, the end of a ten-year negotiation process only led to a proposal for declaration of a "Palestinian surrender" in the name of conflict resolution.[6] The failure of the Camp David II peace deal led to the violent years of the Intifada II. The Second Intifada saw 1,100 Israelis and close to 4,000 Palestinians killed. Palestinian suicide bombers attacked Israeli buses, cafes, and restaurants and other public places, Israel's crackdown, and closures in response cost the Palestinians in the West Bank dearly. Ironically, years later, some still blame Yasir Arafat for its failure![7]

Today, the PNA is in charge of merely 18% of the West Bank, where it can exercise respectable but not complete sovereign control in the designated Area A. Areas B (22%) and Area C (60%) are outside PNA's sovereign control, where Israel has the ultimate say in matters of security and all that falls within its security parameters, including communication, transportation, and all matters of governance in general. The Palestinian people remain divided between those living in the West Bank under the PNA jurisdiction and those living under Hamas control in the Gaza Strip. Israeli settlements have expanded in the West Bank and East Jerusalem, where settlers' population now exceeds over half a million. Gaza is a vast prison camp surrounded by Israeli and Egyptian soldiers and at the mercy of political events happening outside its borders. Political division between the PNA and Hamas has also complicated the Palestinian polity; thus, there is no one voice speaking for the Palestinian people, including millions of refugees spread throughout the region. If prospects for a Palestinian political unification through new parliamentary and National Council elections remain hopeful, the political and ideological rift between the PNA and Hamas (and the Islamic Jihad) remains paramount. President Mahmoud Abbas has also ruled through extensions for 14 years and the last legislative elections were held in 2006.[8] Syria's Golan Heights and its precious water resources also remain under Israeli control and outside of Palestinian reach.

Wider regional and global events have overshadowed and marginalized the plight of the Palestinian people. These events include but are not limited to the September 11, 2001 terrorists attacks on America; the U.S. invasion of Afghanistan (2001) and Iraq (2003); the Israeli invasion of Lebanon (2006) and Gaza (2008, 2014, 2018); the rise of Hamas in Gaza (2006); the Arab Spring (2011–present); U.S. and NATO intervention and regime change in Libya (2011); political change in Egypt and the 2015 military Coup d'état with silent U.S. approval; the Saudi Arabian intervention in Bahrain (2011) and Yemen (2015); the ongoing, devastating war in Syria since 2011, and the regional rivalry between Saudi Arabia and Iran and their respective allies.

The latest blow to the Arab States and the Palestinian leadership and people is the destruction of Iraqi and Syrian states and infrastructure and the threat of Daesh and instability to Lebanese and Jordanian national cohesion, as well as the Palestinian refugees. The Arab world, for the most part, remains divided and uncertain over domestic and regional "security threats," only to show frivolous unity in the Arab League meetings. The rise of Iranian power is the Arab States' latest excuse to deflect their endemic problems in governance by inflaming a Sunni-Shi'a divide and the fabrication of Iran as a security threat to their respective states.[9]

The security threat to many Arab governments originates from within these countries. Many Arab regimes have for decades neglected their own population and have ruled with impunity, pillaging national treasures in the service of the elite and the privileged. Gilbert Achcar,[10] explaining Arab states' political economies, argues that the peculiar modality of the capitalist mode of production dominant in the Arab region is a mix of patrimonialism, nepotism, and crony capitalism and a pillaging of public property, swollen bureaucracy, and generalized corruption. All of this occurs against a background of great sociopolitical instability and impotence or even nonexistence of law.

The central threat to Arab regimes' existence is due to the archaic nature of Arab states' governance, where people are treated as subjects and not as citizens. The Arab Spring movement in 2011 was a manifestation of Arab peoples' frustration with governance that unfortunately has since produced more hardship instead of liberation. Arab populace has long been kept marginalized. The Iranian threat to Arab regimes is not due to its military might and/or threat of an invasion. Despite all its shortcomings, the majority of Iranians today consider themselves as participatory citizens in Iran's political economy, and not as mere voiceless subjects of the ruling elites. Iran's foreign policy since the revolution has championed "national self-reliance." This has been to the detriment of U.S. military and political presence and interest in the Persian Gulf and the wider region. The rise of Iranian power is also at the heart of Arab regimes' hostility toward Iran. The Arab political elites view Iran as a threat to their own existence and not as a source with potential for positive regional security cooperation and development.[11] The Palestinian leadership, for its part, has failed to either chart its struggle separate from the Arab States or maintain a degree of independence free from the Arab regimes' control. So, the Palestinian Liberation Organization (PLO), and later the PNA, have remained dependent on the Arab regimes' largesse and political whims and power play. The history of the conflict testifies in many occasions when Palestinians have been victimized by the Arab regimes' armies and their cronies. Yasser Arafat endlessly struggled to keep Palestinian national aspirations for statehood alive while facing Jordanian, Syrian, and Lebanese military and militia onslaughts and resisting Israeli war machine, control, and occupation.

The end of the cold war pushed a desperate Palestinian leadership into a process of negotiation that was paved from the beginning with insurmountable obstacles, destined to failure. The Oslo process only neutralized the Jordanian threat and left the Palestinian leadership at the mercy of the Israeli protagonists and their American supporters. The failure of the Camp David II (2000) showed the total weakness and dependence of the Palestinian leadership on their Arab patrons and the United States Abandoned by the Arab States, Yasser Arafat could not betray the Palestinian people's trust and agree to the terms of the agreement, to effectively forsake the dream of statehood and control over East Jerusalem and the right of return of the Palestinian refugees. The rise of Hamas and the split in leadership since 2006 has also eroded the Palestinian position. President Mahmoud Abbas' term ended in 2009 and he has ruled since without a mandate from its people—the irony of Arab leaders' political legitimacy. There is also no united front in support of the Palestinian people in the Arab League. Unsurprisingly, Iran, and not Israel, is declared as a threat to the Arab states. In reality, the politically bankrupt Arab regimes' failure in good governance, along with the threat of the Daesh, sectarian violence, chaos of war and refugees, and extra-regional invasion and intervention are the real threats to Arab regimes!

Israel has been transformed in the past seventy years from a small state with a population of less than one million to a regional hegemon with the 15th most[12] powerful military in the world, nuclear weapons, an advanced economy, and a democratic political system, imperfect as it is. The cold peace with Egypt and Jordan still is holding, and the flux of over one million Russian Jews in the 1990s brought more economic vigor, as well as challenges, to its political economy. Israel, with a population of just over seven million in 2016, had a GDP of $312 billion and ranked 34th in the world.[13] Israeli democracy has many faults, including the ambiguity over its secular and religious divide and its overall treatment of its 20 percent non-Jewish citizens. Yet, Israeli citizens' participation in politics and civil society is highly valued.

Israeli politics have shifted to the right since the demise of the Oslo process and the years of increased violence in the 2000–2005 period, coinciding with America's declared war on global terrorism in 2001. The Obama years of presidency were a disappointment to many Israeli pundits: Obama met with Prime Minister Netanyahu 17 times, approved in 2016 a sizeable $38 billion aid for the decade ahead, and yet could not convince Israeli leadership to stop its settlement activities in the occupied territories, effectively killing any prospects for meaningful negotiations.[14]

The unbiased and keen observer notices that the United States has not been completely an honest broker throughout the years of the conflict. The United States pursued a four-tiered policy of anti-communism, stability, and a free flow of cheap oil and ensured Israeli security throughout the cold war. Such umbrella policy goals often meant U.S. support for authoritarian Arab regimes, and in Iran a large cache of arms transfer and political, covert, and overt military interventions. The U.S. policy in the region since 1990 has continued the tradition of strong support for Israel and the defense of authoritarian but friendly Arab regimes, significant arms transfers, and a "declared war" on terrorism that has effectively brought chaos and destruction to much of the region.

The United States' policy preferences have helped perpetuate a dominant Israeli position in its relations with the Arab states and the unresolved Palestinian dilemma. The U.S. continues to overlook Israeli stockpile of nuclear weapons, its illegal occupation of Arab lands and settlement activities, and its repeated violation of its Arab neighbors' national sovereignty through military incursions. This has been occurring in defiance of international law and in violation of the United States' declared core values: human rights, democracy, and the rule of law.

What has remained constant in U.S. Middle East policy since 1945 is inattention paid to the legitimate will of the Arab populace for popular participation and democracy and for national development and pride! Therefore, Arab peoples' frustration with authoritarian rule, corruption, military defeat on the battlefield (1967, 1973, 1991, 2003, 2011), and low level of socioeconomic development in human capital, technological penetration, and innovation instigated the Arab Spring revolt in 2011.

Today, the U.S. policy in the Middle East is viewed as unpopular, biased, and even hostile to the welfare of the people in the region. The U.S. remains extremely unpopular in the Arab world, despite millions spent on efforts at public diplomacy during the G. W. Bush and Obama administrations. A 2016 survey on Arab public opinion of the United States' policy in 12 Arab countries, that included face-to-face interviews with 18,310 respondents, finds that that 63 percent of respondents believed the United States to be the greatest threat to stability in the Arab region, beating out Iran, Russia, and China, while falling short behind Israel. Over a quarter of respondents believed the United States' policy toward Palestine, Syria, and Iraq to be either negative or very negative, while almost a quarter believed the same of the U.S.' policy toward Yemen and Libya.[15] The November 2018 Zogby poll also reminds us that "people in the region for the most part (outside of Saudi Araba and the UAE) really dislike US policy."[16]

The resolution of the Arab (Palestinian)—Israeli conflict is intimately related to the political and socioeconomic realities in Arab countries, Israel, and the U.S. view and policy practices in the region. Arab politics and international politics matter. The optimism expressed by President Trump and Armin Rosen is thus unwarranted. The Israeli-Palestinian peace process is not primed for a newcomer's fresh thinking, and U.S. involvement in the conflict has not been spearheaded by a quarter century of careful, deliberative, and well-intentioned professional U.S. diplomacy.

In the absence of a viable two-state solution to the conflict, while also resolving the Jordanian concerns and the Syrian and Lebanese apprehensions over their territorial disputes, a one-state solution may be, by default, emerging. Palestinians, like others in Arab countries, yearn for political expression and the right to have a say in determining their lives. The millennial Arab generation deserves a better future. Despite their differences and grievances, many Israeli Arab citizens still view the Israeli state with a high degree of legitimacy to rule. A surprisingly two-thirds of Israel's Arab citizens are pleased with the situation of the state in Israel. Their rating of its achievements (except in defense issues) is even higher than that of the Jews. A very large majority (86%) of the Jews and a small majority (51%) of the Arabs are proud of being Israelis. This is perhaps because, despite it all, what matters most in governance is that people everywhere wish to be free from severe socioeconomic hardship and/or political conditions that humiliate them on daily basis.

Notes

1. "Donald Trump Tells Abbas" We Will Get It Done" on Israel-Palestinian Peace Deal," *The Guardian*, May 4, 2017, https://www.theguardian.com/world/2017/may/03/trump-abbas-peace-deal-israel-palestinians

2. Armin Rosen, "Trump's Israel-Palestine Negotiator Is Perfectly Unqualified And that might be exactly why he pulls off a peace deal," *Foreign Policy*, May 1, 2017, http://foreignpolicy.com/2017/05/01/trumps-israel-palestine-negotiator-isnt-qualified/

3. Gilbert Achcar, *The People Want: A Radical Exploration of the Arab Uprising* (Berkeley: University of California Press, 2013).

4. "Positive Peace Report, Institute for Economics and Peace," Vision of Humanity, http://visionofhumanity.org/app/uploads/2017/02/Positive-Peace-Report-2016.pdf

5. "The Palestinian Authority: History and Overview," *Jewish Virtual Library,* http://www.jewishvirtuallibrary.org/palestinian-authority-history-and-overview

6. Charles D. Smith, *Palestine and the Arab-Israeli Conflict: A History with Documents*, 8th edition (Boston, Bedford, St. Martins, 2019).

7. Dennis Ross, "Did Camp David Doom the Palestinians," *Foreign Policy*, October 19, 2018, https://foreignpolicy.com/2018/10/19/did-camp-david-doom-the-palestinians-israel-palestine-yasser-arafat-menachem-begin-jimmy-carter-reagan-bush-clinton-middle-east-peace/

8. "Hamas announces terms for new Palestinian elections," *Middle Eastern Monitor,* January 24, 2019, https://www.middleeastmonitor.com/20190124-hamas-announces-terms-for-new-palestinian-elections/

9. "Iran is seeking 'to control Islamic world', says Saudi Arabian prince," *The Guardian,* Tuesday, 2 May 2017, https://www.theguardian.com/world/2017/may/02/iran-is-seeking-to-control-islamic-world-says-saudi-arabian-prince

10. Achcar, 2013.

11. Ali R. Abootalebi, "40 Years on, Is Iran a Status Quo Power or a Threat to ME Regional Security?" *Informed Comment*, January 31, 2018, https://www.juancole.com/2019/01/threat-regional-security.html

12. Global Firepower.com, https://www.globalfirepower.com/countries-listing.asp

13. "World GDP Ranking, 2017," *Knoema.com*, https://knoema.com/nwnfkne/world-gdp-ranking-2017-gdp-by-country-data-and-charts

14. "The Historic Disappointment of Barack Obama and the Israeli-Palestinian Conflict," *Haaretz,* September 23, 2016 https://www.haaretz.com/opinion/the-disappointment-of-obama-and-the-conflict-1.5441716

15. Daniel Gil, "Trump's Middle-East Trip Takes Policy Priority Despite Arab Disdain for American Involvement," *Arab America*, May 10, 2017, http://www.arabamerica.com/trumps-middle-east-trip-takes-policy-priority-despite-arab-disdain-american-involvement/

16. Zogby Research Services, "Middle East Public Opinion," November 2018 https://static1.squarespace.com/static/52750dd3e4b08c252c723404/t/5c0fcb2e758d461f72dc37ca/1544538926539/2018+SBY+FINAL+WEB.pdf

17. Armin Rosen, "Trump's Israel-Palestine Negotiator Is Perfectly Unqualified," *Foreign Policy*, May 1, 2017, http://foreignpolicy.com/2017/05/01/trumps-israel-palestine-negotiator-isnt-qualified/

DISCUSSION QUESTIONS

1. How would you summarize the main argument of the article in a sentence or two?

2. Why is the author critical of the U.S. policy in the Middle East? What sort of evidence does he provide to demonstrate U.S. disapproval in the Middle East region?

3. President Barack Obama met Israeli Prime Minister 17 times to promote peace between the Arab States, the Palestinians, and Israel. How is President Donald Trump's approach different from the previous administration, and in what way?

4. The author argues that the Arab states' failure in governance is a major cause of the failure of peace in the Middle East. What sort of argument does the author provide for his claim?

5. What evidence can you provide to validate the author's claim that the U.S. policy toward the Palestinian-Israeli conflict is biased?

6. The author suggests that U.S. policy to settle the Palestinian-Israeli conflict has not been helpful and can even be construed as a contributing factor in the perpetuation of the conflict. Do you agree or disagree with him, and why?

Building on the Iran Deal: Steps Toward a Middle Eastern Nuclear-Weapon-Free Zone

By Alexander Glaser, Zia Mian, Seyed Hossein Mousavian, and Frank von Hippel

The July 14 agreement between Iran and the six-country group known as the P5+1 established a set of important limitations and related transparency measures on Iran's nuclear activities. Approved unanimously by the UN Security Council on July 20, the agreement, formally known as the Joint Comprehensive Plan of Action, aims "to ensure that Iran's nuclear program will be exclusively peaceful" and thus to reduce the risk of nuclear proliferation. To this end, it imposes limits for a decade or more on Iran's use of the key technologies required to make highly enriched uranium (HEU) and to separate plutonium, the fissile materials that are the critical ingredients in nuclear weapons.

Other states in the Middle East, especially Egypt and Saudi Arabia, are planning to establish their own nuclear power programs during the period that the Iran deal is expected to be in force. This has led to concerns about how Iran and other countries in the region will act when restrictions on Tehran's nuclear program end. To address such concerns, this article proposes that the P5+1 and the states of the Middle East use the next decade to agree on region-wide restraints based on the key obligations of the Iran deal as steps toward establishing a Middle Eastern nuclear-weapon-free zone, preferably as part of a regional zone free of all weapons of mass destruction (WMD).[1] These measures would ban the separation of plutonium, limit the level of uranium enrichment, place enrichment plants under multinational control, and cap and reduce Israel's existing stocks of fissile materials available for use in nuclear weapons, in time eliminating its arsenal through a step-by-step process.

These are intermediate steps to a nuclear-weapon-free zone that would establish strong, new technical and political barriers to any future attempts by countries in the region to seek a nuclear weapons capability. Although different Middle Eastern states may favor different sequencing of these and other steps, all of the intermediate steps presented below have nonproliferation and disarmament value in their own right. Individually and in groups, states in the region should be encouraged to adopt these steps as way stations toward the larger goal of a nuclear-weapon-free Middle East. They also should be pursued globally as steps toward global nuclear disarmament, especially by the five

Alexander Glaser, et al., "Building on the Iran Deal: Steps Toward a Middle Eastern Nuclear-Weapon-Free Zone," *Arms Control Today*, vol. 45, no. 10, pp. 14-20. Copyright © 2015 by Arms Control Association. Reprinted with permission. Provided by ProQuest LLC. All rights reserved.

permanent members of the Security Council (China, France, Russia, the United Kingdom, and the United States), who all have nuclear weapons and with Germany make up the P5+1.

As in the Iran deal, verification arrangements will be important. Covert proliferation has a long history in the Middle East, starting with Israel's nuclear program in the 1960s and continuing with the violations by Iraq, Libya, and Syria of their commitments under the nuclear Nonproliferation Treaty (NPT) and most recently the confrontation over Iran's nuclear program. Given this history and the deep mutual suspicions of countries in the region, a robust regional safeguards, monitoring, and verification regime may add to the confidence provided by the International Atomic Energy Agency (IAEA) nuclear safeguards system.

Principles and Building Blocks

A nuclear-weapon-free zone in the Middle East was first proposed in the UN General Assembly in 1974 by Iran and Egypt. In 1990, the proposal was broadened by Egypt to include a ban on chemical and biological weapons—that is, to create a WMD-free zone in the Middle East. A 1991 study commissioned by the UN secretary-general proposed that such a zone encompass "all States directly connected to current conflicts in the region, i.e., all States members of the League of Arab States ... the Islamic Republic of Iran, and Israel."[2] As of late 2015, all of these countries but two—Israel and Syria—had sent letters to the UN secretary-general confirming their support for declaring the Middle East a region free from nuclear, chemical, and biological weapons.[3]

Most of the states expected to join a Middle Eastern WMD-free zone have signed and ratified the Chemical Weapons Convention (CWC) and the Biological Weapons Convention (BWC), and all but Israel have joined the NPT as non-nuclear-weapon states. Many also have signed and ratified the Comprehensive Test Ban Treaty (CTBT). Some are members of the African nuclear-weapon-free zone, created by the Treaty of Pelindaba, which entered into force in 2009 (Table 2.1).

Ban on the separation of plutonium. As part of the nuclear deal, Iran agreed that, for 15 years, it "will not, and does not intend to thereafter" carry out any separation of plutonium from spent nuclear fuel, an operation known as reprocessing. Iran also pledged not to build a facility capable of reprocessing or to carry out any research and development activities in that area. In addition, Tehran affirmed its intent to ship out to another country, presumably Russia, all spent nuclear fuel from all present and future power and research reactors.

Israel is the only country in the region that has separated plutonium from spent nuclear fuel. Its nuclear arsenal is based on plutonium that was produced by irradiating natural uranium fuel in a reactor that uses heavy water as a neutron moderator. The reactor, which Israel built with French assistance in the 1950s, is located at the Negev Nuclear Research Center near Dimona.[4]

Israel's plutonium has been separated from the irradiated uranium in an underground reprocessing plant adjoining the reactor. As its first step toward a Middle Eastern nuclear-weapon-free zone, Israel

Table 2.1: Weapons of Mass Destruction Treaties and Possible Members of a Middle Eastern Nuclear-Weapon-Free Zone

	CWC	BWC	NPT	CTBT	Treaty of Pelindaba
Algeria	1995	2001	1995	2003	1998
Bahrain	1997	1988	1988	2004	–
Comoros	2006	–	1995	1996	2012
Djibouti	2006	–	1996	2005	1996
Egypt	–	1972	1981	1996	1996
Iran	1997	1973	1970	1996	–
Iraq	2009	1991	1969	2013	
Israel	1993	–	–	1996	–
Jordan	1997	1975	1970	1998	
Kuwait	1997	1972	1989	2003	
Lebanon	2008	1975	1970	2008	
Libya	2004	1982	1975	2004	2005
Mauritania	1998	2015	1993	2003	1998
Morocco	1995	2002	1970	2000	–
Oman	1995	1992	1997	2003	–
Palestine	–	–	2015		–
Qatar	1997	1975	1989	1997	–
Saudi Arabia	1996	1972	1988	–	–
Somalia	2013	1972	1970	–	2006
Sudan	1999	2003	1973	2004	1996
Syria	2013	1972	1969	–	–
Tunisia	1997	1973	1970	2004	1996
United Arab Emirates	2000	2008	1995	2000	–
Yemen	2000	1979	1979	1996	–

Notes: Dates indicate ratification/accession or signature (gray shading) to the Chemical Weapons Convention (CWC), Biological Weapons Convention (BWC), nuclear Nonproliferation Treaty (NPT), Comprehensive Test Ban Treaty (CTBT), and Treaty of Pelindaba on an African nuclear-weapon-free zone.

Source: Organisation for the Prohibition of Chemical Weapons, Comprehensive Test Ban Treaty Organization, and UN Office for Disarmament Affairs.

could shut down the Dimona reactor and end reprocessing of the accumulated discharged fuel. These steps could be verified with fair confidence at first without access to the site and later under an arrangement that would give IAEA inspectors what is known as managed access, which would

Chavosh Homavandi/AFP/Getty Images

Iranian students form a human chain outside the site of the Fordow uranium-enrichment facility near the northern Iranian city of Qom during a demonstration to defend their country's nuclear program on November 19, 2013.

allow them to determine that the facilities were indeed shut down while allowing Israel to protect sensitive facility information.

Even if Middle Eastern countries pursue ambitious civilian nuclear power programs, they need not develop reprocessing capabilities. No sound economic or environmental justification exists for separating and stockpiling plutonium.[5] Of the 30 countries with operational commercial nuclear power reactors, only six have active civilian reprocessing programs, and five of those six states are nuclear-weapon states. Japan is the only non-nuclear-weapon state with a civilian reprocessing plant, but the plant is not operating and is the subject of extensive debate over its utility, risks, and cost.[6]

Restrictions on uranium enrichment. Centrifuge enrichment plants pose significant proliferation concerns because they can be quickly reconfigured for HEU production.[7] This is why a major part of the nuclear deal focuses on Iran's gas-centrifuge uranium-enrichment facilities and activities. Iran agreed that it will keep its operating enrichment capacity limited to one site and to a total of 5,060 first-generation centrifuges for 10 years and limit for 15 years the enrichment of its product to less than 3.67 percent uranium-235 and its stock of low-enriched uranium hexafluoride, the gaseous form that could be fed into the centrifuge cascades for further enrichment, to a very low level (less than 300 kilograms). These limitations would extend the time it would take Iran to produce enough weapons-grade HEU for a first nuclear weapon from about two months to about a year.

After the limits expire, however, Iran plans to expand its enrichment capacity by a factor of more than 20 in order to produce at least the 27 metric tons per year of 3.7 percent-enriched uranium required to fuel the Russian-supplied Bushehr power reactor.

Weapons-grade HEU is typically enriched to a U-235 level of 90 percent or greater. For safeguards purposes, however, the IAEA treats uranium enriched above 20 percent as a direct weapons-usable material. Even 20 percent is a much higher level of enrichment than the less-than-5-percent-enriched uranium that is used to fuel commercial nuclear power reactors worldwide today.

The only operating uranium-enrichment plant in the United States is licensed to enrich up to 5 percent U-235.[8] France's Georges Besse II enrichment plant, which began operating in 2009 and supplies enriched uranium for France's nuclear power plants, is licensed to produce up to 6 percent U-235.[9] It also supplies France's nuclear submarines. Enrichment in a Middle Eastern nuclear-weapon-free zone therefore could be limited to less than 6 percent and still accommodate states wishing to develop nuclear naval propulsion. Some policymakers and officials in Iran have already expressed such ambitions.[10]

The United States, the UK, Russia, and India use HEU for naval fuel, unlike France and, it is believed, China. They should be pressed to shift to low-enriched uranium (LEU) fuel as part of a strengthened global nonproliferation and disarmament regime.

Only three countries in the potential Middle Eastern WMD-free zone—Iran, Israel, and Syria—have reactors that use HEU as fuel. These are research reactors, all of which are under IAEA safeguards. Israel's U.S.-supplied Soreq reactor is scheduled to be shut down in 2018.[11] The HEU-fueled research reactors in Iran and Syria, supplied by China, contain only about 1 kilogram of HEU each, much less than the 25 kilograms of U-235 that is the figure the IAEA uses as a rough measure of the quantity required for a simple nuclear weapon. China has developed a new fuel for such reactors that could be used to convert them to LEU fuel.

Several other research reactors in Middle Eastern states, including the U.S.-supplied Tehran Research Reactor, use fuel enriched to 19.75 percent. Russia and the United States have enough excess HEU to down-blend and use to supply the fuel needs of these reactors and similar reactors worldwide for many decades. Iran already has agreed to import such uranium as other countries do.

Iran is the only country in the Middle East with plans for a significant commercial uranium-enrichment program. Israel may now have or might have had a small-scale, centrifuge-based uranium-enrichment capability.[12] No other state in the region is believed to have this technology. Saudi Arabia, however, has been unwilling to rule out seeking an enrichment capability.

To address the latent proliferation capability of enrichment plants, uranium enrichment in the Middle East and preferably globally should be placed under multinational control.[13] One-third of global uranium-enrichment capacity, including the only commercial enrichment plants currently operating in two of the five NPT nuclear-weapon states (the UK and the United States), already is operated by Urenco, a company owned jointly by the Netherlands, the UK, and two German utilities, with senior management and an oversight body of government officials drawn from all three countries.[14]

A multinationally managed and operated enrichment plant, bringing together Iran and regional partners, would undercut incentives for Middle Eastern states to follow Iran and build national enrichment facilities. Senior Iranian officials have indicated that Iran is ready to partner with other countries in the region so that they do not have to build their own enrichment plants and to help set up a system to guarantee the fuel supply of nuclear power plants in the Middle East. A strategy of including as partners one or more members of the P5+1, all of whom already hold centrifuge enrichment technology, could maintain extra transparency with regard to Iran's enrichment operations, uranium acquisitions, and centrifuge manufacture after the extra transparency established under the nuclear deal expires. As a first step, Iran and the P5+1 could establish a working committee on multilateralization of Iran's enrichment program. They could invite other partners of the region to join and set a five-year deadline to reach agreement.

Declarations of fissile material stockpiles and step-by-step safeguards. Dealing with Israel's stockpiles of nuclear weapons and fissile materials will be a key part of achieving a Middle Eastern nuclear-weapon-free zone. Israel, the only non-NPT state in the region, keeps the existence of its stockpiles cloaked in secrecy.[15]

A step toward enabling a Middle Eastern nuclear-weapon-free zone and nuclear disarmament would be for Israel to declare the size of its stocks of unsafeguarded fissile materials. Israel initially need not disclose what portions reside in its nuclear weapons or any other information about its nuclear weapons program and arsenal. Israel would be called on to reduce and eventually eliminate the quantities of plutonium and HEU that it has available for use in weapons by placing increasing portions under international safeguards for verified disposal.

Verification Arrangements

Any Middle Eastern nuclear-weapon-free zone will need robust verification. The parties to a zone treaty almost certainly would want a regional monitoring regime to buttress IAEA inspections. Such an arrangement exists in Europe in the form of Euratom. In Latin America's nuclear-weapon-free zone, Argentina and Brazil have a joint organization, the Brazilian-Argentine Agency for Accounting and Control of Nuclear Materials, through which they monitor each other's nuclear activities.

Measures could go beyond standard IAEA safeguards to include the new transparency obligations accepted by Iran under the July 2015 agreement, such as monitoring of uranium mining and purification, uranium imports, and production of nuclear materials and nuclear-related technology such as centrifuges. Some other elements of a possible verification regime are discussed below.

Additional protocol and transparency measures. Under the July agreement, Tehran is to implement on a provisional basis an additional protocol to its IAEA safeguards agreement and to seek ratification of the protocol when the IAEA reaches the conclusion that all of Iran's nuclear material is in peaceful uses or after eight years, whichever comes first. An additional protocol requires parties to declare all of their nuclear-related activities, including centrifuge manufacture—not just those involving nuclear materials—and to give IAEA inspectors access to check those declarations.[16]

Thirteen of the 23 countries that could be part of a Middle Eastern nuclear-weapon-free zone (Egypt, Iran, Israel, Lebanon, Oman, Palestine, Qatar, Saudi Arabia, Somalia, Sudan, Syria, Tunisia, and Yemen) have not ratified an additional protocol.[17] Like Iran, all of these states could bring an additional protocol into force pending ratification.

Israel's safeguards agreement, which has been in force since 1975, covers only the Soreq research reactor. Once this reactor is shut down and the U.S.-origin fuel is returned, no IAEA safeguards of any kind will exist in Israel. As part of the confidence-building process, Israel and the IAEA could negotiate a safeguards agreement that would cover all of Israel's peaceful nuclear-related activities and fissile material withdrawn from its nuclear weapons stockpile. Israel would not be the first nuclear-armed state to do so. The five NPT nuclear-weapon states and India have signed and ratified additional protocols with the IAEA that are much more limited in coverage than those signed by the NPT non-nuclear-weapon states.

Although full transparency and on-site inspections will be indispensable elements of a successful regional and IAEA verification system, some of the initial steps outlined above for moving toward a Middle Eastern nuclear-weapon-free zone could be verified initially with fair confidence without direct access to the sites in question. Among the conditions that could be verified with standoff detection methods could be the shutdown of the reactor and reprocessing plant at Dimona, as described below.

Shutdown of the plutonium-production reactor. Satellite or airborne infrared sensors should be able to verify the operational status of Israel's Dimona plutonium-production reactor by detecting the reduction of the temperatures of the outside of the reactor containment building or the reactor's cooling towers (Figure 2.1) once the reactor shuts down. Likewise, the sensors could help detect heat produced by any undeclared reactors in the region.

Shutdown of the reprocessing plant. The absence of reprocessing should be verifiable by off-site monitoring for the gaseous fission product krypton-85, which is released when irradiated nuclear fuel is cut open in the first stage of reprocessing. Because the gas is chemically nonreactive, reprocessing plants have not bothered to try to capture it. An analysis of measurements of krypton-85 at a distance of 60 kilometers from Japan's Tokai pilot reprocessing plant demonstrated a high detection probability.[18] Unless Dimona has installed a highly effective capture system, it should be possible to detect, with sensors placed around the Dimona site, any emissions of krypton-85 against the krypton background from reprocessing activities elsewhere in the world (Figure 2.2).

FIGURE 2.1 Remote Detection of Thermal Signatures

Infrared sensors on satellites, aircraft, or drones could reliably confirm the operational status of the Dimona reactor. Such sensors are allowed, for instance, as part of the 1992 Open Skies Treaty, an arms control and transparency agreement that has 34 states-parties and covers the United States, Russia, and Europe. The infrared picture shows a train carrying casks of high-level radioactive waste. The peak surface temperature indicated by the pattern on the leading cask was 30 degrees Celsius (86 degrees Fahrenheit).

Source: Greenpeace. The original color-coded version of this image with a temperature scale is available at http://news. nationalgeographic.com/news/2011/01/pictures/110119-nuclear-waste-train-castor-antinuclear-protest-germany-power-energy-pictures.

Shutdown of enrichment. Uranium enrichment using centrifuges is much more difficult to detect from a distance than reprocessing. There is very little leakage from centrifuge plants, so detecting undeclared uranium hexafluoride production might be a more promising approach.[19] The difficulty of detecting clandestine uranium enrichment highlights the potential role and importance of cradle-to-grave approaches to the nuclear fuel cycle.[20]

One immediate opportunity for collaborative efforts to build verification capacity could be for Middle Eastern countries to set up a regional data-sharing, analysis, and technical training process focused on existing or planned CTBT monitoring stations. Of special interest could be the radionuclide monitoring stations that look for radioxenon and other isotopes and particles from nuclear explosive tests. There currently are stations in Kuwait City; Misrata, Libya; and Nouakchott, Mauritania. A station is planned for Tehran. Mobile platforms could look for krypton-85 from reprocessing as part of the verification network for a nuclear-weapon-free zone.

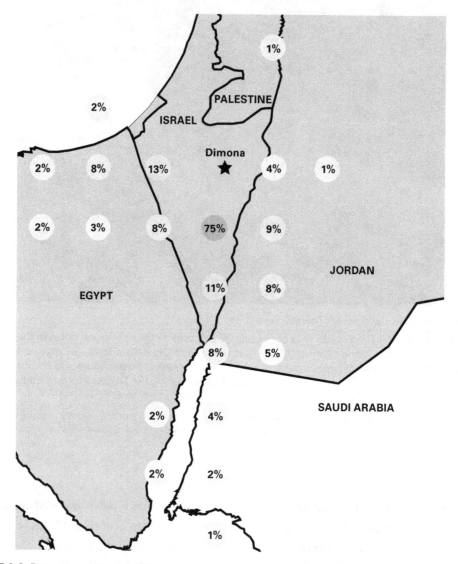

FIGURE 2.2 Detection of Krypton-85

Even a small number of krypton-85 detector stations in the Middle East could enhance confidence that Israel had ended reprocessing at its Dimona site. Based on computer simulations of atmospheric transport, the circles show the percentage of the time over the course of a year that sensors at the center of the circles could detect Kr-85 releases from Dimona associated with the separation of weapons-grade plutonium at a rate of 18 kilograms per year. Sensors located at the boundary of the Dimona site would detect releases of this scale whenever they occurred.

Source: Michael Schoeppner, Program on Science and Global Security, Princeton University

The Dimona nuclear reactor in the Israeli Negev Desert is shown in this September 2002 photo.

One particularly important aspect of a verified nuclear-weapon-free zone in the Middle East will be to obtain confidence in the completeness of Israel's fissile material declaration. This total could be checked after Israel had placed all of its declared fissile material under international safeguards. Israel's historical production of plutonium could be checked using techniques of "nuclear archaeology." These would include measurements of isotopic changes of certain trace elements in the permanent metal structures supporting the core of the Dimona reactor.[21] The measurements would reveal the cumulative flow, or fluence, of neutrons through the core over the lifetime of the reactor, which would provide the basis for an estimate of the total production of plutonium by the reactor. By committing publicly to this goal in advance, Israel could contribute to a regional confidence-building process and help set the basis for a verifiable Middle Eastern WMD-free zone.

Conclusion

The Joint Comprehensive Plan of Action provides an unprecedented opportunity for an international effort to make progress toward a Middle Eastern nuclear-weapon-free zone, possibly as part of WMD-free zone in that region. Building on the foundation created by that agreement, the measures proposed here constitute the essential technical steps toward a nuclear-weapon-free zone.

Although it is unlikely that such a zone can be established anytime soon, it should be possible to make progress on a number of the building blocks for it. Region-wide commitments to refrain from separating plutonium for any purpose, to limit uranium enrichment to the levels required for power reactors, and to conduct any enrichment activities only as part of a multinational arrangement would be major achievements. International and regional verification of such commitments would provide enhanced confidence against possible proliferation risks.

Notes

1. For a longer discussion, see Frank N. von Hippel et al., "Fissile Material Controls in the Middle East: Steps Toward a Middle East Zone Free of Nuclear Weapons and All Other Weapons of Mass Destruction," International Panel on Fissile Materials (IPFM), 2013.

2. UN Department for Disarmament Affairs, "Effective and Verifiable Measures Which Would Facilitate the Establishment of a Nuclear-Weapon-Free Zone in the Middle East," A/45/435, 1991.

3. UN General Assembly, "Letters Received From Member States Confirming Support for Declaring the Middle East a Region Free From Weapons of Mass Destruction, Including Nuclear, Chemical and Biological Weapons: Note by the Secretary-General," A/68/781, March 6, 2014.

4. For a detailed discussion of various estimates of Israel's plutonium production, see IPFM, "Global Fissile Material Report 2010; Balancing the Books: Production and Stocks," December 2010, ch. 8, http://fissilematerials.org/library/ gfmr10.pdf.

5. "Plutonium Separation in Nuclear Power Programs: Status, Problems, and Prospects of Civilian Reprocessing Around the World," IPFM, July 2015.

6. Masafumi Takubo and Frank von Hippel, "Ending Reprocessing in Japan: An Alternative Approach to Managing Japan's Spent Nuclear Fuel and Separated Plutonium," IPFM, November 2013.

7. Alexander Glaser, "Characteristics of the Gas Centrifuge for Uranium Enrichment and Their Relevance for Nuclear Weapon Proliferation," *Science and Global Security*, Vol. 16, Nos. 1–2 (2008): 1–25.

8. U.S. Nuclear Regulatory Commission (NRC), materials license SNM-2010 issued for the Louisiana Energy Services National Enrichment Facility near Eunice, New Mexico, June 23, 2006, http://pbadupws.nrc.gov/docs/ML0617/ ML061780384.pdf.

9. Areva, "Expanding the U.S. Nuclear Infrastructure by Building a New Uranium Enrichment Facility" (presentation at pre-application meeting with the NRC, May 21, 2007), http://pbadupws.nrc.gov/docs/ML0716/ ML071650116.pdf.

10. The deputy head of the Iranian navy said in 2012, "Since we possess peaceful nuclear technology, therefore we can also put on our agenda the construction of propulsion systems for nuclear submarines." "Iran Plans to Build N-Fueled Submarines," *PressTV*, June 12, 2012.

11. Shlomo Cesana, "Israel's Soreq Nuclear Reactor to Shut Down in 2018," *Israel Hayom*, March 21, 2012.

12. IPFM, "Global Fissile Material Report 2010," p. 115.

13. Mohamed ElBaradei, "Towards a Safer World," *Economist*, October 16, 2003; Alexander Glaser, Zia Mian, and Frank von Hippel, "After the Iran Deal: Multinational Enrichment," *Science*, June 19, 2015.

14. The centrifuges used in Urenco plants, including the Urenco USA plant, and in Areva's plant in France are made on a "black-box" basis by the Enrichment Technology Company, which is jointly owned by Urenco and Areva.

15. Israel is believed to have clandestinely obtained about 300 kilograms of weapons-grade uranium from a U.S. naval fuel fabrication facility during the 1960s. Victor Gilinsky and Roger J. Mattson, "Did Israel Steal Bomb-Grade Uranium From the United States?" *Bulletin of the Atomic Scientists*, April 2014. See also Victor Gilinsky and Roger J. Mattson, "Revisiting the NUMEC Affair," *Bulletin of the Atomic Scientists*, Vol. 66, No. 2 (March 2010).

16. International Atomic Energy Agency (IAEA), "Model Protocol Additional to the Agreement(s) Between State(s) and the International Atomic Energy Agency for the Application of Safeguards," INFCIRC/540 (Corrected), December 1998.

17. IAEA, "Status of the Additional Protocol; Status as of 03 July 2015," November 13, 2015, https://www.iaea.org/safeguards/ safeguards-legal-framework/additional-protocol/ status-of-additional-protocol.

18. R. Scott Kemp, "A Performance Estimate for the Detection of Undeclared Nuclear-Fuel Reprocessing by Atmospheric [85]Kr," *Journal of Environmental Radioactivity*, Vol. 99, No. 8 (August 2008): 1341–1348.

19. R. Scott Kemp and Clemens Schlusser, "Initial Analysis of the Detectability of UO_2F_2 Aerosols Produced by UF_6 Released From Uranium Conversion Plants," *Science and Global Security*, Vol. 16, No. 3 (2008): 115–125; R. Scott Kemp, "Source Terms for Routine UF_6 Emissions," *Science and Global Security*, Vol. 18, No. 2 (2010): 119–125.

20. Such a cradle-to-grave approach was proposed by Austria in 2009. IAEA "Communication Dated 26 May 2009 Received From the Permanent Mission of Austria to the Agency Enclosing a Working Paper Regarding Multilateralisation of the Nuclear Fuel Cycle," INFCIRC/755, June 2, 2009.

21. Alex Gasner and Alexander Glaser, "Nuclear Archaeology for Heavy-Water-Moderated Plutonium Production Reactors," *Science and Global Security*, Vol. 19, No. 3 (2011): 223–233.

DISCUSSION QUESTIONS

1. How would you summarize the main argument of the article in a sentence or two?

2. What agency is most responsible for nuclear nonproliferation and what are some of its responsibilities?

3. What is the idea behind a "nuclear weapon-free Middle East," and what countries are its major proponents and opponents?

4. How would multilateralization of Iran's enrichment program help with the Iran nuclear deal, aka, the Joint Comprehensive Plan of Action (JCPOA)?

5. What did the JCPOA achieve when it was signed on July 14, 2015?

6. The Iran nuclear deal was the result of years of negotiations between the P5 +1 and Iran. Who are the members of the P5 +1? Why are these countries so important in negotiating Iran's nuclear deal and in any future nuclear deal negotiations?

What Is Missing in the Sunni-Shi'a Divide Narrative?

By Ali R. Abootalebi

A s a student of social sciences, and now a professor of political science, I persistently urge my students to pay close attention to the underlying context in which events take place; to remain cognizant of socioeconomic, political, cultural, historical, and international contexts in explaining human interactions and events in varying settings. So, it is puzzling as to why intelligent people in the media and those in charge of U.S. foreign policy persistently ignore this simple proposition. Whatever the motivation behind such disregard and/or ignorance, there are important consequences. The late Edward Said[1] told of the "Orientalism" disease that poisoned the minds of both the intellectual and the common observers of Middle Eastern peoples and societies: Designated as "the other," the Oriental people are marred with peculiar and traditional sociocultural values, setting them apart from the "rational" Occidental mind, and are resistant to modernity and political democracy. The cultural essentialists thus claimed that Islam, traditionalism, and tribalism are central variables in explaining the prevalence of what is indeed structural. As such, historical colonialism and imperialism and persistent external covert, and overt interventions in the Middle East and Northern African region (MENA) were largely ignored, downplayed, or justified. Political authoritarianism and social stagnation "must have been" endemic to the Arab world, if less so in the westernizing Turkey and Iran. Even the harshest critics of Said's works cannot dismiss the cultural divide between the West and the East has structural components.[2]

The Sunni-Shi'a schism provides for different narrative and prescriptions for arriving at the "utopian Islamic society" and the incoming of the Messiah, *al-Mahdi*. The theological, doctrinal, and jurisprudential differences between the two main branches of Islam have translated into two different visions on the role of the clerics, the *'Ulema*, in religious and political arenas. Overall, the Shi'a *'Ulema* are better positioned to act as the custodian of the (Islamic) state in the name of the people. The hierarchical Shi'a version of the *Sharia* provides for justifications to bestow its highest ranking *'Ulema*, the *Ayatollahs,* with religious (and political) authority in charge of the state. The Islamic Republic of Iran is the living example of the late Ayatollah Khomeini's legacy, insisting that the *'Ulema*-led Islamic government in Iran is the embodiment of Islam itself. This has positioned

Adapted from Ali R. Abootalebi, "What Is Missing in Our Sunni-Shi'a Conflict Narrative?" *Informed Comment*, 2018.

the Shi'a *'Ulema* as claimants to leadership in both the religious and the temporal worlds![3] The Ayatollah's counterparts in the Sunni tradition, the *Muftis,* on the other hand, are limited in playing such a role. For example, The Sunni community in Iraq today[4] does not follow a single *Marja* (source of authority and emulation) that funds religious leaders independently, like the Najaf-based Shiite authority. The historical Sunni political doctrine of the Islamic state necessitates the presence of a *Caliphate* (Emir or Sultan), the last of who was the last Sultan of the Ottoman Empire, and whose House of the Caliphate was abolished in 1924.

The Sunni or the Shi'a understanding of the "proper" social, theological/jurisprudential, and political framework promoting Islamic governance differ, but such disagreements cannot be understood outside its broader and prevalent national and international contexts. The last wave of Islamic revivalism of the late 1800s, for example, occurred when both the Ottoman and the Safavids dynasties were at the mercy of their European colonial powers and the existing socioeconomic and political environment were marred with severe levels of underdevelopment and poor governance. The mushrooming Islamic question for *revivalists* and *reformers* like Jamal al-din al-Afghani or Muhammad Abdu or Muhammad Iqbal was, then, over the discovery of an Islamic path to recovery considering the Muslim humiliation in the hands of the Christian West and the corrupt, incompetent rulers within. The burgeoning inquiry was over the question of effective (Islamic) governance and not the Sunni-Shi'a divide *per se.* This wave of Islamic movement differed from, for example, the *al-Khawarij* movement in early Islam that reflected the turbulent years of civil war in the Islamic community over the question of succession and the legitimacy to rule in the years after the death of the Prophet Muhammad (632–661AD). The political and social dissension and divide between the political elite in Damascus and the religious and spiritual leadership in Mecca and al-Najaf in Iraq had caused a political and religious gulf between a heretical vision of the political and military leadership in Damascus and the opposition who demanded their share in the distribution of wealth and political power (later known as the Shiite, or partisans of Ali, those followers of the bloodline heirs to the prophet Muhammad, led by the Prophet's son-in-law and later the fourth Caliphate of Islam, Ali ibn Abi Talib).

The ongoing propagated Sunni-Shi'a divide narrative proposes the sectarian divide as the cause of both national and inter-state problems in the region. The Sunni-Shi'a divide has been a dominant theme in explanation of events in the MENA region since the Iranian Revolution, including the root cause of the revolution—as a Shi'a-Islamic-revolution—to the Iraqi (Sunni-Arab dominated) invasion of a revolutionary (Shi'a) Iran, to the historical and modern sectarian divide causing conflict and war in Iraq, Lebanon, Syria, and Yemen, to the (Sunni) Saudi and (Shia) Iranian rivalry in the Persian Gulf region over a Sunni or a Shi'a alternative and vision for the future of Islam and Muslim societies. However, the root cause of the constructed Sunni-Shia conflict in Libya, Syria, Yemen, Iraq, Tunisia, Egypt, Sudan, Somalia, Bahrain, and other members of the Arab League, rests with poor governance, including the presence of illegitimate, authoritarian states. Sectarian mobilization and counter-mobilization is only a manifestation of the larger contest over political power and socioeconomic resources; in other words, it is over the control of the state and matters of governance.

The State and Governance

It is only natural to think of national governments once the question of governance arises.[5] After all, national governments are endowed with tremendous power, legitimate or not, and with resources to govern over matters of significance to the population, including law and order, national security, social and economic development, and the preservation of cultural heritage and overall social harmony. State capacity[6] has two broad components: protecting the safety and security of people and its ability to implement public policies, collect revenue, and deliver basic goods and services to enhance social welfare and economic growth. But, governance is about power, and it is broader than just the ruling government; it is about who has the political authority to make decisions and influence policy, and how resources and wealth are allocated within society. Good governance signals the ability of governing institutions to deliver the key public goods needed to maintain order and stability. Furthermore, governance is "good"[7] and also more likely to advance peace when "it is inclusive, participatory and accountable; when it is characterized by fair procedures and performs well in delivering necessary public goods." Democracy is an essential element of good governance; its presence may not be a guarantee of peace, but its absence and attempts to suppress it are significant risk factors for war.[8]

Democracy is not about culture, religion, or religious sectarianism *per se,* but the management of political power and the competition over socioeconomic resources within agreed-upon normative principles and values and institutional arrangements, whereby individual citizens, through elections and other forms of political participation, determine their own choices through elected representatives. In other words, political democracy is (can be) an instrumental method in the resolution of "identity conflicts" over cultural and nationalistic issues by providing legal and institutional venues for resolution of differences and conflicts to groups in competition over socioeconomic resources and political power. The competition among cultural groups in a given society is not so much about the superiority or inferiority of certain value system or way of life *per se* (e.g., designation of one's identity as Sunni or Shi'a, but how the competition translates into control over local, regional, and national resources while realizing the ambitions and aspirations of all cultural groups. This is especially true, where legal and institutional venues for dispute settlement and conflict resolution and power sharing among competing cultural groups are weak or are seriously lacking. In such cases, it becomes natural for a dominant culture to try imposing its ethos and belief systems, through cooperation or coercion, on minority groups, monopolizing control over socioeconomic resources and political power.

The inadequacies of the state and its institutions and bureaucracy and the presence of weak and divided society have been a prominent problem in the Arab MENA region. The state authoritarian rule and traditional value systems and institutions still pose serious challenges before Arab societies striving for democratic rule and social justice. The opposition in Arab countries also has failed to mobilize the populace around a common ideology to challenge the state. Instead, the state has manipulated ethnoreligious divisions to further divide and paralyze the opposition. Civil society in the Arab World remains underdeveloped. As Gilbert Achcar argues, the deep roots of the Arab uprising, for example, are manifold: First, almost all Arab states take their place on a scale running from patrimonial to neopatrimonial regimes, further accentuated by their rentier economies, and the state is merely a cash cow. Second, sociopolitical instability and the absence of any real rule of law in virtually all Arab countries means the development of speculative or commercial capitalism with the specific variant of a capitalist mode of production being politically determined. So, the peculiar modality of the capitalist mode of production—a mix of Patrimonialism, nepotism, and crony capitalism, pillaging of public property, swollen bureaucracy, and generalized corruption, against a background of great sociopolitical instability and the impotence or even nonexistence of the rule of law, is dominant in the Arab region. The Arab region on the eve of 2011 lacked organized political forces capable of moving popular protest and stood little chance of peacefully overturning Arab patrimonial regimes that were protected by a praetorian guard with tribal, sectarian, and regional loyalties. [9]

Corruption is the antithesis of good governance; it undermines the conditions that favor peace, economic development, stable governing institutions, and social trust,[10] and nothing does more to erode public trust and the legitimacy of government than public officials abusing their authority for illicit gain. Economic growth is dependent on policies that protect and support free markets, but markets flourish best in governance systems that promote equality of access, provide social safety nets, enhance human capital, respond effectively to market failures and guard against exploitation and abuse.[11] So, as Marwan Bishara in "The Invisible Arab"[12] observes, pillars of liberty and justice reconciled with religion and nationalism form the bedrock that will allow stability and progress to flourish in the Arab world and beyond.

The state of the Arab world is in turmoil. The rise of the so-called Islamic State in Iraq and Syria (al-Sham)' or the ISIL—the Daesh in Arabic—was (is) fundamentally the result of both the poverty of Arab politics and the failure of the Islamic clerical leadership in formulating and institutionalizing the mechanics necessary for modern governance. This failure is more pronounced in the Sunni Arab countries. Arab politics experimentation with Ba'athism, Pan-Arabism, secular nationalism, and monarchism have all failed, paving the way for Islamic movements, mostly colored with radical solutions to empower society and to thwart foreign influence. Although some Arab states have done better than others in the promotion of socioeconomic change, they all have fallen short in the political arena. The failure of the Arab Spring movements since 2011 only testifies to the entrenched power of Arab political elites and their foreign supporters who have thus far played the sectarian card and the war on terrorism mantra to secure regime survival and maintaining the status quo. The Shi'a clerics' takeover of the state in Iran since the 1979 revolution has allowed them the opportunity to formulate, institutionalize, and practice an Islamic Republicanism, with many successes and failures, but at least avoiding violent dissident religious movements. The simultaneous competition and cooperation between the religious and political establishment has resulted in tangible settlements, still evolving, of some seemingly intractable issues involving Islam and the operation of modern society, economy, and polity. As Bruce Rutherford elaborates on Islamic democracy, the interaction between liberal constitutionalism and Islamic constitutionalism is likely to produce a *distinctive form of democracy* that resembles Western democracy in institutional terms but differs about the purpose of the state, the role of the individual in politics and society, and the character and function of law. That is, the place and duties of the Islamic State remain controversial since it is the state that must ensure the presence of Islam in society, sanctioning rules and laws that can violate the individual rights of the citizen (e.g., hijab, minority rights, women rights, inheritance, family planning, testimonials, and role of judges, etc.).[13]

The contemporary Sunni-Shi'a schism dates back to the 1979 Iranian Revolution. Iran's foreign policy prior to, and since, the revolution has been driven, for the most part, by pragmatism; the sectarian card is played as a reaction to the rise of militant Sunni movements in Afghanistan, Pakistan, and the greater Arab world to protect the new revolutionary state and its ethos. Recall that Iran, before the revolution and unlike Egypt, Jordan, Saudi Arabia, or Pakistan, lacked any serious religious movement or religious political parties challenging the state, and it resembled its neighboring Turkey in its secular political orientation. Yet, the first 20th-century Islamic revolution in (Shi'a) Iran implied that Islam is indeed a potent sociopolitical contender in governance. The seizure of the Grand Mosque in Saudi Arabia in 1979 crystalized the threat of an "Islamic challenge" in the Arab world that diverted a great deal of wasted Saudi national treasure to thwart a Shi'a threat and promote militant Salafism in Pakistan, Afghanistan, and beyond, while protecting the prevailing sociopolitical and economic status quo. Hitherto, the sectarian card became currency in the constructed debate over not so much the deficiencies of good governance but over the supposed threat of all Islamic movements as a terrorist menace to societies everywhere! Iran's policy in support of national sovereignty and integrity of Iraq, Lebanon, Syria, and Yemen falls in line with its support of empowering the historically suppressed Shi'a political and religious establishments in Iraq and Lebanon, while its support for Syrian government and the Houthis in Yemen, though a limited one, counters the United States' and its allies' hostilities and their not-so-secret push for regime change in Tehran. Iran's foreign policy since the revolution has championed national self-reliance. This has been to the detriment of U.S. military and political presence and interest in the Persian Gulf and the wider region. The rise of Iranian power is also at the heart of Arab regimes' hostility toward Iran. The Arab political elites view Iran as a threat to their own existence and not as a source with potential for positive regional security cooperation and development.[14]

Marwan Bishara contends how Israel, oil, terrorism and radical Islam have affected the interior identity of the region as well as Western projections upon it. Protection of Israel, Western imperial ambition, a thirst for oil, and fear of radicalism have caused many Western regimes and media to characterize Arab countries and people as unreceptive to democracy or progress. First, Arab people stand apart from their governments. Then, the question must be asked as to why the West can perpetually manipulate Arab political leaders since the end of First World War. How far have the Arab politics really traveled in the past one hundred years? Are the Arab states and peoples truly victims of an Iranian-conspired sectarianism in the region? Or, is it that the Arab peoples are a victim of archaic and parochial politics and continuously manipulated by Western powers? In the end, let the evidence speak for itself: What is portrayed as the hallmark of relations between the leading Western countries and the modernizing Arab political allies has brought the Daesh, civil wars, death and destruction and humiliation, unprecedented to the region since the Mongol invasion or modern colonialism.

Notes

1. "Edward Said, Life and Career," http://www.edwardsaid.org/

2. Joshua Muravchik, "Enough Said: The False Scholarship of Edward Said," *World Affairs*, March/April 2013.

3. Ervand Abrahamian, *Khomeinism: Essays on the Islamic Republic* (Berkeley: University of California Press, 1993).

4. Ali Mamouri, "Will Iraq's Sunnis Get Own Political-Religious Authority?," *Almonitor,* February 23, 2018, https://www.al-monitor.com/pulse/originals/2018/02/iraq-sunni-marja-kubaisi-humim. html#ixzz58mh126it

5. David Cortright, Conor Seyle, and Kristen Wall, *Governance for Peace: How Inclusive, Participatory and Accountable Institutions Promote Peace and Prosperity (Cambridge:* Cambridge University Press, 2017).

6. Pippa Norris, *Making Democratic Governance Work: How Regimes Shape Prosperity, Welfare, and Peace* (Cambridge: Cambridge University Press, 2012).

7. Cortright et al., p. 47.

8. Ibid., 176.

9. Gilbert Achcar, *The People Want: A Radical Exploration of the Arab Uprising* (Berkeley: University of California Press, 2013).

10. Cortright et al., p. 130.

11. Ibid., 193.

12. Marwan Bishara, *The Invisible Arab: The Promise and Peril of the Arab Revolutions* (Nations Book, 2012).

13. Bruce Rutherford, "What Do Egypt's Islamists Want: Moderate Islam and the Rise of Islamic Constitutionalism," *Middle East Journal,* 60, no. 4 (Autumn, 2006): 707–731.

14. Ali R. Abootalebi, "40 Years on, Is Iran a Status Quo Power or a Threat to ME Regional Security?," *Informed Comment,* January 31, 2019, https://www.juancole.com/2019/01/threat-regional-security.html

DISCUSSION QUESTIONS

1. How would you summarize the main argument of the article in a sentence or two?

2. Why does the author believe that what appears as an ethnic conflict is in its core a conflict over socioeconomic resources and political power?

3. According to the article, what is the root cause of the failure of Arab politics?

4. How does the author explain the failure of the Arab Spring movement since 2011?

5. What does the author mean by "good governance," and why is it so important in explaining the failure of politics in dealing with identity conflict in the Arab world?

6. How is political democracy relevant in the quest for "good governance"?

PART III

Sources of Peace

Is There a Future for the United Nations?

By Karen A. Mingst, Margaret P. Karns, and Alynna J. Lyon,

T he United Nations today leads what seems at times like a double life. Pundits criticize it for not solving all the world's ills, yet people around the world are asking it to do more, in more places, than ever before.

> —*Secretary-General Ban Ki-moon,*
> Sydney Morning Herald, *December 31, 2010*

Secretary-General Ban Ki-moon's words echo a refrain often heard from supporters of the UN: "If the UN did not exist, a similar institution would have to be created." In this ... chapter, we explore some of the ways in which the UN has made a difference over more than seventy years and identify areas where it has failed. We examine factors that have shaped its successes and failures and the question of whether, in fact, the UN can be reformed to play an even more vigorous role in global governance.

As former UN secretary-general Kofi Annan wrote in reflecting on his experience, "To say the world is interdependent had become the worst kind of cliché. ... True in the literal sense, but unable to generate the kinds of multilateral engagement befitting a world where no threat was limited to one country or region."[1] The UN may have more reach than any other IGO, but that has never meant that it has had the resources, authority, competence, and coordination capabilities needed to address the many challenges it has faced.

Does The Un Make A Difference?

You might imagine in a book on the UN that the automatic, unequivocal answer to this question would be "of course." If you were to pick up literature from the UN's Department of Public Information, you would find it filled with a list of UN achievements over the years, including the positioning of peacekeepers along fragile borders in the Middle East and Cyprus, energizing the voices of newly independent colonies on behalf of self-determination and economic development, pushing an international human rights agenda for marginalized peoples, and improving global

Karen A. Mingst, Margaret P. Karns and Alynna J. Lyon, "Is There a Future for the United Nations?" *United Nations in the 21st Century*, pp. 335-347. Copyright © 2017 by Taylor & Francis Group. Reprinted with permission.

health through the WHO's eradication of smallpox and UNAIDS partnerships. Some books that dwell on the UN's achievements also note its shortcomings, much as we have. Still others are critiques of the UN or even polemics that emphasize that the institution is overtly politicized, criticizing states such as Israel and not others or responding to threats to the peace emanating from smaller states while neglecting those posed by the P-5. These critics point to the UN's failures: its inability to halt genocides, to stop weapons proliferation, and to close the gap between the rich and the poor. For some American pundits, the only logical response is for the United States to pull out and withdraw its support.

In weighing these questions of success and failure, it is important to acknowledge that the world of the twenty-first century is very different from the world of 1945. The scale and nature of today's problems go far beyond those envisioned by the UN's founders. The speed of changes, from the growing effects of climate change and numbers of refugees and migrants flooding into Europe in 2015 to the rapid spread of Ebola and the sudden emergence of ISIS in 2014, demand new ways of thinking as well as timely action. UN agencies, like bureaucracies everywhere, are not geared to handling rapid change and generating new thinking. They tend to be "silos"—created to deal with a particular category of problems, but now operating in a world of interconnected and interdependent problems with far fewer resources at hand.

Yet before examining what the UN can and cannot do, we must return to the notion that there is not just one UN but three UNs, each of which plays and has played a role in shaping what the UN does. As three experts put it, there is "the UN of governments, the UN of staff members, and the UN of closely associated NGOs, experts, and consultants."[2] It is the third UN that has been most neglected by scholars, diplomats, and governments because of the long-standing state-centric focus of international relations. And it is the third UN that has grown immensely in recent years, with NGOs and civil society organizations taking active roles in shaping new norms and policies and challenging notions of representation, accountability, and legitimacy; with for-profit corporations being drawn into UN activities with the establishment of the UN Global Compact; and with foundations such as the Gates Foundation now funding a significant portion of global health needs. All three UNs have influenced what the UN has and has not been able to do over the years, although it is admittedly difficult to differentiate between them in the area of one of the UN's major accomplishments, the development of new ideas.

Developing New Ideas

Over the decade 1999–2009, the United Nations Intellectual History Project (UNIHP) produced fifteen books and seventy-nine in-depth oral history interviews that trace and document the history of key ideas and concepts about security and economic and social development within the UN system. Thanks to UNIHP, we have important insights into those areas where the UN has had a major impact. The final volume, *UN Ideas That Changed the World*, brings together the wealth of insights that emerged from the project. The authors conclude that ideas are among the most significant contributions the UN has made to the world and to human progress. And all three UNs have played various roles "collectively ... sometimes in isolation and sometimes together or in parallel" in generating ideas, providing a forum for debate, giving ideas legitimacy, promoting adoption of ideas for policy, implementing or testing ideas and policies at the country level, generating resources for implementing ideas, monitoring their progress, and sometimes burying them.[3]

In the area of peace and security, the UN has advanced an idea that has proven to be of tactical importance to the UN's own role and has shown itself as flexible enough over time to encompass a variety of tasks. *Peacekeeping*—the idea that military personnel, police, and civilians from states acting on behalf of the international community, wearing the UN's blue berets, could insert themselves into conflict situations—represents an institutional innovation that was not explicit in the UN Charter. Peacekeepers can separate, disarm, and demobilize combatants; police cease-fires; and, in limited circumstances, even use more coercive measures under Chapter VII mandates to preserve international peace and security. They can protect aid workers, monitor human rights violations, undertake security sector reform, repatriate refugees, and provide interim civil administration. The idea has been implemented on six continents, using small to large contingents, some with pronounced effect and others deemed as mixed successes or even failures. Peacekeeping has become an integral part of the UN's approaches to addressing threats to peace and security, along with mediation, preventive diplomacy, and enforcement. ... However, the UN has now encountered serious problems of sexual abuse by some peacekeeping contingents that are jeopardizing the UN's and peacekeeping's reputations; this is compounded by the failure of the UN to take responsibility for the cholera epidemic in Haiti that has been traced to peacekeepers from Nepal.

The UN has also been instrumental in expanding the very concept of security from state security to *human security*. Humans, too, need to be secure in their own person, protected from violence, economic deprivation, poverty, infectious diseases, human rights violations by states, and environmental degradation. While it is governments' responsibility to provide for security within the state, some states may need assistance in controlling cross-border arms, human trafficking, and drug trafficking, and may need funding for economic development, monitoring disease, and adaptations to reverse or protect against environmental threats. In implementing the idea of human security, then, the UN can help states protect individuals and carry out the responsibilities of sovereignty.

Following from this, the UN legitimized the norm of states' *responsibility to protect* their own citizens, particularly from war crimes or crimes against humanity. This particular idea introduced a new interpretation of both state sovereignty and the obligations of the international community. As Edward Luck, the first assistant secretary-general for R2P (2008–2012), notes, "For all its ups and downs in practice, in political and normative terms the progress of R2P has been remarkably rapid, especially compared to other human rights and human protection norms. Among the member states, there are still questions about implementation—as well there should be—but not about the validity and legitimacy of the prevention and protection principles that lie at the heart of R2P. The level of understanding, not just acceptance, today is much deeper and much wider." But, Luck cautions, "knowing that we need to protect and knowing how to protect are two different things. ... The credibility of norms can be gained only in the field and in the lives of the vulnerable."[4]

In the area of economic development, the UN has benefited from the creativity of innovative economists who have at one time or another been employed by the UN or served as consultants and who have contributed to key UN ideas. *Sustainability*, as enunciated in the Brundtland Report, clearly showed that economic development cannot occur without consideration of the future, resources cannot be exploited without assurance that there are not detrimental side effects, and resource uses need to be managed with an eye to future generations. As a result, the UN and other development institutions have attempted to weigh development needs against environmental imperatives. And with the approval of the SDGs in 2015, sustainability figures in the majority of the goals that are intended to serve as the focus of UN development-related operations until 2030.

Development has also been reconceived as *human development*. Introduced in the 1990s, this idea represented a sea change in thinking from traditional economic theory that measured development in terms of growth in a state's GNP over time and in comparison to that of other states. Instead, UNDP and some of the specialized agencies began to think of development in terms of how it affected people: their health, educational level, income, and overall well-being, and the differential effects of gender. Thinking about human development led to the MDGs, then the SDGs, and to concerted action to eliminate extreme poverty and improve human well-being.

Universalizing *human rights for all* represents a key normative idea where all three UNs share credit. NGOs, in particular, were instrumental in getting human rights provisions into the UN Charter, and they continue to play critical roles in the promotion and monitoring of human rights. As one noted scholar has said, "Among the most improbable developments of the previous hundred years or so is the spectacular rise of human rights to a position of prominence in world politics. This rise cuts across the grain of both the structure of world order and the 'realist' outlook of most political leaders acting on behalf of sovereign states."[5]

And in human rights, as well as in peace and security and development, new categories of individuals as well as groups have been recognized as needing protection, including the disappeared, migrants, indigenous peoples, and lesbian, gay, bisexual, and transgender (LGBT) persons. The UN system has devoted particular attention to enhancing the status and role of women, but the UN itself did not initiate these efforts—key states and NGOs played that role—and the League of Nations provided the first international forum for promoting women's rights. But as the founding director of UNIFEM has said, "The global women's movement would be lost or at least much weaker without the UN."[6] Indeed, the four UN-sponsored world women's conferences played a major role in the creation of the global women's movement. And countless UN resolutions "have forced ... governments to be more accountable .... showing that this is the way that governments should behave, or corporations should behave, or men should behave."[7] Another major achievement on the long road for gender equality was the creation of UN Women in 2010.

Developing ideas is, therefore, an important way in which the UN has made a difference, but ideas alone are inadequate. Furthermore, some ideas took hold, while others did not. The UN itself sometimes implemented ideas, sometimes buried them. What, then, are other ways in which the UN has made a difference?

Filling Knowledge Gaps, Gathering Data

In the early years, the UN played a key role in helping states gather basic data and measure outcomes. That data collection largely reflected the perspective and methods of liberal economists and dominant states. But as new ideas emerged, the data collected had to change. Just as critical as monitoring deaths and refugee flows from interstate wars is knowing death rates and displacements during civil wars and monitoring flows of those forcibly displaced by climate change. Did economic development projects really benefit everyone, as liberal economists anticipated? We did not know the answer until data were collected comparing women and men on various development indicators. We now have a variety of indicators and data that help us to provide numbers to assess the impact of new ideas, and also help us to set goals, another key UN contribution. Data gathering and reporting have been core elements of the MDG process, as they will be in the SDG process now under way.

Setting, Promoting, and Monitoring Goals

The UN is often criticized as a forum for empty rhetoric and hot air, for resolutions and declarations that make no difference. One of the surprising conclusions from the UNIHP is the importance of goal setting; indeed, setting targets for economic and social development is seen as a "singular UN achievement."[8] More than fifty economic and social goals in all, beginning with the First Development Decade in 1960 and including the most recent ones—the MDGs for poverty reduction and the SDGs—have been set, promoted, and monitored. Despite concerns, for example, that many of the MDGs would not be met by the deadline in 2015 ... the final report showed that the proportion of people in dire poverty worldwide was more than halved ahead of the target year. The long list of human rights treaties negotiated under UN auspices established the normative foundation for global human rights and, hence, a set of goals of rights for all. The UN has established international machinery for their promotion through the OHCHR, as well as the Universal Periodic Review mechanism and treaty review processes for monitoring states' human rights records and the implementation of the various treaties. In the areas of arms control and counterterrorism, the UN has also set goals and provided assistance for both state and international monitoring. The IAEA plays a central role in the nuclear nonproliferation regime monitoring processes, as does the OPCW for chemical weapons. With the 2015 Paris climate change agreement, states agreed to five-year review cycles for their emission reduction targets. In short, "goals have also served over the years as a focus for mobilizing interests, especially the interests of NGOs, and for generating pressures for action."[9]

Agenda Setting: The UN's Value as a Forum

The value of the UN as a general forum, and particularly the General Assembly as a voice of the "peoples of the world," means that member states have used it to raise and act on new issues, thereby setting agendas for the UN itself, for other IGOs, for NGOs, and for states themselves. No one doubts the forum's value over time for promoting self-determination and decolonization in the 1950s and 1960s, calling attention to apartheid and pressuring South Africa to change over more than forty years, negotiating the comprehensive UN Convention on the Law of the Sea over nine years in the 1970s, recognizing the unique position of small island states in the climate change debate, or putting on the agenda the rights of the disabled, migrant workers, LGBT persons, and indigenous peoples. For more than forty years, the Palestinians have used the General Assembly and other UN agencies as forums to gain recognition of their existence and rights. In 2011, Palestine was admitted as a member of UNESCO, and in 2012, it was granted nonmember observer state status by the General Assembly—a de facto recognition of sovereignty. To be sure, in the eyes of some, the forum has been abused, as when it was used to repeatedly link Zionism with racism in General Assembly resolutions over many years. Still, it is valuable for the international community to have a place where issues can be raised, resolutions can be put forward, and consensus can be built or votes taken, both as a way to set agendas and to let off steam. The General Assembly's vote in 2015 calling for a more transparent process for selecting the next secretary-general illustrates well the frustration of a majority of UN member states with the stalled process of UN reform.

Partnerships

The UN's various organs, programs, and agencies increasingly work with a variety of partners to accomplish their objectives, making partnerships an important modus operandi. UN specialized agencies and programs not only work in tandem but also work with NGOs, local community groups, corporations, and foundations. The UN Joint Programme on HIV/AIDS, established in 1996, is a partnership of seven UN specialized agencies along with UNDP, WFP, national governments, corporations, religious organizations, grassroots groups, and NGOs to meet the multifaceted challenges of HIV/AIDS. It tracks the epidemic, monitors responses, distributes strategic information, mobilizes resources, and reaches out to diverse groups. It also illustrates that not all UN partnerships are effective: while it continues its work, it is supplemented by the independent Global Fund to Fight AIDS, Tuberculosis, and Malaria. And it underscores how the UN increasingly works with the private sector, including in improving labor and environmental policies (UN Global Compact, Green Energy Fund) and in tackling specific health threats (pharmaceutical companies and the Gates Foundation). Partnerships are essential for augmenting financial resources and marshaling expertise for global problem solving, for providing broader participation from donors, and for improving buy-in and, hence, legitimacy for recipient states and individuals.

Former UN secretary-general Kofi Annan, who initiated the Global Compact with corporations, asks, "Can it [the UN] confine itself, in the twenty-first century, to the role of coordinating action by States? … Is it not obliged, in order to fulfill the purposes of the Charter, to form partnerships with all these different actors? To listen to them, to guide them, and to urge them on?" As Thomas Weiss notes, "Such partnerships represent a new way to govern the world … that is underresearched and poorly understood, especially the role of transnational business."[10] In peace operations, the UN has also undertaken partnerships with regional and subregional organizations, especially the African Union, ECOWAS, the EU, and NATO, as well as with coalitions of the willing.

Yet as much as the UN has demonstrated how it has made a difference, history has also made evident what the UN cannot do. Identifying these lessons is critical to considering what changes are needed in UN operations and in the expectations of member states and UN supporters.

Lessons About What the Un Cannot Do

At its core, the UN remains a product of the state system, an IGO whose member states retain sovereignty and whose policy outcomes must reflect state agreement. As John Ruggie reminds us, "International organizations remain anchored in the state system. … Their role in actual enforcement remains tightly constrained by states."[11]

Enforcement

Referring to the UN, Thomas Weiss and Ramesh Thakur acknowledge that "no ways exist to enforce decisions and no mechanisms exist to compel states to comply with decisions."[12] Although that may sound extreme, the fact is most UN bodies can only make recommendations. Hence, as the same authors explain, "One of the main tactics used in the face of these constraints has been to embarrass those who do not comply. This tactic is used when UN secretariats or NGOs generate and publicize information and data about noncompliance."[13] In the human rights area, this tactic has been successful *if* it is accompanied by strong domestic measures for compliance, particularly in the form of NGO pressure. On other issues, however, publicly naming and shaming states for noncompliance may not yield the desired results. The practice will be tested in the years ahead with the implementation of the 2015 Paris climate change agreement.

The UN Security Council, under Chapter VII, can clearly authorize sanctions and direct, coercive military action if the P-5 concur (or do not exercise their vetoes). Although sanctions have been extensively used since the Cold War's end, there have been a number of key lessons learned, as … . For one, comprehensive sanctions are not effective. Sanctions must be carefully targeted based on knowledge about the targeted country, key individuals, and groups; they must also be monitored and adjusted over time, and sanctions violators must be held accountable. It is also clear that each sanctions case is unique and prior experience is not necessarily a predictor of future outcomes. UN sanctions on Iran do appear to have been a factor in securing the 2015 agreement on its nuclear program, but sanctions have not worked with North Korea.

Military enforcement action is still rare, despite the greater use of Chapter VII authority in mandates for peace operations. Even if there is consensus on some type of enforcement, it may be for a relatively brief period of time, and member states may not back up that commitment with sufficient resources to ensure success. A clear lesson is that the UN must rely on major powers, a coalition of the willing, or NATO with its alliance capabilities for joint action. States are unwilling to provide the UN with the types of military resources necessary for major coercive action. And, as the Syrian civil war has tragically demonstrated, member states are also often reluctant to see the UN intervene in some situations. This particular failure has clearly damaged the UN's reputation and especially that of the Security Council. Too little attention has been given to precedents that may be set with UN authorized enforcement actions in the DRC and Mali that threaten to put peacekeepers at further risk and compromise the UN's ability to serve as an impartial broker …

Responding to Crises

As illustrated by the Ebola outbreak and the refugee/migration crisis, the UN system does not have a good track record in recent years in responding to emergencies. WHO has shown itself not to be the global health responder that it needs to be, and it is hobbled by bureaucratic and structural problems. UNHCR, WFP, and other parts of the UN humanitarian aid system are woefully underfunded to meet current needs, and there is no agency within the UN system (or outside) with a mandate to address larger migration issues.

Similarly, despite numerous calls over the years for the UN to create a rapid- reaction force to prevent the outbreak of armed conflict or secure an end to fighting pending deployment of a regular peacekeeping force, member states have failed to act on this except for where individual states have earmarked peacekeeping contingents. Multilateral military interventions, be they organized under the UN, NATO, or the EU, require time: time to get the consent of the P-5 in the case of the UN; time to organize the military units from member states; time to transport troops and equipment to the crisis area. A small UN rapid-reaction force could be designed for quick deployment, pending organization of a larger force. Boosting the UN's early-warning, intelligence-gathering, and analysis capabilities has long been promoted as a way of strengthening its ability to anticipate crises and undertake timely preventive diplomatic or other actions. Yet member states have been reluctant to permit this. So as Luck asserts, despite the UN's extensive field presence, "the United Nations has never been structured to do the kind of dynamic, candid, detailed, and layered cross-sectoral analysis of developments in states under stress that is needed to craft effective policy responses to early signs of trouble."[14]

Coordinating the Activities of a Variety of Agencies

As numerous UN staff and NGOs have remarked, "Everyone is for coordination, but nobody wants to be coordinated."[15] This has been a chronic problem, as seen in ECOSOC's coordination or lack of coordination of the multiple overlapping economic and social programs and agencies. It can also be seen in the problems of uncoordinated responses to complex humanitarian crises or the late and feeble responses to HIV/AIDS and Ebola. Weiss refers to the "spaghetti junction" of the UN organizational chart ... and suggests that it creates either "productive clashes over institutional turf and competition for resources, or paralysis. Both are less-than-optimal outcomes resulting from the structure of decentralized silos instead of more integrated, mutually reinforcing, and collaborative partnerships among the various moving parts of the United Nations."[16] Further evidence of the problems of coordination within the UN system come from looking at UN operations in developing countries, where there may be twenty or more different UN organizations with separate offices and staff—a problem that has been remedied only in a handful of cases by the creation of a single country representative, office, program, and fund. One small, encouraging sign came with the creation of UN Women, when four entities were merged—a rare occurrence at the UN.

Yet if the UN cannot coordinate itself, how can it participate effectively in broader partnerships involving regional organizations, NGOs, or the private sector that are requisite for addressing the challenges of the twenty-first century? Will it be able to form the partnerships so necessary to address the refugee/ migration crisis or to achieve the SDGs? With these lessons of what the UN cannot do, is it possible to judge success and failure?

Factors In Un Success and Failure

How can we judge success and failure of the UN (or of any institution)? What criteria can be employed? What measures can be used? Did the UN meet the objectives of the founders as reflected in the Charter? Is the UN meeting the demands of the second decade of the twenty-first century? What frame of reference should we use—an individual program or a particular period of time? And for whom has the UN been a success or a failure—for dominant states, small states, or certain groups or individuals? For an institution with many moving parts, can we really measure success or failure as a whole, or should we evaluate particular parts? Although it is not up to us to set evaluation criteria, we can set forth some generalizations about the probability of success and failure.

First, if the UN's actions reflect consensus among member states and have financial backing from key donor states, corporations, or private foundations, then they have a greater likelihood of success. Second, if the relevant UN program or agency takes responsibility and seizes the initiative for an action, then there is a greater probability of success. Third, endorsement and support of professionals, outside experts, scholars, and NGOs—that is, the third UN—will increase the probability of success even more. Yet, given the size of the UN's diverse membership of sovereign member states, getting these conditions right is rare.

The UN's actions are more likely to lead to failure when they try to tackle an issue that, by institutional design, the founders did not intend. That includes having a strong role in international economic relations. If major powers oppose UN action, it will likely fail, as the case of Syria has so tragically demonstrated. Barring Security Council reform, P-5 power is ensured. Barring finding independent sources of funding, economically strong states will wield the power of the purse, leading to greater likelihood that their policies will be followed. If member states turn to new institutions and programs that bypass the UN, this will marginalize the UN and undermine its legitimacy as the primary global institution. States may do this because they do not approve of UN actions, because they anticipate weak UN performance, or because of the effects of the changing distribution of power. Or other global institutions will replace the UN because the demands of the twenty-first century may really outrun the capacity of the UN in any form.

Can the Un Be Reformed?

Because the UN has rarely lived up to the full expectations of all member governments, its own staff, and its supporters as well as critics, the topic of reform has been what Mark Malloch Brown, former deputy secretary-general under Kofi Annan and former administrator of UNDP, calls "an occupational obsession."[17] This has been particularly true with regard to Security Council reform and the perception for many years that the council's makeup reflects a world long gone. As we discussed in Chapter 2, however, Security Council reform is only a small part of the puzzle, and although there has been no change in its makeup, there have been other changes in the Security Council's operation and many types of changes in the Secretariat and other parts of the first and second UN. There have been a host of reforms in peacekeeping since the early 1990s as well as in human rights institutions, as noted in earlier chapters.

To make more substantial reforms, Brown asserts, there is no alternative "to a real commitment by member states to a better UN. ... Real reforms will require major concessions from powerful and weak countries alike. The intergovernmental gridlock between the big contributors and the rest of the membership concerning governance and voting is the core dysfunction. To overcome it, both sides would have to rise above their own current sense of entrenched rights and privileges and find a grand bargain to allow a new, more realistic governance model for the UN."[18]

What will it take to break the deadlock and change the political equation for a major overhaul of the UN? Will it take some type of international crisis? In Brown's view: "When politicians reach for a solution for climate change or a war and cannot find it, this absence will build the case for a better UN."[19] Indeed, it took the outbreak of World War II to make possible the creation of the UN as a replacement for the League of Nations—a stronger League, if you will. Brown adds, "Until the sense of crisis at the UN is strong enough to make governments let go of their own agendas, there cannot be the kind of cathartic recommitment and renewal of the UN proper that is required."[20] So what might such a crisis look like? The expansion of ISIS as a protostate controlling territory in North, East, and West Africa in addition to the Middle East? An environmental catastrophe? A global recession or depression greater than the financial meltdown in 2008? The outbreak of war in the Middle East involving Iran, Israel, Saudi Arabia, Turkey, Russia, the United States, and others, or perhaps a war in Northeast Asia involving North and South Korea, Japan, the United States, and China?

To undertake major reform of the UN will require member states—both powerful and weak—to be willing to make major concessions. They will need to create a new system of representation in the Security Council and other bodies that not only accommodates today's emerging powers but also is flexible enough to adjust to future power shifts. They will have to overcome their reluctance to bring modern management principles and procedures into the UN Secretariat, empower the secretary-general to exercise more authority, and establish a more open, competitive process for selecting the secretary-general. They will need to devise a means for the third UN—civil society, NGOs, the private sector—to be involved in the work of the organization, recognizing the major contributions (including financial resources) to be gained and the value of inclusiveness. Or, one might ask, will they scrap the UN itself and create an entirely new institution for global governance?

Linking The Un to Global Governance

The fact is that the UN must reform to meet the demands for governance and the challenges of diminished sovereignty, to find states and coalitions able and willing to lead, and to establish partnerships that provide the human and financial resources required to address contemporary global problems. Unless those dilemmas are addressed, the UN will become increasingly irrelevant. Global governance—rather, pieces of global governance to manage a wide variety of international issues and problems—is a reality, with many different actors, including the UN, having authority, resources, and processes in place. Yet none of these other actors, be they regional security organizations, the G-20, NGOs, various types of networks, public-private partnerships, MNCs, or even powerful states, can begin to replace the UN in its entirety. The real question for the UN is whether it will be a central player or a marginal one in global governance in the twenty-first century.

Notes

1. Kofi Annan, *Interventions: A Life in War and Peace* (New York: Penguin, 2012), 144.
2. Richard Jolly, Louis Emmerij, and Thomas G. Weiss, *UN Ideas That Changed the World* (Bloomington: Indiana University Press, 2009), 32–33.
3. Ibid., 34–35.
4. Edward C. Luck, "R2P at Ten: A New Mindset for a New Era?" *Global Governance* 21, no. 4 (2015): 500–501.
5. Quoted in Thomas G. Weiss, "The John W. Holmes Lecture: Reinvigorating the International Civil Service," *Global Governance* 16, no. 1 (2010): 52.

6. Jolly, Emmerij, and Weiss, *UN Ideas That Changed the World,* 73.

7. Ibid., 75.

8. Ibid., 43.

9. Ibid., 44.

10. Thomas G. Weiss, *Governing the World? Addressing "Problems Without Passports"* (Boulder, CO: Paradigm, 2014), 85.

11. John Gerard Ruggie, foreword to *Global Governance and the UN: An Unfinished Journey,* by Thomas G. Weiss and Ramesh Thakur (Bloomington: Indiana University Press, 2010), xvii.

12. Weiss and Thakur, *Global Governance and the UN,* 21.

13. Ibid.

14. Luck, "R2P at Ten," 502.

15. Quoted in Thomas G. Weiss, *What's Wrong with the United Nations and How to Fix It,* 2nd ed. (Malden, MA: Polity Press, 2012), 14.

16. Ibid., 14.

17. Mark Malloch Brown, "The John W. Holmes Lecture: Can the UN Be Reformed?" *Global Governance* 14, no. 1 (2008): 1.

18. Ibid., 6.

19. Ibid., 7.

20. Ibid., 11.

DISCUSSION QUESTIONS

1. How would you summarize the main argument of the article in a sentence or two?

2. How has the UN expanded our understanding of security from "state security" to "human security"? Why is this significant?

3. Authors believe that one major problem with the UN agencies is the lack of coordination of the multiple, overlapping economic and social programs and agencies. What do they mean by this, and can you name some of these programs and agencies?

4. According to the authors, among challenges facing the UN are "diminished state sovereignty," "increased number of NGOs and Transnationals on the word stage," and the "the question of governance." What do they mean by these challenges?

5. How has the UN responded to the rising number of business entities, NGOs, and transnationals? Hint: Think about the UN attempt at building partnership.

6. According to the authors, the UN agencies have successfully brought the world attention together for debate and consensus building in different areas, ranging from human rights to environment, to development, to communicable and infectious diseases. What are the main UN agencies involved in such efforts? Have they really been successful?

European Union Trade Policy and the Prospects for a Transatlantic Trade and Investment Partnership

By Panagiotis Delimatsis

Amid the most severe refugee crisis the European continent has seen in decades and the increasing fears that European integration is in peril, the expansion of European Union (EU) trade policy continues. Jean-Claude Juncker, the president of the European Commission, and his administration have prioritized the conclusion of comprehensive economic agreements with strategic partners, including the United States, Japan, and China. These negotiations are currently conducted by the European Union, showcasing the dramatic change of global trade politics in the last ten years.[1]

A clear shift away from the World Trade Organization (WTO) as the predominant trade negotiating forum is taking place. The fact that the recent WTO Ministerial Conference in Nairobi expressly recognized not only the centrality but also the primacy of the WTO system does not seem to affect these dynamics.[2] Particularly, this shift has manifested itself in the increasing emphasis the EU is placing on concluding bilateral trade agreements with strategic partners—which, while occurring within the framework of WTO obligations, occurs outside of the WTO as a negotiating forum.

Against this backdrop, this note assesses the current state of affairs and future prospects for a balanced transatlantic trade deal. Absent any significant progress within the WTO and multilateral negotiations, larger economies are seeking to redefine the agenda of trade rules for the medium run out of the acknowledgement that new production methods and business models also require creative legal engineering. This note outlines the current trajectory of EU trade policy under the Juncker administration, analyzes the importance and challenges of concluding the Transalantic Trade and Investment Partnership (T-TIP) between the EU and the United States, and concludes with a review of the current state of global trade regulation.

Panagiotis Delimatsis, "European Union Trade Policy and the Prospects for a Transatlantic Trade and Investment Partnership," *The Fletcher Forum of World Affairs*, vol. 40, no. 2, pp. 29-40. Copyright © 2016 by The Fletcher School of Law and Diplomacy. Reprinted with permission. Provided by ProQuest LLC. All rights reserved.

The Direction of Eu Trade Policy

Focusing on the future of EU trade policy, the European Commission has made clear the shape of the EU agenda in coming years:[3] it will seek to become more effective and more transparent, as well as attempt to export EU values to the rest of the world. These three elements—effectiveness, transparency, and values—constitute the three pillars of the revitalized EU trade policy. Effectiveness means that EU trade policy will become more results-oriented, focusing on the facilitation of value chains, the inclusion of digital trade in prospective negotiations, and the easing of rules governing movement of high-skilled professionals. Transparency, the second pillar, has been a recurring theme in trade negotiations, and EU institutions have been the recipients of numerous calls for increased access to documents previously regarded as confidential. In a significant policy turn toward more openness vis-à-vis civil society and the public in general (which, admittedly, was also the result of a more hands-on approach to the issue of access to confidential documents by the Court of Justice of the European Union, the EU's highest court), the EU started publishing key negotiating texts shortly after they were discussed at the table with the EU's partners. This is in stark contrast to the policy the United States administration has adopted, turning a deaf ear to the demands for more transparency in the negotiations for the Trans-Pacific Partnership (TPP) or in the current T-TIP negotiations.

> *These three elements—effectiveness, transparency, and values—constitute the three pillars of the revitalized EU trade policy.*

The third pillar of the EU's new approach to trade matters rests on the idea that EU values can be "exported" through trade negotiations. In EU foreign policy, this has previously included the exporting of concepts relating to public services (so-called "services of general interest") to the EU's partners in Eastern Europe, but also the exporting of concepts relating to competition law. In its new policy, the EU aspires to enrich this agenda with new concepts such as enhanced corporate social responsibility to ensure a high level of protection for European consumers, increased legitimacy for investment arbitration systems used by the EU in its international agreements, and a more targeted system of autonomous preferences given to developing and least developed countries.

T-Tip's Importance for the Eu

Whereas the EU claims to remain focused on the conclusion of the Doha Round, it seems that the Doha negotiating mandate has been abandoned.[4] The multilateral round of negotiations that was launched with high hopes in 2001 in the Qatari capital largely failed to meet the expectations of developing and developed countries. After fifteen years of negotiations and procrastination, the WTO Ministerial Declaration in Nairobi confirmed the indifference of many key members regarding the conclusion of the Doha Development Round. It is worth noting that despite the sluggish progress in the WTO negotiations, trade liberalization—notably through the decrease of tariffs on goods—continued apace, showing that trade liberalization occurs, but increasingly outside the WTO. The EU trade agenda, announced in October 2015, had already signalled the arrival of a new era for the WTO by suggesting that, rather than focusing on comprehensive (and thus time-consuming) negotiations on an ever-increasing array of issues, issue-based negotiations and early harvesting may be the most sustainable future for the WTO.

> *Rather than focusing on comprehensive (and thus time-consuming) negotiations on an ever-increasing array of issues, issue-based negotiations and early harvesting may be the most sustainable future for the WTO.*

This approach is being tested with the negotiations for a Trade in Services Agreement (TiSA), currently negotiated by twenty-five WTO members (counting the EU as one member). TiSA has been promoted by the biggest services exporters globally, including the EU, the United States, Japan, Canada, and the Republic of Korea. Brazil, Russia, India, China, and South Africa (the BRICS) have largely distanced themselves from this initiative, but any signal by China suggesting its participation would quickly alter these dynamics. With the current slowdown of trade in goods and the rather mediocre prospects in the short run,[5] China will soon need to further diversify its economy. The potential of the service sector remains untapped for the most part.

> *Concluding comprehensive and balanced trade agreements with the United States, China, Russia, Japan, India, and Brazil became a top priority for EU trade policy.*

With a combined transatlantic trade volume of around €400 billion in 2014, representing over half of all global trade in services, services are a key component of a future transatlantic deal between the EU and the United States. In both goods and services trade with the United States, the EU as a bloc currently enjoys a small but steady surplus, notably in goods. However, this does not mean that the EU will not benefit from such a deal with the United States; to the contrary, T-TIP forms part of the EU's considerable shift in external trade policy to focus on the conclusion of trade agreements that can have a significant impact on EU trade. Thus, under the instructions of the European Council,[6] the European Commission's interest shifted towards the launch of negotiations with its strategic partners, who are at the same time important global trade partners. Within this framework, concluding comprehensive and balanced trade agreements with the United States, China, Russia, Japan, India, and Brazil became a top priority for EU trade policy.[7]

There are varying degrees of progress in these negotiations. For instance, negotiations with India have witnessed sluggish progress with no real prospect for the conclusion of a trade and investment agreement any time soon. The same appears to be the case with MERCOSUR, a trade bloc of South American economies, of which Brazil is a member. It is unclear whether the EU still favors the initial idea of concluding the EU-MERCOSUR association agreement before any separate agreement with

Brazil. On the other hand, the United States and Japan appear to be the top political priority for the new Juncker administration, as an agreement seems to be more feasible in the short run.[8]

In his State of the Union speech, the president of the European Commission reiterated his willingness to conclude a reasonable and balanced agreement with the United States in the coming years.[9] The EU leadership had hoped to conclude the transatlantic negotiations as early as 2015, but negotiations are still ongoing, notably because they were put on hold until the TPP was concluded in October 2015. However, the most recent statements by the lead negotiators of the two partners suggest that a conclusion of the negotiations during the Obama administration is desirable and feasible.[10] At the same time, the EU recognizes that the recently concluded TPP also needs to enter into force. Obama has faced criticism for this agreement from various sides, including reluctant statements by members of the United States Congress and every presidential candidate of both parties. Thus, it may be more challenging than in 2015 for the Obama administration to conclude an additional trade deal of even greater magnitude. Calls that this should be left to the incoming United States president increase. The fact that the EU has increasingly insisted on adding its new concept of investor-state arbitration into the final deal its new concept of investor-state arbitration after convincing Canada to add it in the final EU-Canada Comprehensive Economic and Trade Agreement (CETA) render slim the prospects of a final deal by the end of 2016.

Even so, this does not seem to change the planning on the EU side. In any case, ratification and enforcement also entail a complicated process within the twenty-eight individual EU member states. Taking into account the most recent views of the Commission, it seems that the EU has opted for immediately prioritizing three agreements: T-TIP, the agreement with Japan, and the investment agreement with China. In all cases, the EU confirmed the importance of concluding WTO-consistent bilateral agreements, although it is no longer conceivable to achieve substantial progress on both the bilateral and the multilateral front simultaneously. Perhaps the only exception where such simultaneous negotiations take place is the area of services, in which the EU expressly confirmed its commitment to the bilateral route (through T-TIP, CETA with Canada, or the EU-Korea Agreement) and the multilateral/plurilateral route (through TiSA within the WTO framework).

Upgrading the cooperation with the United States on all fronts is the clear message from European leaders. For many observers, the Transatlantic Economic Council (TEC) that preceded the T-TIP negotiations did not achieve as much as was expected, but for others, it did set the foundations for a more comprehensive collaboration and understanding, in particular on regulatory matters.

T-TIP has drawn public attention since the very beginning of the announcement that transatlantic negotiations would start. Legally speaking, T-TIP represents an interesting legal construct under the the lens of EU external relations law. It is not the first free trade agreement that the EU has negotiated, nor is it the first free trade agreement that the EU will conclude since the entry into force of the Treaty of Lisbon. The Comprehensive Economic Trade Agreement (CETA) with Canada will also be concluded under the relevant new Common Commercial Policy (CCP) provisions of the

Treaty on the Functioning of the European Union (TFEU). The EU Free Trade Agreement with South Korea, the EU's first with an Asian economy, was also concluded recently.[11] This agreement was concluded as a "mixed agreement," which, in EU jargon, designates that both the EU and its member states together shall conclude the agreement. In practice, such a mixed agreement requires ratification by all member states before it can produce any legal effects. In the case of the Korea free trade agreement, though, the Council had decided to provisionally apply the free trade agreement as of July 2011. This is the first agreement of what the Commission calls the new generation of EU free trade agreements. However, both free trade agreements were concluded based on respective mandates that were addressed to the European Commission *prior* to the entry into force of the Lisbon Treaty, with much confusion surrounding the normative character of the changes brought about by the then forthcoming introduction of the new Lisbon treaty rules.

The T-TIP mandate was approved by the Council of the EU in 2013.[12] Thus, all related decisions and acts were adopted after the entry into force of the Lisbon Treaty. Another, less mediatized agreement that has similar characteristics is the free trade agreement with Singapore, negotiations for which were finalized in October 2014, absent political will to conclude a broader agreement with all ASEAN countries. The free trade agreement with Singapore, however, is not as prominent as T-TIP in terms of trade flows because Singapore is the EU's seventeenth largest trading partner. Still, the free trade agreement with Singapore is of high constitutional significance for the evolution of EU external relations law, as the European Commission decided to go a step further and claim exclusive competence for the conclusion of this agreement based on the then-new Lisbon framework. The new Article 207 TFEU appears to suggest that CCP, including investment, is an exclusive EU competence with varying decision-making procedures (that is, qualified majority combined with unanimity when liberalization of the audio-visual sector or public services is at stake). The Commission's request for an Opinion by the Court of Justice of the European Union (CJEU) based on Article 218:11 TFEU is pending and awaited with great interest, as it may constitute a yardstick for all subsequent EU free trade agreements, including the T-TIP.

Hence, just in terms of sheer trade size, T-TIP is at the epicenter of the public debate regarding trade and regulatory matters on both sides of the Atlantic. The United States is the EU's top trading partner, representing over 15 percent of extra-EU trade flows. For the United States, the EU is the second most important trading partner after Canada. In the United States, a recurring discussion about the benefits of NAFTA, and lately TPP, instigates suspicion against mega-regional agreements of this type. In the EU, on the other hand, the debate about T-TIP is even more heated due to the trauma that the *EC Hormones* saga caused, but also due to the EU-specific concept of public services, that some see being put in jeopardy if a trade agreement with the United States is to occur, even though there is agreement between the EU and the United States to exclude public services from the agreement. In addition, statistics show that, even in times of crisis, the EU has had a steadily positive trade balance with the United States the last decade, making the case for further integration a "tough sell" to EU citizens anxious about their standards of living and the future of their welfare state so much hit by the recent Great Recession that followed the global financial crisis.[13]

> *In terms of sheer trade size, T-TIP is at the epicentre of the public debate regarding trade and regulatory matters on both sides of the Atlantic.*

Harnessing public opposition against T-TIP is not a given in the EU, as recent events show. Civil society groups and other non-governmental organizations (NGOs) started collecting signatures of EU citizens who were willing to support the interruption of any trade negotiations with the US. A central argument is that the agreement would possibly jeopardize the status quo with respect to the supply of public services in Europe. Just as over 3 million signatures in favor of stopping the T-TIP negotiations were collected, the central organizers of the movement attempted to unsuccessfully register this initiative as a European Citizen initiative pursuant to Article 11 TEU and the corresponding regulation. Accordingly, the persons in charge decided to launch a lawsuit before the CJEU.

To reassure citizens and NGOs that were mobilized, the EU and the United States recently pledged to take into account the important preferences and values that underlie the provision of public services.[14] Water, education, health, and social services are mentioned as mere examples of sectors in which important sensitivities on both sides of the Atlantic exist. This statement confirms a consistently reluctant stance that the EU has taken in its free trade agreements with respect to public services (a so-called "public utilities exception") in line with the negotiating guidelines by the Council.[15] Other sensitive areas for the EU in terms of liberalization include the opening of audio-visual services to the United States service suppliers. Due to traditional sensitivities associated with this sector that have been expressed already at the moment that the most-favored nation (MFN) exemptions to the WTO General Agreement on Trade in Services were discussed in the early 1990s, the Council of the European Union recommended the overall exclusion of the sector from the transatlantic discussions.[16]

Once the negotiations started drawing public attention, European Parliament involvement also increased, signalling the type of deal and ensuing commitments that it would be unable to approve. Recall that in the case of T-TIP, no agreement can be binding for the EU unless the European Parliament gives its consent. Recently, the European Parliament invited the Commission as the lead negotiator to exclude from the scope of T-TIP public services to ensure that "national and, if applicable, local authorities retain the full right to introduce, adopt, maintain, or repeal any measures with regards to the commissioning, organisation, funding, and provision of public services as provided in the Treaties as well as in the EU's negotiating mandate; this exclusion should apply *irrespective of how the services are provided and funded*" (emphasis added).[17] Notably in the case of public healthcare services, the Parliament suggested the exclusion of the sector from the negotiations due to the differing approaches between the EU and the United States. Whereas the EU is very keen to add in the final text a horizontal chapter on regulatory cooperation, its proposed text excludes services of general interest (i.e. public services) from the scope of that chapter.

In addition, the Parliament agreed with the Council regarding the exclusion of the audio-visual sector. The Parliament even pushed this carve-out further by asking the Commission to actively pursue the introduction of a provision that would allow the EU and its member states to continue subsidizing and providing financial support to cultural industries and cultural, educational, audio-visual, and press services. However, the Parliament was no less ambitious in its final recommendations. According to the Parliament, an ambitious and balanced deal with the United States would entail the removal of United States restrictions on foreign ownership of transport services and airlines, better access to United States telecommunications markets (without disregarding the EU high level of data protection and conditions for data flows), and liberalization of the United States public procurement market at all levels of government. In the area of financial services, the Parliament underlines the importance of cooperation within international fora such as the Financial Stability Board (FSB), but urges the European Commission to negotiate meaningful commitments on market access. In addition, both the Council and the Parliament agree with the Commission that such commitments would only be useful if accompanied by strong rules on regulatory cooperation in financial services, including exchange of financial information. Finally, the Parliament calls for the convergence of regulations relating to professionals that still hamper mutual recognition of equivalent standards. Therefore, facilitating mobility should be an important objective of the EU to the benefit of both partners.

> *An ambitious and balanced deal with the United States would entail the removal of United States restrictions on foreign ownership of transport services and airlines, better access to United States telecommunications markets, and liberalization of the United States public procurement market at all levels of government.*

A Critical Juncture for Global Trade Negotiations

The regulation of global trade has never been more in flux than it is now. The emergence of mega-regional agreements such as TPP and T-TIP and the long-lasting difficulties in finalizing the Doha Development Agenda agreed upon in 2001 reveal a more fragmented future as far as trade regulation is concerned. One cannot help but observe the dynamics developed in the last fifteen years that followed the high hopes created by the adoption of the Doha Mandate. Fragmentation and variable geometry is the order of the day and the prospects for a more inclusive approach have faded. The ecology of global trade is characterized, on one side, by a group of countries, mostly developed and advanced developing ones, which have come together to set more specific rules that aim at the facilitation of supply chains, trade in intermediate goods, digital trade, state trading, or the movement of high-skilled personnel and, on the other side, by a larger group of developing and least developed countries (LDCs), whose reluctance to join the trend transforms them into takers of trade liberalization pledged in a rather patchy way within the WTO.

Indeed, whereas the most recent WTO Ministerial Declaration in Nairobi confirmed the indifference of many key developed-country members regarding the conclusion of the Doha Development Round, members still felt compelled, after several years of procrastination, to finally go after the low-hanging fruits to the benefit of the developing world: members agreed to alleviate diachronic injustices in the trade of cotton and to address, decisively, the issue of export subsidies in the agricultural sector. With respect to market access in the cotton sector, members (developed countries and developing countries that are able to do so, including China) pledged to offer duty-free, quota-free access to imports of cotton from LDCs.[18] Most crucially, members satisfied a recurring request by the cotton-producing countries by prohibiting cotton export subsidies. This prohibition has immediate effect for developed-country members and shall be applicable to developing countries no later than January 1, 2017. This pledge is part of a broader obligation made by developed countries to finally abolish export subsidies in agriculture (except for a very limited number of agricultural products) immediately. For developing countries and LDCs, this obligation is set for a later date.[19] If one adds to these obligations the LDC waiver in the area of services, allowing deviation from the MFN obligation to grant to LDCs preferential access to domestic services markets, and the agreement on trade facilitation, the deliverables of the Doha negotiations are not negligible. Nevertheless, they are still not as ambitious as they were at the moment the multilateral trade negotiations started.

For the EU, such deliverables at the multilateral level are quintessential for the stance in international trade matters (and international relations, more generally) that the EU28 bloc advocates a more inclusive and responsible approach to trade matters, focusing on sustainable development and benefits for all. After some considerable delays in the conclusion of Economic Partnership Agreements (EPAs) with Asian, Caribbean, and Pacific trade partners to replace the WTO-inconsistent Cotonou Agreement, the EU has managed to conclude trade deals with African regional and multilateral communities, including West Africa, the Eastern African Community (EAC), and the South African Development Community (SADC). Additional EPAs with the remaining African countries and the Pacific partners are in advanced stage. However, T-TIP is the most ambitious and strategic trade agreement ever undertaken by the EU. If successful, these negotiations will certainly shape multilateral trade rules in the not so distant future. If seen through this angle, then both the EU and the United States have an interest in a comprehensive bilateral trade and investment agreement.

> *T-TIP is the most ambitious and strategic trade agreement ever undertaken by the EU. If successful, these negotiations will certainly shape multilateral trade rules in the not so distant future.*

Notes

1. Discussions with Bernard Hoekman, Petros Mavroidis, Hal Scott, Joel Trachtman and Mark Wu have allowed me to sharpen the ideas developed here. Any errors are the author's alone. Contact: p.delimatsis@uvt.nl.

2. WTO Nairobi Ministerial Declaration, December 19, 2015, WT/MIN(15)/DEC, para.19.

3. European Commission Communication, "Trade for all: Towards a more responsible trade and investment policy," COM(2015) 497 final, October 14, 2015.

4. Shawn Donnan, "Trade talks lead to 'death of Doha and birth of new WTO'," *Financial Times,* December 20, 2015.

5. Shawn Donnan, "Global trade: structural shifts," *Financial Times,* March 2, 2016.

6. European Council Conclusions of 16 September 2010, EUCO 21/1/10, October 12, 2010, para. 4.

7. European Commission Communication, "Trade for all: Towards a more responsible trade and investment policy," COM(2015) 497 final, October 14, 2015.

8. The conclusion of the transatlantic deal is one of the 10 top priorities that Jean-Claude Juncker set for his term as European Commission's president.

9. *Jean-Claude Juncker,* "State of the Union 2015," September 9, 2015, available at: http://ec.europa.eu/priorities/soteu/docs/state_of_the_union_2015_en.pdf (visited November 22, 2015). See also President Juncker's political guidelines addressed to the next Commission, "A New Start for Europe: My Agenda for Jobs, Growth, Fairness and Democratic Change," July 15, 2014.

10. Leo Cendrowicz, "T-TIP talks 'could be competed before the end of 2016'," *The Independent,* February 26, 2016.

11. Council of the European Union, "EU-South Korea free trade agreement concluded–Press release," October 1, 2015, available at: http://www.consilium.europa.eu/en/press/press-releases/2015/10/01-korea-free-trade/ (visited November 22, 2015).

12. Council of the European Union, "Press Release—3245th Council meeting," 10862/13, June 14, 2013. The document was declassified in October 2014: see "Council Directives for the negotiation on the Transatlantic Trade and Investment Partnership between the European Union and the United States of America," ST 11103/13, June 17, 2013.

13. *See,* for instance, Eurostat, "US EU international trade and investment statistics," Statistics in focus 2/2015, September 11, 2015.

14. "Joint Statement on Public Services by Ambassador Froman (USTR) and EU Commissioner Malström (DG Trade)," March 20, 2015.

15. *See* Panagiotis Delimatsis, *Services of General Interest and the External Dimension of the EU Energy Policy,* in Services of General Interest Beyond the Single Market–External and International Law Dimensions, 345ff (Markus Krajewski, ed, 2015).

16. With respect to both audiovisual services and public services, see the European Parliament "Resolution on the opening of negotiations on a plurilateral agreement on services (TiSA)," 2013/2583(RSP), July 4, 2013.

17. EU Parliament Resolution, "Recommendations to the European Commission on the negotiations for the Transatlantic Trade and Investment Partnership (T-TIP)," 2014/2228(INI), July 8, 2015, para. 2(a)vii.

18. WTO, "Ministerial Decision of 19 December 2015 on Cotton," WT/MIN(15)/46 and WT/L/981, December 21, 2015.

19. WTO, "Ministerial Decision on Export Competition," WT/MIN(15)/45 and WT/L/980, December 21, 2015.

DISCUSSION QUESTIONS

1. How would you summarize the main argument of the article in a sentence or two?

2. Why does the author believe that a clear shift away from the World Trade Organization (WTO) as the predominant trade negotiating forum is taking place?

3. Why are such major trading entities and "blocs" across the Atlantic and the Pacific (e.g., WTO, CETA, TPP, TPIP, BRICS) so important in facilitating global trade? How do they contribute to global trade outside the WTO framework?

4. What are the three pillars of the EU trade policy?

5. According to the author, many Europeans agree that trade between the U.S. and the EU must exclude the public sector. Why is this the case?

6. What are the issues (obstacles) facing a successful EU and U.S. trade deal? Hint: Think about ownership, accessibility to market, and liberalization issues of some market areas.

Human Security as a Prerequisite for Development

By Nsiah-Gyabaah, Kwasi

....

S ecurity and development are not new concepts. The right to life and security of all persons are basic rights that were enshrined in article 3 of the 1948 UN Declaration. However, since the publication of the World Commission on Environment and Development report *Our Common Future* by Gro Harlem Brundtland of Norway (WCED 1987), and the United Nation Development Programme's 1994 Human Development Report (UNDP 1994), security and development have been interpreted in many different ways. "Human security" and "sustainable development" have emerged as new paradigms for understanding different threats to security and development. Recently, human security and governance and sustainable development have become important fields of study, which are taught in universities as part of international relations, environmental science, peace, and human rights studies (UNDP 1994; Tadjbakhsh and Chenoy 2006).

In spite of the popularity and extensive use of the human security and "sustainability" concepts in research and development (R&D), there is no consensus on their actual meaning or the links between them (Redclift 1987, 1992; Adelman 2000; UNDP 1994, 1998; Sen 2000). What one country perceives as human security and sustainable development may not be another's perception because of the wide range and complexity of the phenomena that are attributed to both concepts. The quagmire of meanings and ambiguity have not only reduced the practical value of the concepts, but have led to fundamental questions being asked about whether it is possible for them to be fully met, and if it is feasible to implement the human security and sustainable development agendas. Fundamental questions such as "what security?," "whose security?," "whose sustainability?," and "for how long?" have not been adequately addressed regarding the identification of the multiple threats and vulnerability and adaptation to the threats of human security and development (Redclift 1987, 1992; Hyden 1998).

In order to ensure global peace, human security, and cooperation, it is important for researchers and the policy community to understand each other's aspirations and perceptions of security and development. Therefore, this chapter sets out to address three issues. First, it examines the meanings

Kwasi Nsiah-Gyabaah, "Human Security as a Prerequisite for Development," *Global Environmental Change and Human Security*, ed. Richard A Matthew, et al., pp. 237-259. Copyright © 2009 by MIT Press. Reprinted with permission.

and scope of human security and development. Second, it presents new perspectives of human security and development and the links between them. Third, it establishes prerequisites for achieving human security and sustainable development. The primary objective is to provide an entry point for researchers and the policy community to formulate policies and implement action programs that address the critical and pervasive threats to human security and sustainable development at the international, regional, and local levels.

What Is Human Security?

Human security is a concept that has evolved since the Cold War from the notion of "national security" or the state protecting its borders from external aggression, to include threats to the physical security of the person and human rights, as well as direct and indirect threats to livelihoods, human dignity, and well-being (UN 1948; Berkowitz and Bock 1968; Brock 1991; UNDP 1994; Matthew 2002). The potential for conflict during the Cold War era shaped the notion of threats to a country's borders and the ability to deter or defeat external aggression. Although the majority of people still see security in terms of state security or militarism, this narrow, state-centered definition has been contested because it leaves out the most elementary and legitimate concerns of ordinary people regarding their health, water, energy, livelihoods, environment, and other securities in their daily lives (Rodney 1982; Ullman 1983: Renner 1989; Westing 1989; Gleditsch 1997). In Africa, where the greatest threats to human security are pervasive poverty, inequality, HIV/AIDS, and bad governance, the traditional definition of human security as "state security" or national sovereignty is too narrow and inadequate for policy formulation and implementation (UNDP 1994; Lonergan, Gustavson, and Carter 1999; Dabelko, Lonergan, and Matthew 2000).

Moreover, globalization, information and communication technology (ICT), and rapid economic development have created more opportunities for conflict resolution and new threats such as terrorism, drug abuse, infectious diseases, and environmental degradation that extend beyond state security. The complexities of the array of these human security challenges are not captured and cannot be resolved by state security instruments such as military force and international sanctions. As a result of the limitations of the traditional definition, a human security paradigm has emerged that is "people-centered" and takes account of the complex and multidimensional causes of threats to human security (WCED 1987; Buzan 1991; UNDP 1994).

New Paradigms of Human Security

A new understanding of people-centered security, which incorporates factors such as poverty, environment, infectious diseases, gender, empowerment, freedom from want, and survival, has become extremely important in policy formulation and implementation because in addition to military threats, nonmilitary threats such as human rights abuses, bad governance, and widespread poverty continue to undermine human security and development in many countries, especially Africa. While in some countries such as Sierra Leone and Liberia, the state has failed its security obligation to protect its citizens from violence, in others such as Darfur, the state has become the instrument of oppression and a major source of threat to the safety, rights, and freedoms of its own citizens (Axworthy 2001; Sanjeev, William, and Raad 2003). Therefore, human security is about the ability of the state to protect both its citizens and its borders from external aggression (Heinbecker 1999).

Recent definitions of human security therefore emphasize the protection and safety of individuals, their fundamental rights and freedoms, gender equality, and promotion of their welfare. In this context, human security needs are paramount, rather than the protection of territorial borders. Human security is therefore people centered and goes beyond state protection to the security of individuals, empowering them and addressing the threats to their lives and freedoms and reducing their vulnerability to poverty, disease, and natural disasters (Axworthy 2001; Commission on Human Security 2003; Leichenko and O'Brien 2005). The Universal Declaration of Human Rights (UN 1948) was one of the first attempts to bring together the political and socioeconomic perspectives into one analytical framework for understanding security. It noted that there is security when people have the right to life and are not vulnerable to the constant threats of hunger, disease, crime, famine, environmental degradation, natural disasters, oppression, ethnic cleansing, and political persecution. It noted further that when citizens are killed by their own security forces or cannot walk the streets because of fear of being attacked, their security is threatened (Rodney 1982; Ullman 1983; Renner 1989; Westing 1989).

The United Nations Development Programme (UNDP 1994) gave a broader definition of human security, which included threats in seven areas: economic, political, food, health, environment, community, and personal security. According to the UNDP, freedom from want and freedom from fear for all persons is the best way to address the problem of global human security (UNDP 1994; 1997). Although each of UNDP's seven areas of threats to human security has received international attention, appropriate mechanisms for achieving them have proved illusive. Other proponents of a broader definition of human security such as Mahbub ul Haq and Steve Lonergan have stressed the importance of a human-centered approach, and the application of sustainability, vulnerability, resilience, poverty, and secured livelihoods concepts in understanding human security. Consequently, they have designed people-centered interventions such as poverty reduction, access to income, and sustainable livelihoods to address the enduring and underlying causes of human security problems (Meyers 1989; UNDP 1994; Rothschild 1995; GECHS 1999; Lonergan, Gustavson, and Carter 1999; Sen 2000; King and Murray 2002; RIVM 2002).

In the last decade, the notions of human security are being transformed in the face of climate change (GECHS 1999; Matthew 2002). The Global Environmental Change and Human Security (GECHS) project has become a core area of research of the International Human Dimensions Programme

(IHDP). GECHS situates environmental change and the capacity of individuals, communities, and regions to cope with and adapt to environmental change within the larger context of human security. GECHS defines human security broadly not only as freedom from conflict, but also as having the means to secure basic rights, needs, and livelihoods, and to pursue opportunities for human fulfillment and development (GECHS 1999; Matthew 2002; Leichenko and O'Brien 2005). It focuses on gender, equity, and how certain individuals, groups, or regions are supported or constrained in their capacity to respond to the multiple processes of change, which can manifest either as shocks or as structural transformation (Leichenko and O'Brien 2005). The GECHS project's conceptualization of human security argues that "human security is achieved when and where individuals and communities have the options necessary to end, mitigate, or adapt to threats to their human, environmental and social rights; have the capacity and freedom to exercise these options; and can actively participate in attaining these options" (GECHS 1999). Challenging the structures and processes that contribute to insecurities is considered key to achieving human security (GECHS 1999). Moreover, "human security embodies the notion that problems must always be addressed from a broader perspective and must include both *poverty* and issues of *equity* (i.e., social, economic, environmental, or institutional) because they often lead to conflict and human insecurity (GECHS 1999; Lonergan, Gustavson, and Carter 1999).

Human security is now widely used to convey a condition in which individual citizens live in freedom, peace, and safety and can participate fully in the processes of governance and decision making. It includes the protection of fundamental human rights and access to resources and basic necessities of life such as health, decent housing, education, and an environment that is not injurious to people's livelihoods and well-being. Researchers, non-governmental organizations (NGOs), and policymakers have found the people-centered, comprehensive human security framework a useful approach for poverty reduction and implementation of sustainable development. This chapter supports the notion of human security as a condition in which the rights and freedoms of citizens are respected; where there is rule of law and good governance; where the basic material and survival needs of citizens are met; where people are not constrained by poverty, disease, ignorance, and hunger; and where the poor and vulnerable groups such as women are able to participate meaningfully in decision making and development.

What Is Development?

Development, like human security, has been interpreted in many different ways (Seers 1977; Simon 2003; World Bank 2004). The evolving vision of development has largely overturned the old assumptions of economic growth-oriented strategies as the path to development and a world divided into "rich" and "poor," "developed" and "underdeveloped." For many years, economists used the concept of development to explain why some countries are *rich* or *developed* while others are *poor* or *underdeveloped*, and how the social, economic, political, and cultural conditions in the poor countries could be changed so that they would become rich. The general perception was that the rich countries such as the United States and Great Britain had achieved certain positively evaluated socioeconomic conditions, which needed to be copied by the poor countries so that they could become rich. This meant that changes in the developing countries so that they resembled the developed countries were regarded as development.

As a result of this, many of the developing countries, especially the former colonies, adopted the Euro-American models of development after independence, with emphasis on industrialization, urbanization, and modernization. The blueprint Eurocentric models of development achieved limited results. This approach to development carried a negative connotation by dividing the world in two: the rich or *developed countries* on one hand, and the poor or underdeveloped (also called backward) countries on the other hand. One of the significant adverse impacts of the dichotomy was the exploitation of natural resources from poor countries to rich countries and the unequal terms of trade between the developed and developing countries (Rodney 1982).

Many writers criticized this definition of development as narrow, value laden, and too ethnocentric. The critics considered the Western-style industrialized society as the standard against which the developing countries were measured inadequate (Warwick 1982; Mertus, Flowers, and Mallike 1999). The definition also portrayed the poor countries negatively: not by what they were but by what they were not; and not by what they had, but by what they lacked. Moreover, it overlooked the miserable history and legacy of colonialism, which were believed to be the root causes of poverty and underdevelopment in the former colonies (Harrison 1993). In order to address the immediate economic concerns in developing countries in the 1980s, it became necessary to shift the emphasis on development away from the post-war classic industrialization, modernization, and Western-style approach to the Marxist and neo-Marxist political and economic growth paradigms, which were defined as *economic growth with or without equity*. Development was seen in economic terms and income per capita was taken as the key indicator of the standard definition of development. Efforts to measure productive capacity and economic growth were limited to income measurements of one kind or another such as gross national product (GNP) and gross domestic product (GDP) (Marx 1976; Sen 1988; Streeten 1994).

These ideas were never unchallenged. In the late 1970s, advocates for women rights and equality argued that development required empowerment of women so they could enjoy greater freedom, power, and security. In the late 1980s, many writers questioned the theoretical adequacy and empirical validity of the growth-centric model because it ignored the social and demographic dimensions of development (Weaver and Jameson 1981). They argued that development cannot be defined purely in economic terms. Although the critics recognized that increased incomes and national economic growth were important in improving the standard of living, they were not the only preconditions for development (Sen 1988). An alternative "welfare-centric" paradigm emerged. Human welfare and poverty reduction became the overall objective and essence of development. The welfare-centric theorists, therefore, urged the pursuit of much broader goals with emphasis on rural development, poverty alleviation, and improvement in human welfare (Griffen 1981; Streeten 1981; Weaver and Jameson 1981: Dreze and Sen 1989). This led to the development of all kinds of infrastructure including water, roads, and energy systems, reflecting the belief of the state as the main agent of investment and development.

However, since the WCED report and the UN 1994 Human Development Report, development has taken a new outlook and the idea of sustainability has become a useful entry point to understanding the environment, human security, and development. By the early 1990s it was becoming clear that decades of misguided growth in the name of development had manifested in environmental degradation, mostly air, water, and land degradation, which posed serious threats to human security and development (WCED 1987; UNDP 1994; Redclift 1987, 1992; Mannion 1992). Although there are over one hundred definitions of *sustainable development*, the most popular definition was submitted by the Brundtland Commission report, *Our Common Future*, which defined it as: "development that meets the needs of the present without compromising the ability of future generations to meet their own needs" (WCED 1987; Blaikie 1996). Sustainable development implies maintaining a delicate balance among human needs to improve well-being while preserving natural resources and ecosystem in the interest of future generations (Department of Environment 1988).

Even though the Brundtland Commission report represented an important shift from the notion of sustainability as primarily ecological, to a focus on environment and equity, not all advocates of sustainable development considered the environment as a primary concern of the sustainability debate. Others, however, maintained that the sustainability of the environment and the security of future generations were the ultimate goals of sustainable development. They also believed that ecological/environmental, political, economic, technological, and technical sustainability as well as participatory democracy were important (Barbier 1989; Brinkerhoff and Goldsmith 1990; Rees 1990; UNCED 1992; UNDP 2003).

In 1994, the UNDP advanced a broader understanding of the human dimensions of development when it introduced the concept of sustainable human development. Sustainable human development emphasized growth, but growth with rather than at the expense of employment, environment, empowerment, and equity. It is pro-poor, pro nature, pro-jobs, and pro women (UNDP 1993). The creators of the Human Development Movement, led by Mahbub ul Haq, introduced the human development paradigm as a holistic development model that focused on people. Human security was defined simply as "a process of enlarging people's choices" (UNDP 1994). In principle, these choices can be definite and can change over time. According to the UNDP report, people often value achievements that do not show up at all, or not immediately, in income or growth figures, including: greater access to knowledge, better nutrition and health services, more secure livelihoods, security against crime and physical violence, satisfying leisure hours, political and cultural freedoms, and a sense of participation in community activities.

The definition embraces every development issue including economic growth, empowerment, the provision of basic needs and social safety nets, political and cultural freedoms, and all aspects of people's lives. It also includes safety from chronic threats such as hunger, disease, and repression as well as protection from sudden and harmful disruptions in the patterns of daily life—whether in homes, in jobs, or in communities. While no aspect of the sustainable development model falls outside its scope, the vantage point is the widening of people's choices and the enhancement of their lives (UNDP 1994). The Millennium Development Declaration also expanded development and human security to include eight key indicators to be achieved by 2015 (UN 2000).

Causes and Threats to Human Security

There is still much to learn about the threats to human security because the causes are many and the relationships among the drivers and how they influence one another are complex and interdependent. Violent conflict is one of the major threats to human security and a barrier to development in many of the world's poorest countries. The post-World War II era has seen the emergence of other nonmilitary threats resulting from poverty, food insecurity, water shortage, natural and human-made disasters, environmental degradation, and climate change. The United Nations Human Security Report (UNDP 1994) has identified seven critical areas of threats to human security for action. They include:

- *Political insecurity* Results from conflict, bad governance, and lack of participation in decision making.
- *Economic insecurity* Mainly owing to the lack of basic needs for a good life and livelihood support for the vulnerable, financial insecurity and volatility, and insecurity of jobs and incomes affecting people in rich and poor countries.
- *Food insecurity* Lack of access to nutritious, healthy, and well-packaged food for all at all times and in all places.
- *Health insecurity* Caused by infectious diseases, with HIV/AIDS, malaria, and tuberculosis the most obvious risks.
- *Community/cultural insecurity* Caused by unbalanced flows of TV, film, and other media that are heavily weighed from rich countries to poor ones.
- *Personal insecurity* Caused mainly by domestic violence, growing crime areas such as rape, drug abuse, armed robbery, and other acts that affect personal safety.
- *Environmental insecurity* Caused by natural and human-made disasters, lack of environmental resources, and climate change.

Political insecurity is mainly caused by inter- and intrastate conflict and bad governance, which contribute to making people unsafe and incapable of adapting and coping with changes that affect their livelihoods and survival. According to O'Reilly, because of violent conflict, about 3.6 million people were killed, 24 million were internally displaced, and 18 million became refugees between 1990 and 1998 (O'Reilly 1998). In Rwanda, between 200,000 to 500,000 people died during the conflict. In 2000, about 10.6 million people in Africa were internally displaced by ethnic conflicts.

In Africa, the major threats to human security are violent conflict, bloody coups, poverty, bad governance, and political instability. These threats have led to the loss of millions of lives. Available statistics show that over four million people have died in violent conflict in the Democratic Republic of Congo (DRC). Between 1999 and 2003, an estimated 10,000 people lost their lives and 800,000 were internally displaced as a result of "localized" conflict in Nigeria (Commission for Africa 2005). In many countries, bad governance has led to human rights abuses, political oppression and persecution of opponents, ethnic cleansing, and lack of citizen participation in governance. Human rights abuses, killing of civilians, and human suffering in Kosovo, Liberia, and Iraq under Saddam Hussein show the effects of bad governance on human security and development and the exaggerated belief that state security is a guarantee for achieving human security and prosperity. In countries such as Sudan (Darfur region) where security forces are killing citizens, and people cannot walk the streets for fear of being killed, human security is threatened.

Another threat to human security is climate change and the systematic destruction of natural resources especially water, forests, and marine resources. At a global scale, the destruction of natural resources is undermining the ability of the poor to secure their livelihoods. In the last two decades climate change has become a global human security issue because of its staggering impacts on health, food security, and water supply. Adverse impacts of climate change on water supply are known to lead to conflict, which can undermine human security (Meyers 1989; ERM 2002). Lack of access to safe drinking water and sanitation is also a major threat to human security. It is estimated that around 3.4 million people die annually from water-related diseases (DFID 2002). In many parts of the world, conflict rages over rights to the use and management of water and as a result of the adverse impacts of climate change these conflicts may become more intense (Gleditsch 1997).

Globalization and growing poverty constitute another cause of human insecurity in the developing countries. The increasing marginalization of Africa, critical limitations to industrial development, lack of technology, low and decreasing levels of production, high level of poverty, illiteracy, and minimal trading power affect the economy and livelihoods and pose major indirect threats to human security. In addition, external factors such as high oil prices, unfair trade between the North and South, and mounting external debts and debt servicing affect local economies, livelihoods, and human security. While globalization is creating unparalleled opportunities for wealth creation and sustainable development in the developed countries, it is leading to diminished human security in the poor countries with limited capacity to compete in the global market. The estimated 1.2 billion people, especially the absolutely poor who live on less than one dollar per day and the 800 million people who go hungry each day, without shelter and good health have minimal security. In the Northern Region in Ghana, pervasive poverty and deprivation are major causes of violent conflict and unsustainable use of natural resources, which also undermine livelihoods and human security. Therefore, poverty, including the lack of access to basic needs for survival such as water, food, health, education, and shelter, are important causes of human insecurity in many developing countries.

In many developed and developing countries, particular social vulnerability configurations such as illegal immigration, rapid population growth, and urbanization and the associated problems of armed robbery and organized international crime have become the greatest threat to human security. Other insecurities that people and societies face include natural disasters, climate change, floods, drought, diseases, wildfire, proliferation of weapons—especially the development of nuclear technology—and HIV/AIDS (Bush 2003). In Africa drought has had human security implications for a variety of livelihood activities. In addition, infectious diseases, especially HIV/AIDS, has affected nearly thirty million people, including three million under the age of fifteen. Although violent conflict and war were the major causes of human insecurity in the 1940s, with the demise of the Cold War and demilitarization other factors such as drought, floods, hurricane, poverty, illiteracy, climate change, and political and religious persecution are among the major threats to human security (Ullman 1983; Renner 1989; WCED 1987; Westing 1989, Buzan 1991). Figure 3.1 shows the complex and

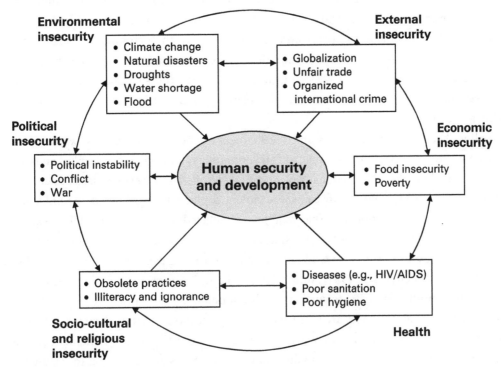

FIGURE 3.1 The Multiple Causes and Threats to Human Security and the Relationships Between Human Security and Development

multidimensional causes of human insecurity. Development is a concept that must be seen within the larger context of household, community, and national economies and, more broadly still within the context of human well-being, human security, basic materials for a good life, good social relations, and freedom of choice or action. Therefore, development and human security are directly and intimately related because the factors that cause human insecurity also undermine the development process and the achievement of development objectives.

However, as new understanding of the meaning and complexity of factors that affect human security and development emerge, establishing the links between human security and development is extremely important for policy formulation and implementation. The main objective of development is to improve human well-being through sustainable livelihoods, and to meet the basic needs of food, water, shelter, clothing, transport, healthcare, education, and productive employment. Other aims include poverty reduction, environmental security, elimination of drugs and diseases, conflict prevention, and sustainable production and consumption patterns. Human security is enhanced when sustainable development objectives are met. However, it is the first casualty when sustainable livelihoods and other development objectives are not achieved.

In this context, Thomas (2000) argues that human security and development are intimately linked because they aim for the same objectives: ensuring human safety, adequate food, health, education, gender equality, participation in decision making, good governance, human dignity, and control over one's life. According to DFID, human security and sustainable development are possible where people live in peace and have a say in how their community is run, and have access to water, food, shelter, education, and the chance to earn a living and to bring up healthy and educated children (DFID 1997). Both human security and sustainable development are enhanced when there is good governance, rule of law, and active citizen participation in decision making and development.

The links between human security and development can be traced to the post-war efforts of the UN General Assembly on global disarmament and nonproliferation of nuclear weapons and weapons of mass destruction. The UN noted that violent conflict affected both personal safety of citizens and socioeconomic development. In Africa, where violent conflicts have occurred, the links between human security and development are clear. In the war-afflicted countries such as Liberia and Sierra Leone, conflicts have led to the loss of lives, destruction of property and basic infrastructure, and refugee problems. Violent conflict has also contributed to growing poverty, food insecurity, diseases, and underdevelopment (Starr 1991; Annan 2001). The UN argues that human insecurity due to conflict is profoundly damaging to sustainable development because resources meant to provide basic infrastructure and services are sacrificed for the protection of national sovereignty. In 1985, about $900 billion was spent on military purposes. The cost in terms of development is what the same resources could have been used to do—for example, it was estimated that to rehabilitate the degraded tropical forests would cost $1.3 billion; to combat desertification would cost $4.5 billion;

to provide water and supply contraceptives for family planning would cost $30 billion and $2 billion respectively (Agarwal et al. 1981; World Bank 1984; ITF 1985; Tolba 1986).

Currently, the war in Iraq and the fight against terrorism cost the United States huge sums of money to protect national security and ensure the safety of U.S. nationals from terrorist attacks. If the money that has been spent since the war had been made available to Africa, the enormous human security and development challenges facing the continent would belong to history. Moreover, the loss of human resources and displacement of people as a result of conflict deprive nations of the human resources they need for development (O'Reilly 1998). Therefore, while human security can promote sustainable development, insecurity and conflict can increase substantially the vulnerability of the poor to diseases and food insecurity and reduce poor people's capacity to mitigate, cope with, and adapt to security threats.

Francis Stewart (2004) has described a three-part relationship for human security and development. First, human security forms an important part of human well-being, which is also an objective of development. Second, human insecurity affects economic growth and development. Third, issues of equity are important sources of conflict, which undermines human security. Therefore, lack of development and growing poverty can lead to conflict and conflict can also lead to lack of development as well as poverty and deprivation. Similarly, high levels of security enhance socioeconomic development, and socioeconomic development promotes human security (ibid.). For example, in Africa, violent conflict, which leads to human insecurity, also results in hunger, poverty, and deprivation. Globally, countries with the highest percentage of poor people are also those that have been affected by conflict. In the 1990s, forty-six countries in the world were involved in armed conflict (primarily civil). This included more than half of the poorest countries (17 out of 33). These conflicts had very high costs because they destroyed development gains, leaving a legacy of damaged assets and mistrust that impeded future gains (UNDP 2003).

As a result of the bidirectional relationships between human security and development, many states and individuals have asserted that human security is the underlying condition and prerequisite for sustainable development. The violent conflicts and human insecurity in countries such as Sierra Leone, Rwanda, Burundi, the DRC, Liberia, Côte d'Ivoire, and Darfur in Sudan best illustrate the direct but complex links between human security and development as well as the importance of ensuring human security as a prerequisite for sustainable development. In these countries, violent conflicts have hampered the development process in many ways. Farmlands have been ruined, houses have been flattened, and basic infrastructure and services, especially schools, hospitals, and water-distribution systems have also been destroyed. The WCED (1987), the 1992 Rio Conference, and the UN Millennium Development Goals (MDGs) (UN 2000) also elaborated, at the highest level, the fundamental relationship between sustainable development and human security when linked to the environment. It was noted that sustainable development and human security largely depend on the creation of a safe and secure environment.

The theories linking development and human security to the environment are based on the feedback that exists between them (Westing 1989). Since many environmental problems are directly linked to human well-being and development, environmental protection has formed the basis for ensuring human security and sustainable development. Environmental problems, particularly air, water, and soil pollution, are seen as a violation of the right to life and a barrier to socioeconomic development. Whether or not we believe that environmental concerns are linked to human security and development, it is difficult to argue that environmental problems have not been important considerations in armed conflicts and peace building, which are important human security and development issues.

Mahbub ul Haq, for example, has noted that sustainable development shares a common vision with human security. "The objectives of development are to enlarge people's choices, protect human freedom and rights, and create an enabling environment for people to enjoy long, healthy and creative lives" (UNDP 1994). For development to occur, people must be free to exercise their choices and to participate in decision making that affects their lives. Development and human security are therefore mutually reinforcing, helping to secure the well-being and dignity of all people, building self-respect and the respect of others. The development aspects of human security relate to poverty eradication, health improvement, education and gender equality, income equality, adequate food and water supply, shelter, employment, and the removal of other types of inequalities. It is in recognition of the direct and intimate relationships between human security and sustainable development that development agencies and advocates for global peace and security must form a strong partnership, with a common agenda, to promote human security and sustainable development.

Human Security as a Prerequisite for Sustainable Development

It is generally acknowledged that on the one hand, sustainable development is impossible in the context of conflict or human insecurity because conflict exposes vulnerable people, particularly women and children, to hunger, poverty, and deprivation. On the other hand, human security is also impossible in the midst of growing poverty, hunger, and deprivation. While threats to human insecurity—especially violent conflict—has led to poverty and deprivation in many other countries, underdevelopment including poverty and the lack of basic infrastructure has increased the vulnerability of individuals, groups, and regions to violent conflict and human insecurity. In addition, threats such as droughts, floods, and storms, which have resulted in loss of lives, displacement, and damage to natural, social, and physical capital, have negatively impacted on development.

While the 1950s witnessed growing recognition that international peace and cooperation were necessary for human security and development, growth-based development models aimed at ensuring long-term sustainability and sharing of economic progress dominated R&D thinking in the 1980s. After World War II, many people held the view that peace was a precondition for economic growth and development. The link between human security and development was seen in terms of loss of lives and property. However, with the emergence of new definitions and perspectives of human security and sustainable development, the direct and indirect links between them have become complex and therefore not clearly understood.

Robert McNamara, who expanded the notion of security to include the promotion of socioeconomic and political development in order to prevent conflicts in Africa and preserve global order and stability, argues that development is a precondition for peace and human security (McNamara 1968). In his opinion, everyone has basic needs for water, food, basic education, and health, which must be available to ensure human security. These basic needs that are the objectives of development enable the poor to take charge of their own future. Consequently, under his leadership as president of the World Bank in the 1970s, the World Bank pursued a policy of massive resource transfers to support socioeconomic development in the developing countries in order to promote global peace and security. Others think that, for a start, sustainable development and progress in ensuring peace cannot be achieved unless everyone's human rights are protected, including those of the poorest and most disadvantaged people (DFID 1997).

Over the years, many African countries have learned from their own experiences that human security is necessary for sustainable development because the countries that have experienced violent conflicts, natural disasters, and environmental degradation are poor and underdeveloped. Of the forty poorest countries in the world, twenty-four are either in the midst of armed conflict or have recently emerged from it. In Africa, where armed conflict has led to massive population displacement, socioeconomic development has been slow. Therefore, many African countries have pledged their support for global peace, environmental security, and good governance to promote human security and sustainable development. Other qualitative elements of human security that African governments consider essential and prerequisites for attainment of the goals and objectives of development include the protection of human rights, rule of law, economic stability, good governance, democratic accountability, and democratic institutions for decision making and policy implementation (Brinkerhoff and Goldsmith 1990).

Although human security is a prerequisite to development, the process of development can also threaten aspects of human security. Development can generate friction or create conflict and become a destabilizing force in communities. It can create problems, contradictions, and social upheavals (PRIO 1999). The social grievances, conflict, and disruptions of traditional ways of life arising from modernization, industrialization, and commercialization in Africa have been discussed extensively by writers such as Huntington (1968) and Olson (1963). Recently, development through science and technology has led to the introduction of new technologies such as nuclear weapons and other weapons of mass destruction, which pose a serious threat to human security in many countries. Human security forms an important part of people's well-being and is therefore an objective of development (Stewart 2004). Insecurity cuts life short and thwarts the use of human potential, thereby affecting the achievement of development objectives.

The experience of many countries in Africa—from the DRC to Sierra Leone, from Ethiopia to Liberia, and from Angola to Côte d'Ivoire—best illustrates the importance of human security as a precondition for sustainable development. The violent conflicts in these countries have had huge direct costs in loss of lives, with serious long-term consequences on development. The conflict in Sierra Leone, for example, represents a good example of the direct link between human security and development. The heinous crimes committed against the people led to three thousand deaths and one million refugees. In addition, three thousand children were abducted and over five thousand buildings were destroyed. Moreover, when stocks of food for development agencies were looted, the agencies abandoned development projects and many local and foreign investors left the country (UNICEF 1996; Lansana 2000). Thousands of professionals including medical doctors, engineers, administrators, and academics also fled to Europe and other safe countries in the subregion. Development suffered immensely and post-war reconstruction has remained an unaccomplished task.

According to the UK Department for International Development (DFID 1997), the right to life and security is a basic human right and key for sustainable development. It is impossible to achieve sustainable development and make progress in reducing poverty unless the rights and freedoms of all citizens are protected (ibid.), and without increased investment to reduce threats to security—especially conflict, environmental degradation, and climate change—the developing countries cannot reduce poverty and make the rapid acceleration in development that people aim to achieve. New policy responses and action programs are therefore required to ensure peace and security and integrate human security and sustainable objectives in a bidirectional relationship to ensure peace and security and create a favorable environment for sustainable development.

Recommendations

Different threats to human security and development require different policy and action response strategies. However, the promotion of peace and stability is indispensable if countries are to attract investment and trade and promote pro-poor development. Today's world offers many opportunities and the developing countries—especially in Africa—should form partnerships and networks with the developed countries for a better future. Long-term global cooperation, good governance, and rule of law are necessary conditions for ensuring human security and sustainable development, and governments should be committed to good governance and the rule of law. In the pursuit of sustainable development and human security, the UN, NGOs, and civil society should refocus their development efforts to eliminate poverty in the developing countries. They should support policies that create sustainable livelihoods for the poor, promote human development, and conserve the environment. All appropriate mechanisms must be strengthened and timely prevention and resolution of conflict are necessary to protect individuals from the effects of conflict.

The wealthy countries must show greater commitment to working with the poor countries by creating an enabling environment in which free trade and sustainable development are possible. The wide range of avenues to promote sustainable development and human security include development and transfer of appropriate technology, prevention and control of diseases, especially HIV/AIDS, environmental protection, and participatory democracy. Given the persistence of poverty, accelerated environmental degradation, especially the threat of climate change, violent conflict, and the growing gap between the developed and the developing countries, comprehensive implementation of Agenda 21, which developed out of the 1992 United Nations Conference on Environment and Development in Rio de Janeiro, and the MDGs remain vitally important (UNCED 1992; UN 2000). Development assistance should focus on the root causes of human insecurity including violent conflict, food insecurity, poverty, and environmental degradation and should promote good governance, sustainable environmental development, and global peace and cooperation.

Conclusion

Two of the most pressing issues facing humankind are human security and development. However, they are fundamentally linked because widespread, chronic, and crushing poverty and underdevelopment negatively impact human security; and threats to human security such as climate change, international crime, food insecurity, conflict, infectious diseases, bad governance, and human rights violations negatively impact development. Therefore, sustainable development objectives can be achieved when poverty reduction, global peace, and cooperation are promoted and threats to human security are eliminated or reduced.

The hope for human security lies in a balanced development approach based on poverty reduction, global peace, and cooperation, in which threats to both development and human security are eliminated. Effective conflict prevention, poverty reduction, and environmental security are not only development goals but also central to the challenges for human security, and will require concerted action and commitment from all stakeholders including the UN, NGOs, the media, and civil society. Moreover, gender equality, and participatory, accountable, and efficient governance can facilitate and harness activities toward the achievement of development objectives. New policies, new expertise, and more resources are required in the face of increasing terrorist attacks and accelerating environmental degradation to meet the challenges of global peace, human security, and sustainable development. Concerted effort by governments, civil society, and the diverse range of development partners would ensure the achievement of sustainable development and human security objectives.

References

Adelman, H. 2000. From refugees to forced migration: The UNHCR and human security. *International Migration Review* 35:17–32.

Agarwal, A., J. Kimondo, G. Morena and J. Tinker. 1981. Water, sanitation, health—for all? Prospects for the international drinking water supply and sanitation decade: 1981–90. London: IIED/Earthscan Publication.

Annan, Kofi. 2001. Report to the UN General Assembly. New York: United Nations.

Axworthy, Lloyd. 2001. Human security and global governance: Putting people first. Global Governance 7:19–23.

Barbier, E. 1989. Economics, natural resource scarcity and development, London: Earthscan.

Berkowitz, M., and Bock, P. 1968. National security. International encyclopedia of the social science, vol. 11. New York: Macmillan and The Free Press.

Blaikie, P. 1996. New knowledge and rural development: A review of views and practicalities. Paper presented at the 28th International Geographical Congress, The Hague, August 5–10.

Brinkerhoff, D. W., and A. A. Goldsmith, eds. 1990. Institutional sustainability in agriculture and rural development: A global perspective. New York: Praeger.

Brock, Lothar. 1991. Peace through parks: The environment on the peace research agenda. Journal of Peace Research 28 (4): 407–424.

Bush, George W. 2003. State of the Union Address. Office of the Press Secretary, The White House, Washington, DC, January 28.

Buzan, B. 1991. Peoples, states and fears: An agenda for international security studies in the post-Cold War era, 2d ed. Boulder, CO: Lynne Rienner Publishers.

Commission for Africa. 2005. Our common interest: Report of the Commission for Africa. Tony Blair (chair), March.

Commission on Human Security. 2003. Human security now. New York: Commission on Human Security.

Dabelko, G., S. Lonergan, and R. Matthew. 2000. State of the art review of environmental security and co-operation. Paris: OECD.

Department of Environment. 1988. Our common future: A perspective by the UK on the report of the World Commission on Environment and Development. London: HMSO.

Department for International Development (DFID). 1997. Eliminating world poverty: A challenge for the 21st century—A summary. London: DFID.

Department for International Development (DFID). 2002. Poverty and environment. March. London: DFID.

Dreze, J., and A. Sen. 1989. Hunger and public action. New York: Oxford University Press.

Environmental Resources Management (ERM). 2002. Predicted impact of global climate change on poverty and sustainable achievement of the Millennium Development Goals. London: Environmental Resources Management.

GECHS. 1999. Global environmental change and human security: GECHS Science Plan. IHDP: Bonn.

Gleditsch, N. P. 1997. Environmental conflict and the democratic peace. In Conflict and the environment, ed. N. P. Gleditsch, 91–106. Dordrecht: Kluver Academic Publishers.

Griffin, K. 1981. Land concentration and world poverty, 2d ed. New York: Holmes and Meier.

Harrison, Lawrence. 1985. Underdevelopment is a state of mind: The American case. Cambridge, MA: The Center for International Affairs, Harvard University.

Heinbecker, P. 1999. Human security. Headlines 56 (2): 4–9.

Huntington, S. 1968. Political order and changing societies. New Haven, CT: Yale University Press.

Hyden, G. 1998. Environmental awareness, conflict genesis and governance. In Managing the globalized environment: Local strategies to secure livelihoods, ed. Tina Riita Granfelt, 150–172. London: IT Publications.

International Task Force (ITF). 1985. Tropical forests: A call for action. Washington, DC: World Resources Institute.

King, Gary, and Christopher Murray. 2002. Rethinking human security. Political Science Quarterly 116 (4): 585–610.

Lansana, Fofana. 2000. Sierra Leoneans know the devastating consequences of conflict on their country's fledging development. Developments, The International IFPRI Development Magazine 12 (fourth quarter): 7–9.

Liechenko, R. M., and K. L. O'Brien. 2005. Double exposure: Global environmental change in an era of globalization. New York: Oxford University Press.

Lonergan, S. C., K. R. Gustavson, and B. Carter. 1999. Developing an index of human security. Global Environmental Change and Human Security Project, Research Report No. 2. University of Victoria, BC (see also AVISO Bulletin 6: 1–2).

Mannion, A. M. 1992. Sustainable development and biotechnology. Environmental Conservation 19:298–305.

Matthew, Richard. 2002. In defense of environment and security research. ECSP Report 8:109–124.

Marx, Karl. 1976. Capital, vol. 1. Harmondsworth: Penguin.

McNamara, Robert S. 1968. The essence of security: Reflections in office. New York: Harper and Row.

Mertus, Julie, N. Flowers, and D. Mallike. 1999. Local action, global change: Learning about human rights of women and girls. New York: UNIFEM.

Meyers, Norman. 1989. Environment and security. Foreign Policy 74 (2): 23–41.

National Institute for Public Health and the Environment (RIVM). 2002. Forum for globally-integrated environmental assessment modeling. United Nations University (UNU), Japan, and the National Institute for Public Health and the Environment (RIVM), the Netherlands. http://www.unu.edu/env/GLEAM/ (accessed March 4, 2009).

Olson, M. 1963. Rapid growth as a destabilizing force. Journal of Economic History 23 (1): 524–552.

O'Reilly, Siobhan. 1998. Conflict and development: Responding to the challenge. World Vision 6 (Spring): 3.

PRIO. 1999. To cultivate peace: Agriculture in a way of conflict. Report 1/99. Oslo: International Peace Research Institute (PRIO).

Redclift, M. 1987. Sustainable development: Exploring the contradictions. London: Methuen.

Redclift, M. 1992. The meaning of sustainable development. Geoforum 23:395–403.

Rees, W. E. 1990. The ecology of sustainable development. The Ecologist 20:18–23.

Renner, M. 1989. National security: The economic and environmental dimensions. Worldwatch Paper 89. Washington, DC: Worldwatch Institute.

Rodney, W. 1982. How Europe underdeveloped Africa. Enugu: Ikenga Publishers.

Rothschild, Emma. 1995. What is security? Daedalus 124 (3): 53–93.

Sanjeev, K., C. William, and D. Raad. 2003. From the environment and human security to sustainable development. Journal of Human Development 4 (2): 289–231.

Seers, D. 1977. The meaning of development. International Development Review 11:2–6.

Sen, Amartya K. 1999. Development as freedom. New York: Knopf, and Oxford: Oxford University Press.

Sen, Amartya K. 2000. Why human security? Paper presented at the International Symposium on Human Security, Tokyo, July 28.

Simon, David. 2003. Dilemmas of development and the environment in a globalizing world: Theory, policy and praxis. Progress in Development Studies 3 (1): 5–41.

Starr, J. R. 1991. Water wars. Foreign Policy 82:17–36.

Stewart, Francis. 2004. Development and security. Centre for Research on Inequality, Human Security and Ethnicity (ORISE), Working Paper 3. London: University of Oxford.

Streeten, P. 1981. First things first: Meeting basic needs in developing countries. New York: Oxford University Press.

Tadjbakhsh, S., and A. Chenoy. 2006. Human security: Concepts and implications. London: Routledge.

Thomas, C. 2000. Global governance, development and human security. London, Pluto.

Tolba, M. K. 1986. Desertification and economic survival. Land Use Policy, 6:260–268.

Ullman, R. H. 1983. Redefining security. International Security 8 (1): 129–153.

United Nations (UN). 1948. United Nations Declaration of Human Rights. New York: United Nations.

United Nations (UN). 2000. United Nations Millennium Development Goals. New York: United Nations.

United Nations Conference on Environment and Development (UNCED). 1992. Agenda 21. Rio de Janeiro.

United Nations Development Programme (UNDP). 1993. Heading for change. UNDP annual report. Oxford: Oxford University Press.

United Nations Development Programme (UNDP). 1994. Human development report. Oxford: Oxford University Press.

United Nations Development Programme (UNDP). 1999. Human development report. Oxford: Oxford University Press.

United Nations Development Programme (UNDP). 2003. Re-conceptualizing governance. Discussion Paper 2. New York: UNDP.

UNICEF. 1996. The state of the world's children 1996. Oxford: Oxford University Press.

Warwick, Donald. 1982. Better pills: Population policies and their implementation in eight developing countries. Cambridge, UK: Cambridge University Press.

Weaver, J., and Jameson, K. 1981. Economic development: Competing paradigms. Lanham, MD: University Press of America.

Westing, Arthur H. 1989. The environmental component of comprehensive security. Bulletin of Peace Proposals 20 (2): 129–134.

World Bank. 1984. World development report. New York: Oxford University Press.

World Bank. 2004. Perspectives on development. Washington, DC: World Bank. World Commission on Environment and Development (WCED). 1987. Our common future. Oxford: Oxford University Press.

DI SCUSSION QUESTIONS

1. How would you summarize the main argument of the article in a sentence or two?

2. What is human security and how is that different from the "traditional" understanding of state security?

3. According to the article, how has our understanding of economic growth and development changed over the years? What is "sustainable development" and how is that different from development? Why have our views of development changed/evolved?

4. According to the United Nations, what are the seven areas of critical threats to human security? How are they related to the issue of human security and development?

5. What is meant by "bidirectional relationships" between human security and development? Explain.

6. What recommendations does the author highlight as central to the cause of human security and development?

The U.S. Mideast Policy and the International Law Imperative

By Ali R. Abootalebi

....

The American foreign policy in general and toward the Middle East in particular has since the demise of the Soviet Union dithered between neoliberalism and neoconservative interventionism. Fundamentally, both neoliberal and neoconservative foreign policy principles and strategies have justified U.S. military adventurism abroad in the name of not only "fabricated" threats to the national interest (e.g., Iraq), but democracy and freedom and the global responsibility to protect (R2P) (e.g., Libya). The result has been nothing short of disastrous for populace living in the targeted countries. Similarly, the historically dominant Realist perspective of U.S. foreign policy has had a state-centric view of the world based on power politics and the pursuit of national interest that is neutral on the State's regime type, treating all states equal in matters of *Realpolitik*. This implies that people's welfare in any state is a matter of national sovereignty and is subject to non-interference by other states and even international actors like the United Nations so long as they are not a threat to global peace. President Donald Trump's "America First" slogan may resonate with some economic nationalists hopeful for less interventionist U.S. behavior abroad except for grave matters of national interest. President Trump's embrace for neoconservative personalities in his cabinet, however, raises questions whether the administration has a coherent alternative foreign policy strategy and principle.

The United States has a long history of foreign interventionism in the name of national interest and in the name of democracy and peace, but with detrimental consequences for the country's long-term national interest as well as the welfare of people of the targeted countries. This is evident nowhere better than in the Middle East and the North African region (MENA). In historical parallel, the Progressive movement of the turn of the last century that sought to further social and political reform at home also failed in its ideals for U.S. policy abroad as a force for positive change. This was despite its adherents' domestic agenda aiming at curbing political corruption and limiting the political influence of large corporations. The result was earlier U.S. interventions and colonialism

Adapted from Ali R. Abootalebi, "Are US Middle East Policies Against the Law?" *Informed Comment*, 2018.

in the form of the American-Spanish war, conquest and the occupation of the Philippines, Puerto Rico, Cuba, and Haiti.

An alternative U.S. approach can rely on international law and diplomacy and organizations, involving an expanded and restructured United Nations and other multilateral institutions and organizations in the service of sustainable development, democracy, good governance, and global governance. International intergovernmental organizations such as the United Nations and its functional agencies (e.g., World Health Organization, International Labor Organization, World Intellectual Property Organization, United Nations Educational Scientific, and Cultural Organization, International Atomic Energy Agency, Organization for the Prohibition of Chemical Weapons, others), the International Monetary Fund, the World Bank, the Asian Development Bank, the Asian Infrastructure Investment Bank, the International Court of Justice, the International Criminal Court, and the European Union can and are central players in global governance. Calls for the reform of the United Nations' Security Council and other IGOs is not new and are needed. (Recall, for example, the only expansion of the UN Security Council occurred in 1965, and there are genuine concerns about the efficacy of the UNSC in safeguarding global peace within the current institutional and legal framework.) The urgency of world politics today demands a more responsible, representative global governance based on international law and through multilateralism and diplomacy to avert looming threats of military adventurism and sociopolitical, economic, and environmental calamities.

The 20th century witnessed the death of 170 million people as victims of war crimes, crimes against humanity, and genocide.[1] The post-cold war alone has witnessed numerous conflicts, wars of aggression, failed states, acts of genocide, war crimes and crimes against humanity, terrifying environmental degradation and climatic concerns, and deregulated, hyper-capitalism with repeated international economic and financial crises (1994 Mexican Tequila crisis; 1997 Asian Economic Crisis; 2000 Dotcom crisis; 2007–20008 (somewhat still ongoing) housing and financial crisis, just to name a few). The 21st century has already witnessed high crimes committed, among others, in Rwanda, Bosnia-Herzegovina, the Sudan, Nigeria, Afghanistan, Iraq, Libya, Syria, and Myanmar. The intention of this article is not to engage in a discussion of how to reform and build mechanisms necessary for a more constructive global governance. Instead, my contention is that strengthening the function and the utility of international law and institutions can greatly enhance global human security and governance. It can also help reduce the risk of major powers' confrontation, evident in the conflictual world politics in the post-cold war aftermath. This can also help the United States to avoid continuously getting involved in global conflicts in the name of humanitarianism while violating international laws and principles. A point of departure for analysis is to review and highlight deficiencies inherent in the U.S. Mideast policy, if not its overall foreign policy behavior, built on paradigmatic assumptions and principles.

The U.S. Mideast policy has ignored the long-lasting crisis of governance that has left most of the populace of the Arab MENA region under authoritarian regimes humiliated by defeat in wars, chronic inefficiencies and corruption, and overall poor governance. Both the neoconservatives and the neoliberals have selectively advocated support for authoritarian regimes and regime change through direct military intervention (the neoconservatives) or through pressure and NATO action in the name of human rights and humanitarian interventionism (neoliberals). Both paradigms' supporters in the U.S. foreign policy establishment are selective in their views on the significance of principles and values in determining policy choices; both are comfortable with supporting authoritarian but friendly regimes in the region (and indeed elsewhere in the world) while ignoring continuing human rights abuses in places like Egypt, Jordan, Saudi Arabia, and the Persian Gulf States.[2]

The United States throughout the 1990s remained the unmatched hegemonic power, supported by a booming domestic economy that saw economic growth throughout the 1990s: Between 1993 and 2000, the United States exhibited the best economic performance of the previous three decades. In 2000, its economic expansion surpassed in length the expansion of the 1960s and thus became the longest on record. During Clinton's second term, real economic growth averaged 4.5 percent per year, and unemployment fell to 4 percent, although by the year 2000 the economy had returned to approximately the same point in the business cycle it had occupied in 1990.

The "successful" Persian Gulf War of 1991 saw Iraqi forces ejected from Kuwait and facilitated U.S. troops' presence in the holiest land of Islam in Saudi Arabia. It emboldened the first post-cold-war American administration to counter Iraqi and Iranian "bellicose" foreign policy posture through a dual containment policy[3] and to also push for the settlement of the long-enduring Arab (Palestinian)-Israeli conflict. Both China and the Russian Federation under Boris Yeltsin acquiesced to the American leadership in the Middle East and cooperated in the United Nations' Security Council. China's eagerness for its further integration into the global political economy after 1989 Tiananmen Square incident ensured their cooperation. The Russian Federation's embrace of an "economic shock therapy" to[4] fix their ailing economy in the 1990s meant their full-fledged cooperation with the United States in the UNSC to pass resolution 660 (1990) to rally the U.S.-led coalition against Iraq to liberate Kuwait. Meanwhile, the United States' push for the Oslo peace process led to the Oslo I (1993) and Oslo II (1995) agreements that also brought along the Jordanian-Israeli peace agreement in 1994, and the Wye River Memorandum in October 1998, outlining further Israeli withdrawal from the West Bank.

The consolidation of U.S. hegemonic presence in the region in the 1990s remained largely insensitive to the continuing worsening of the socioeconomic and political situation in much of the Arab World. The 1990s witnessed the U.S. dual containment policy of Iraq and Iran, resulting in the additional death of one half million of Iraqi infants in addition to its natural rate of mortality, and the expansion of Israeli settlement activities in the occupied territories despite Oslo agreements. The U.S. military presence in the region throughout the 1990s also ensured support for notorious regimes such as those in Tunisia, Egypt, Saudi Arabia, and the Persian Gulf states, while anti-American sentiments remained widespread in the region. Terrorists' attacks on U.S. interests continued throughout the 1990s, culminating in the 1996 Khobar Tower attack in Saudi Arabia, the 1998 attacks on U.S. embassies in Kenya and Tanzania, and the attack on USS Cole in Yemen in 2000.

The September 11, 2001 terrorists' attacks set the tone for the "new" U.S. policy in the MENA region. The neoconservative camp in the George W. Bush administration did not hesitate to use the American military might in a new push to "rejuvenate" the American hegemonic moment that had since 1990 dominated the world but had remained underutilized. The United States in the post 9/11 world had the military and economic means, but it now had the ideological backbone behind a new strategy to change the world in its own image: to export democracy and to punish those opposing it, birthing the Bush Administration's "Preemption Doctrine."[5] The declared war on terrorism only "legitimated" a broader policy of interventionism, continuing support of authoritarian regimes and solidifying support for the state of Israel while securing access to the region's lucrative oil, natural gas, and consumer and financial markets, including the ever-pervasive arms market.

Modern militant movements like the Wahhabi's,[6] dating back to the 18th and 19th centuries in tribal Arabia, the Muslim Brotherhood beginning in the 1920s, the Taliban in Afghanistan, al-Qaeda since the 1980s, and a plethora of other militant movements in the past few decades, have aimed to take over the state to "restore" justice and harmony through Islamic governance. The U.S. policy of regime change (Afghanistan 2001, Iraq 2003, Libya 2011, and Syria 2011) and the expansion of a perpetual war on terror to Yemen, Somalia, Afghanistan, and parts of the African continent has opened the gates of political rivalries and open conflict. It has strengthened the resolve of militant Muslim groups in countering the U.S. military presence and its support for political status quo in the name of stability. Mainstream and militant Muslim groups alike have taken full advantage of the chaos to claim their own space as alternative visionaries in matters of politics and governance. The prolongation of American military occupation, political wrangling among competing Iraqi Shi'a and Sunni elites and groups, and al-Qaeda-inspired terrorism initially targeted the U.S. and its allies. However, Iraqi chaos created the environment for the rise of Abu Musab al-Zarqawi, who broke off from al-Qaeda with a deliberate strategy of inflaming sectarian and communal violence. In October 2004, Al-Zarqawi declared himself the "emir" of Al-Qaeda in Iraq. His followers broke from al-Qaeda, renaming itself the Islamic State of Iraq in late 2006, about four months after al-Zarqawi was killed by a targeted American airstrike.[7] This, along with the ineptitude of the Shi'a-dominated government in Baghdad and the foreign occupation, ensured the rise of extreme ideologies, facilitating the rise of the Islamic State in Iraq and Syria. Daesh has thrived on ultra-conservatism and sectarian killings in the name of its "true" version if Islam ever since, while supported by the very authoritarian regimes responsible for its creation through ideological, financial, and political support, and under the U.S. protection!

The U.S. Mideast policy is short-sighted, inconsistent, and fundamentally ignores the welfare of the people in the region in pursuit of pragmatic national interest, or often in the interest of special interest groups and constituencies like the AIPAC, the oil industry, the arms manufacturers and the like, and in defiance of a realistic foreign policy. The gap between the rhetoric and policy encapsulated in selective and inconsistent behavior in matters of human rights and principles remain problematic. If the Iraqi invasion of Kuwait in August 1990 proved Saddam's butchery and adventurism to the West, he was only praised and supported for his war against the Iranians! The eight years of a bloodbath in Saddam's war against Iran throughout 1980s and the use of chemical weapons against Iranian troops and Iraq's Kurdish population, and the massacre of Shi'a and Kurdish population in March and April 1991, became only footnotes in the overall strategy of stability, security, and the protection of the State of Israel. Fast-forward to Syria in April 2017 and again April 2018, when the use of chemical weapons is used as justification of two U.S. and allies' missile attacks on Syrian territory in the long-running civil war since 2011. The message of such strikes does not escape the sharp mind: U.S. (and the UK and France) can break the international law while acting as the judge, the jury, and the enforcer. The outcry over the death of over one hundred victims of chemical attacks, by still undetermined entities, as horrible as that is, fails to raise outrage over the death of half a million in the Syrian civil war, instigated and illegally intervened by multiple rivaling parties! (Recall, U.S. presence in Syria without a UNSC mandate or a Syrian government invitation is illegal.) This is while the use of phosphorous and cluster bombs by Saudi Arabia in Yemen and Israel in Lebanon and Gaza are totally ignored. The war on Yemen lacks any legal foundation and the United States has played a large role in providing weapons, intelligence, targeting expertise, and logistical support to the so-called Saudi-led coalition. The United Nations blacklisted the coalition for killing and injuring 683 children in Yemen and attacking dozens of schools and hospitals in 2016 alone.[8]

There is no doubt that political underdevelopment in the Arab world itself invites and facilitates foreign manipulation and interventionism. The absence of political democracy, corruption, lack of transparency and accountability in the political arena, and the presence of a weak civil society impede active and effective citizen participation in governance. This situation has resulted in the humiliation of Arab people's dignity, *al-hogra or ihtiqaar,*[9] and culminated in the still-unresolved Arab Spring movements since 2011. Some Arab societies like Tunisia and Egypt have embarked on a desperate journey for political freedom, economic opportunity, and human dignity. This has happened while Islamic movements (e.g., Muslim Brotherhood),[10] have been unable to fill the political/ideological void in gaining the trust of popular support in national movements for freedom, prosperity, and dignity. Western military interventions have not brought security and democracy and have failed to resolve the deficit of good governance in places like, among others, Libya, Syria, Yemen, Afghanistan, Iraq, and Somalia.

Conversely, good governance at national and international levels can help avoid conflicts and settle them peacefully when they occur. Good governance signals the ability of the governing institutions to deliver the key public goods needed to maintain order and stability. Governance is good" and also more likely to advance peace when "it is inclusive, participatory and accountable; when it is characterized by fair procedures and performs well in delivering necessary public goods."[11] Decision making rests at the heart of governing and governance, particularly given the complexities of globalization and the changing dynamics of state-society relations. Similarly, good governance at the international level implies the presence and effective functioning of legitimate institutions aimed at management of global relations to provide "human security" for all.

In closing, imagine if the U.S. hegemonic moment in the 1990s had invested money and energy in reforming and strengthening international institutions and the meaningful rule of international law and diplomacy in the elevation of human security and liberty. Instead, the first UN intervention in the service of collective security since the Korean War in 1950 saw the restoration of Kuwaiti sovereignty, but the death of hundreds of thousands of Iraqis through the war and the subsequent sanctions led to no attempt at reforming the UN. Kuwait also reverted back to its authoritarian rule after its liberation and the restoration of the government. Similarly, the U.S. invasion of Afghanistan, that remains unresolved 17 years later, could have been averted: An international tribunal could have tried members of al-Qaeda responsible for their crimes against humanity based on the existing international law. Later, the fabrication of the Iraqi regime in pursuit of weapons of mass destruction in 2003 led to an illegal war, causing regional and extra-regional interventions and the lives of millions adversely affected. The U.S-led NATO illegal operation in Kosovo in 1999 only emboldened its operation over Libya in 2011 that expectedly proved the initial calls for liberty and freedom in Libya hollow.

While the United States has spent hundreds of billions on perpetual wars, the Europeans have tried promoting the cause of integration and cooperation through international mechanisms: The creation of the European Union (1993), the World Trade Organization (WTO) (1995), the Kyoto Protocol (1997), the adoption of common monetary union (1999), and the creation of the International Criminal Court (1998). Conversely, the United States has continued to defy conducting its foreign policy within the framework of international law, institutions, and norms while preaching it loudly: the Bush administration's withdrawal from the 1972 Anti-Ballistic Missile (ABM) Treaty in June 2002—that led to Russia's withdrawal from the Strategic Arms Reduction Treaty (START II) in the same year—its refusal, until today, to ratify the Law of the Sea Treaty (LOST), its withdrawal in 20017 from the 2015 Iran nuclear deal agreement (also known as the Joint Comprehensive Plan of Action (JCPOA)) and its June 2017 withdrawal from the mainly voluntary adherence to the 2015 Paris climate agreement only demonstrate a unilateral and detrimental approach to global governance. The latest blow to global security, at the time of this writing, is the U.S. suspension and planned withdrawal from the 1987 Intermediate Nuclear Force (INF) treaty. The United States and the global community must do much better to secure a more peaceful, cooperative, and harmonious world that ensures human security for people everywhere, especially for the long-embattled peoples of the MENA region.

Notes

1. R. J. Rummel, *Death by Government* (New Brunswick, NJ: Transaction Publishers, 2009). See also https://www.hawaii.edu/powerkills/NOTE5.HTM

2. Jeffrey Frankel and Peter R. Orszag, "Retrospective on American Economic Policy in the 1990s: Taxes, U.S. Economy, Monetary Policy, Federal Budget," *Brookings Institution,* Nov. 2, 2011.

3. F. Greogry Gause, "The Illogic of Dual Containment", *Foreign Affairs*, March/April 1994, https://www.foreignaffairs.com/articles/iran/1994-03-01/illogic-dual-containment

4. "Shock therapy—With Emphasis on Shock," *Newsweek*, January 12, 1992, http://www.newsweek.com/shock-therapy-emphasis-shock-197912 ; Jeffrey Sachs, "What I Did in Russia," March 14, 2012, http://jeffsachs.org/2012/03/what-i-did-in-russia

5. "The Bush Administration's Doctrine of Preemption (and Prevention): When, How, Where," *Foreign Affairs*, Council on Foreign Relations, February 1, 2004, http://www.cfr.org/world/bush-administrations-doctrine-preemption-prevention-/p6799

6. "Islamic Radicalism: Its Wahhabi Roots and Current Implications," Islamic Supreme Council of America, http://www.islamicsupremecouncil.org/understanding-islam/anti-extremism/7-islamic-radicalism-its-wahhabi-roots-and-current-representation.html

7. Ted Kemp, "Abu Musab al-Zarqawi Is the Man Who Founded ISIS," *CNBC*, Thursday, 11 August 2016, http://www.cnbc.com/2016/08/11/who-founded-isis-abu-musb-al-zarqawi-started-the-terror-group.html

8. Michelle Nichols, "UN blacklists Saudi-led Coalition for Killing Children in Yemen," *Reuters*, October 5, 2017, https://www.reuters.com/article/us-yemen-security-saudi-un/u-n-blacklists-saudi-led-coalition-for-killing-children-in-yemen-idUSKBN1CA2NI

9. Sain Ilahiane, "Why Do Protests Keep Happening in North Africa? It's 'al-Hogra,'" *Informed Comment*, January 22, 2019 https://www.juancole.com/2019/01/protests-happening-africa.html

10. Patrick Kingsley, "How Mohamed Morsi, Egypt's First Elected President, Ended Up on Death Row," *The Guardian*, June 1, 2015, https://www.theguardian.com/world/2015/jun/01/mohamed-morsi-execution-death-sentence-egypt

11. David Cortright, Conor Seyle, and Kristen Wall, *Governance for Peace: How inclusive, Participatory and Accountable Institutions Promote Peace and Prosperity (Cambridge University Press, 2017)*, p. 47. See also, chapter 16.

DISCUSSION QUESTIONS

1. How would you summarize the main argument of the article in a sentence or two?

2. What does the author mean by the MENA region's long-lasting crisis of governance? How is that related to the rule of law and international law?

3. Why is the author critical of the American post–Cold War policy of neoliberal and neoconservative interventionism?

4. The author claims that the U.S. Mideast policy is short sighted, inconsistent, and fundamentally ignores the welfare of the peoples in the region? Explain why?

5. What kind of evidence does the author provide for his claim that the U.S. Mideast policy outcomes would have been different had it invested its efforts in strengthening international institutions and the pursuit of meaningful rule of international law and diplomacy?

6. Why does the author see a connection between the U.S. military intervention in Iraq in 2003 and the rise of Daesh, aka the Islamic State, in Iraq and Syria (ISIS)?

PART IV

Global Challenges

Globalization and Development Options

By Richard Lagos and Osvaldo Rosales

There is no political future or economic scenario that is predetermined. That was the bold proposal former Brazilian President Fernando Henrique Cardoso and Enzo Faletto made over 40 years ago in the midst of dependency theory's determinism.[1] A very influential analytical framework in Latin America between the 1950s and 1970s, dependency theory asserts that the world economy is organized in an industrial core and a commodity-producing periphery. Countries in the periphery (mostly developing ones) remain stuck in the production of low-value primary products for the consumption of the industrial core and are thus unable to significantly close their development gaps with the industrialized countries. Cardoso and Faletto's statement has even more relevance today in light of the profound transformations in the global economy and the surprises brought by the first decade of the twenty-first century.

After the fall of the Berlin Wall, the world seemed to enter a phase of "hyperpower" in which the exercise of American "soft power" would be enough to assure peace and American hegemony. The EU aspired to transform itself by 2010 into the main technological power of the knowledge society. On the other hand, the incorporation of China into the World Trade Organization (WTO), not without its tensions, was interpreted as a mechanism for both disciplining China and motivating its adjustment to the global economy.

The results have been unexpected. China has exceeded expectations. It is already the second largest economy in the world in GDP terms and was the key player that saved the world from a deeper recession. Its massive stimulus program in response to the 2008 financial crisis allowed for the maintenance of high levels of demand for commodities and industrial inputs, favoring the growth of Africa, Asia, Latin America, Australia, and Canada, among others. China has been strengthened by the crisis, which has even had an institutional consequence in China's presence in the G20; the increase in its IMF voting share; and a whirlwind of international seminar, business, and diplomatic activities carried out in Beijing or Shanghai with first-rate players from all areas of the world. At the end of the first decade of the twenty-first century, the conclusion is the world has to begin "adapting" to China.

Richard Lagos and Osvaldo Rosales, "Globalization and Development Options," *The Brown Journal of World Affairs*, vol. 19, no. 2, pp. 283-301. Copyright © 2013 by Brown Journal of World Affairs. Reprinted with permission. Provided by ProQuest LLC. All rights reserved.

This is a peculiar moment of hegemonic transition that will last for decades. The United States faces a medium-term fiscal crisis that will affect its potential economic growth. The EU will end this decade with serious economic and social decline. Meanwhile, China, East Asia, and the emerging economies have been responsible for two-thirds of the world economic growth in the first two decades of the twenty-first century. Together, the accumulation of disequilibria between globalization and rapid technological changes, the emerging countries erupting with force in the global economy, and the multilateral institutionalism no longer functional for the development of these tendencies open new possibilities and unprecedented negotiation leverage for developing countries. In this decade, the emerging economies have taken unthinkable steps in their convergence with OECD incomes and have transformed themselves into the engine of the global economy. In just a few decades they will account for 60 percent of world GDP and constitute the most dynamic segment of international trade. Small- or medium-size countries can diversify their partners and markets as well as participate in international alliances of variable dimensions according to specific issues of interest. Today it is more valid than ever to say that the destiny of developing countries is not predetermined and that they are not condemned to waiting for the resolve of the main international players.

It is true that the playing field continues to be uneven and, in particular, the disparity between the military power of the United States and the rest of the world is colossal. However, one of the peculiarities of this globalization, driven by the command of finance, technological change, and market openness, is that it tends to reduce the relevance of weapons or military alliances. In fact, these do not help solve the difficulties of innovation or competitiveness, the fragility of the financial systems, or the high public debt—issues that are to varying degrees affecting the main industrialized economies.

In light of this scenario, Cardoso and Faletto's theory becomes more relevant than ever because none of these tendencies could have been deduced from the dependency framework. It is true that there are a set of political, economic, and social factors that when intertwined establish the conditions through which the future emerges. However, the future of a society is based not only on objective conditions that shape power relations in the political, economic, and social spheres but also on how these relations interact with social forces and with politics. As a consequence, there is no determinism, and there is room for political maneuvering, both in the domestic and international spheres.

Two Walls in Crisis and Epochal Change: From Iron Wall to Wall Street

Globalization has produced two radical changes in the political sphere. First, the current globalization process is different from the one that dominated in the bipolar world until the fall of the Berlin Wall. During this period, there was not only economic but also political and military competition among the blocs seeking hegemony in the world. The fall of the Berlin Wall marked the transition from a bipolar world to one where a *Pax Americana* would be implemented, one which assumed a radical reordering of the world. However, the Iraq War and the difficulties in Afghanistan after the attack on the World Trade Center in 2001 have introduced limitations with regard to the present meaning of a unipolar world. In fact, an "American Peace" has not emerged with the force that was expected. What has emerged instead is a scenario where, on the one hand, the United States is not capable of imposing its authority on the rest of the world and, on the other hand, the will of the United States remains indispensable for achieving solutions to global challenges. This is the perception transmitted by the Obama administration to the rest of the world, a departure from the unilateralism of the previous administration and the reason why a negotiation space has opened in the global political sphere.

The second radical change is, without a doubt, the economic crisis that started in the financial sphere in 2007, worsened in 2008, and generated a global quasi-recession in 2009.[2] This has been the equivalent of the fall of the Berlin Wall in terms of its consequences for the ideas and praxis of international relations in this globalized world.

Indeed, the crisis has been located in industrialized economies and in the financial sector, the most dynamic segment of the globalization. With increased trade and economic links between developing economies themselves, they could resist the financial crisis well and recover sooner and faster than industrialized economies. In the last five years, in comparison with developed economies, developing economies are growing more, their fiscal accounts are more orderly, their financial systems are most healthy, their exports more dynamic, their poverty indicators are declining, and even in a large group of developing areas their distributional indicators are improving.

The magnitude of the financial crisis led former U.S. President George W. Bush to convene 19 countries in October 2008 in order to collectively address the problem, giving rise to the G20. This represented the most convincing proof that the G7, created 30 years earlier as a privileged space for the main industrialized countries to monitor and govern international economic relations, was unable to deal with the magnitude of the global crisis by itself. In fact, the G7 was a substantial part of the public and private debt problem and of the vulnerability of the financial system, while growth, savings, and economic solidity were produced by China and the emerging economies. It has thus become necessary to sit other relevant economies—all emerging economies—at the table of global decision making. The G20, which emerged as a result of the crisis, will certainly transcend it. It will eventually subsume the G7 and the G8, illustrating explicitly the new distribution of global power that is emerging.

The crisis revealed that deregulated financial markets do not self-regulate or enhance economic and social efficiency. In a global financial context, regulation cannot be strictly national because finance moves internationally. Any regulatory reform should cover taking care of capitalization levels, avoiding excessive dependence on short-term financing, restricting risk taking, limiting the use of complex instruments and opaque operations, implementing effective accountability of operations through firms' balance sheets, increasing transparency, modernizing normative frameworks, and enhancing the technical capabilities of financial supervisors. These substantial modifications to financial laissez-faire must be undertaken on a global scale.

What has collapsed is more than the so-called Washington Consensus of privatization, liberalization, and deregulation. Now concerns focus on speculative and deregulated capitalism and the more extreme version of the neoconservative project that includes supply-side economics, the concept of the minimal and passive state, and aggressive and unilateralist geopolitics. With this collapse, spaces have opened for a new paradigm of economic organization that provides greater room for nonconservative visions. However, in order for progressive projects to become a viable alternative, it is necessary for governments to carry them out with innovative proposals and a good understanding of previous shortcomings, including those of progressive forces. These projects must also be relevant in a global economy marked by intensified technological change, the emergence of new players, and the challenge of climate change. In Latin America, any proposal must additionally take on the baggage of still high poverty levels and unequal income distribution.

The Rise of The Emerging Economies

The main transformation of the first decade of the twenty-first century is the drastic change in the composition of world economic growth and international trade. The weight of the emerging economies has grown, placing India and China in an increasingly more relevant role. The Asia-Pacific region has become the engine of the world economy, while the relevance of South–South trade (that is, trade among developing countries) has increased significantly. As a result, the West has lost economic and demographic momentum, accentuating the gradual transition of the world economy's center of gravity from West to East and from North to South.

A structural trend that was already clear before the crisis but has been heightened by it is the greater weight of China in the world economy. To a lesser degree, this tendency is accompanied by India, Russia, Brazil, and South Africa (the other BRICS countries). Besides being the world's second largest economy, China is since 2010 the first global exporter of goods. It consumes one-fourth of the world's supply of steel, aluminum, copper, and iron and one-third of the supply of petroleum. Furthermore, it is the gravitational center of the world's industrial sector. With its enormous investments in education, infrastructure, and innovation, China is becoming one of the strongest competitors at a global level. In the next few years, China will be an even more important player and, as a consequence, will claim a major role in the reforms of the international financial system and more broadly in the governance of the international economic system.

> In the next few years, China will claim a major role in the governance of the international economic system.

For Latin America the global crisis means that India, Asia, and—above all—China will become the main source of export growth. Commodity-exporting economies—such as those of South American and African countries—have been less affected, taking advantage of China's high growth rate, which has kept international demand for these products high. In the case of Mexico and Central America, by contrast, accentuated competition with Chinese manufacturers for the United States market could accelerate structural changes in certain industries, especially the *maquila* in textile industry and other labor-intensive manufactures.

In the last 20 years, the center of gravity of the world economy shifted from the OECD toward the emerging economies. In 1990 the OECD economies represented 62 percent of world GDP, measured in purchasing power parity. Presently these countries account for half of world's GDP and by 2030 will account for only 43 percent. Conversely, in 2030 emerging and developing economies will account for 57 percent of the world's production. Furthermore, these countries accounted for almost three-quarters of global economic growth in the first decade of this century. In that same period, 65 of these countries doubled the growth rate of the OECD countries, while only 12 of them had achieved this in the 1990s.[3] Such an accentuated trend of convergence toward OECD income has not been observed since the 1970s. This is the main economic trend of the past decade and everything indicates that it will continue in the coming decade.

A great part of the explanation for this structural transformation of the global economy is related to the rise of China. The numbers show that for many developing countries, economic growth is beginning to depend more on the relationship with China than with the G7.[4] Between 2001 and 2009, the growth elasticity of the emerging economies vis-à-vis growth in the G7 was 0.26, while it was 1.11 vis-à-vis China.[5] In the case of the middle-income economies, like most Latin American countries, 0.37 growth points are added for every additional Chinese GDP growth point.[6] As a result, China has not only unleashed a gigantic impulse toward growth in the developing economies but also, through this impulse, has become the most important force for poverty reduction in the history of humanity.[7]

Because growth has spread widely across the developing world, South–South trade has become more important in the world economy, increasing from 8 percent of world trade in 1990 to 19 percent at present, although 75 percent of that amount is intra-Asian trade. The high demand for commodities by China, India, and other Asian economies impacts their international prices as well as the prices of the assets linked to the emerging economies. Those countries whose economies are more complementary with the increased Chinese and Asian demand—such as the South American ones—face favorable prospects in their terms of trade and their trade balances. By contrast, those nations that compete with Asia's industrial production—such as Mexico and the Central American countries—tend to be harmed and must rethink their strategies to position themselves in the global economy. Nevertheless, since the increasing wages in China and Mexico have been recovering their comparative advantage and their industrial production is going up, now the Mexican economy is expanding fast.

Developing countries should thus pay more attention in their economic strategies to the liberalization of South–South trade flows. These exchanges will be an increasingly important source of growth; however, they are often subject to higher tariffs than those between the South and the North. Furthermore, the creation of South–South value chains should be explored, as should possibilities for regional integration and cooperation, especially because greater profit potential is associated with South–South trade liberalization.[8]

The current debate centers on how permanent the favorable impact of Chinese dynamism will be on prices of commodities supplied by countries in the Global South. If this boom turns out to be a long-term phenomenon, it would oblige a careful revision of the possibilities of industrialization based on natural resources. Some authors even predict a long cycle of high commodity prices, a "commodity super-cycle" that could rival the one that occurred in the United States between the end of the Civil War and the First World War.[9] Still, even if the current commodity boom were to last not 40 years but only 20, Latin America would cease to be, on average, a middle-income region and would begin to enter the range of income of developed countries.

Of course, this scenario of commodity-led development raises concerns about the impact of commodity prices on the production and exporting structure, a phenomenon known as Dutch disease. A sustained period of high prices for the main export goods will tend to increase the real exchange rate, thereby hindering the profitability of nontraditional exports. Economic history indicates that successful cases of convergence with industrialized economies tend to coincide with long periods of total factor productivity growth in conjunction with production and export diversification that, together, increase the relative weight of manufactured products and high-skill services. This process could be threatened in Latin America by a return to its past reliance on commodity exports. Such a scenario could jeopardize the possibility of socially inclusive growth, given the limited productive and technical linkages associated with the export of natural resources.[10]

We are not proclaiming a "natural resource curse" here. Instead, we wish to call attention to the need to make the most of this favorable historic moment by investing in infrastructure, human resources, and the creation of clusters of productive economic activities associated with natural resources by adding value and knowledge to them. If a "commodity super-cycle" does occur, this will require a redoubled and intense effort to link natural resource exports with the rest of the economy, strengthening production, technological, and job-generating linkages. Without such efforts, a curse will prevail—not the curse of natural resources, but that of bad policies.

In sum, it is necessary to revise and update the framework for understanding center–periphery relations. The experience of China and other Asian economies over the last three decades illustrates that convergence with the levels of income of the developed "core" economies, although gradual, is possible. Contrary to one of the main postulates of dependency theory, several of these peripheral economies have reached the technological frontier in different areas and now play an important role as exporters of manufactured products, services, and technology. Some of those economies are also among the main holders of international reserves and suppliers of global savings, something that is especially evident in the case of China. It is time to incorporate these new facts into the analysis of developmental options, hereby acknowledging the existence of heterogeneity in the periphery. This is exemplified by two groups of countries: a traditional group limited to exporting commodities with little value added and an innovative one able to compete successfully with the global leaders of the knowledge economy. A key line of inquiry concerns whether the expansion of South–South relations has a negative and marginalizing effect on the traditional peripheral economies that still export low value-added goods.[11] This concern is ever more relevant, considering that South–South trade is becoming the engine of the world economy and that Latin America and the Caribbean are increasing their economic and commercial ties with China.

Latin America's Opportunity

After a process of transformation spanning the last 20 years, Latin America today is fundamentally different. Three elements are at the heart of this transformation.

A process of democratic consolidation has allowed the countries of Latin America to be part of a globalized world. It is hard to imagine a reversal of this process. With national differences, today there are elections, political parties, and respect for the rule of law. Of course, there is still a long way to go to achieve a civic culture like the one seen in more advanced countries.

In Latin America today, there is a better understanding of what can and cannot be done with economic policies. Although there are still some populist tendencies—protectionist temptations, inflationary pressures, easing in fiscal discipline, and some administrative controls over foreign trade—it is clear that these trends are the minority.

The crisis came at an extraordinary moment of growth for Latin America. The regional terms of trade were tremendously favorable as a result of the expansion of international trade and the increase of world growth rates, in particular those of emerging countries such as China and India. These elements partly explain the growth rates observed between 2003 and 2008, which amount to six years of growth at an annual rate of five percent. This allowed Latin America to decrease its population living under the poverty line from 44 percent in 2003 to 34 percent in 2007. This growth was also accompanied by low inflation and a significant expansion in employment. As a result, the crisis affected Latin America far less than the rest of the world.

After an interruption in 2009 due to the world economic crisis, Latin America is again on a clear path toward economic growth. Thus in 2011 the regional poverty rate reached 29.4 percent, its lowest level in three decades. Those countries that used the favorable economic cycle of 2003 to 2008 to consolidate their fiscal situation, increase their international reserves, and even save transitory resources from high export prices were better able to apply countercyclical policies that cushioned the impact of the crisis and helped spur a faster recovery than in the industrialized economies. The region also benefits from the stable Chinese demand for its exports. For example, Chile—which since 2000 has carried out a countercyclical policy through a structural surplus rule regarding its fiscal budget—was able to draw on its savings and low debt to implement a broad package of economic stimulus when the financial crisis struck. The package amounted to nearly four percent of GDP—one of the largest in the world by this standard—and was financed completely by what had been saved in previous years. In sum, Latin America emerges from the international economic crisis as a strengthened region with better prospects for growth and with room to implement development policies.

Most Latin American countries today are classified in the middle-income category and therefore do not qualify for some official loans and Official Development Assistance. Therefore, they must be capable of financing their own development. This generates important challenges because the level of savings in Latin American countries is insufficient. As a consequence, foreign investment becomes an essential ingredient to achieve levels of savings above 25 percent of GDP. This is a level that many middle-income countries such as those in Latin America are not reaching.

The great Achilles' heel for sustainable development in Latin America is the distribution of income. It is one thing to lower the levels of poverty and quite another to improve the income distribution. The region continues to be highly unequal and its fiscal systems, as has recently been pointed out by the OECD, are not establishing the right targets. Proof of this is that the distribution of income before and after taxes is practically the same. However, public spending does seem to have a positive effect on the distribution of income because a great majority of the countries in the region target their fiscal expenditures toward creating a social safety net in the realm of social security and the health, education, housing, and justice systems, as well as through specific programs that directly help citizens living in extreme poverty. Hence some, such as former President of Brazil Fernando Henrique Cardoso, refer to globalized countries as having social democracy, or "globalized social democracy."

> *The great Achilles' heel for sustainable development in Latin America is the distribution of income.*

There is a political space for strong social policies in most Latin American countries today. Political will allows the modification of the initial distribution of income and the possibility of improving it through targeted expenditures. Most countries in the region with these types of programs—including Mexico, Colombia, Peru, Argentina, Chile, Brazil, and Uruguay—experienced a rise in the equality of income distribution in the first decade of this century. As a consequence, the space for political action, to which Cardoso and Faletto referred to in their work over 40 years ago, aided by a favorable international commodity cycle, has proved that it is possible to grow, reduce poverty, and improve the distribution of income. Although this is not the first favorable international cycle experienced by Latin America, it is the first that has produced such strong results in terms of improving social justice.

Some raise doubts about the sustainability of these distributive advances because they are rooted in an export structure dominated by commodities, which favors a climate prone to rent seeking and low taxes.[12] These phenomena will indeed occur if economic policy do not supplement export structures in order to defend against the volatility of international prices, and if tax policy does not correct the high concentration of income that can be generated by the exploitation of such resources. The economic history of Latin America shows that more conservative governments have faced strong temptations to respond to favorable prices for export commodities by lowering taxes on firms and individuals. This generates a permanent downsizing of public sector revenue, financed by a transitory revenue windfall, which is a recipe for future fiscal crisis. The problem is even more pressing because, as the economy grows and income per capita increases, the demand for public goods—such as education, health care, social security, infrastructure, and environmental protection—increases. Therefore, the current challenge—in the context of what will likely be a long period of high global commodity prices—is to reach a national consensus on fiscal priorities (a "Fiscal Covenant") that uses revenues from favorable global conditions to bolster competitiveness, innovation, and social justice. The present and expected favorable prices in commodity markets allow Latin America to think about these great challenges. Working toward this new Fiscal Covenant should thus be an essential part of the political conversation in Latin America.

Seizing the opportunity for sustainable development offered by the commodity boom requires balanced budgets, a stable macro economy, trade openness, and a willingness to compete in the global economy, as well as the political will to improve the distribution of income and pursue adequately financed social policies of a broad scope. Serious social policies should be financed by economic growth within more progressive tax structures than the ones currently in place, and these should be sustained by political consensus. This will allow governments to address structural issues related to inequality, such as the lack of equal access to quality services like education, health, housing, and welfare. It is up to the political system and the citizens to determine the magnitude of the transfer of the wealth generated by economic growth to the poorer sectors of society. Expecting these issues to be resolved by market forces is naive and even dangerous, because in the best-case scenario, in theory, the market will take several generations to resolve them. In practice, the unregulated action of the market, without correcting policies, tends to perpetuate inequalities.

There exists maneuvering room for politics and this is a fundamental aspect of Latin America's future. The contours of this maneuvering space will be different from the one that allowed the Asian miracle of the 1970s and 1980s, for at least three reasons. First, there are new conditions imposed by globalization, including the regulatory framework of the WTO. Second, Latin America today is starting with a higher per capita income than the Asian countries had at the time. Third, the political and institutional conditions of democracy in Latin America force the process of development to occur with greater social justice.

How Much Growth and How Much Equality?

The premise that it is necessary to grow first and then redistribute is false, as is the argument that it is necessary to redistribute first and grow later. What has been learned in Latin America is that it is necessary to simultaneously grow and redistribute. It is higher growth that allows for improvements in income distribution and equality. If both growth and redistribution are maintained year after year, a revolution will occur in the long run comparable to these last 10, 15, or 20 years. The experience of Chile illustrates this point. Once democracy was reestablished, between March 1990 and March 2010 (the period during which the "Concertación de Partidos por la Democracia" coalition was in office) the average annual growth rate was five percent, while poverty was reduced from 47 percent of the population to 11.5 percent in 2009.[13]

From an economic perspective, two distinct options are available for improving equity and equality. First, a welfare state could provide public and merit-based goods such as pension coverage, unemployment insurance, basic access to healthcare, and quality education financed with a high tax rate. Second, a production-centered model could improve the distribution of income through the creation of quality jobs with high productivity in a large enough quantity so individuals could finance their own social services. Of course, these are theoretical and polar options. National realities conform to a combination of these alternatives in variable proportions depending on the political and institutional context. Still, focusing on these two contrasting possibilities is useful to illustrate that it is necessary to avoid an overemphasis on these options because the challenge is to find the right combination for each national context. The important thing to point out is that without improvements in the productive structure, any social policy oriented toward reducing inequalities will have limited effects.[14] Likewise, a production-oriented model that underestimates the relevance of social policy—design, objectives, management, financing, and results—will fail to reconcile growth with equality.

Moreover, overcoming structural heterogeneity—such as reducing the excessive differentials in productivity and income across firms and sectors—through the "deliberate and systematic incorporation of technical progress" in the productive phase raises demands both of greater scale and productive diversification that rapidly leads to the necessity of developing exports.[15] The presence of competitive markets should result in productivity improvements that translate in higher labor incomes. However, asymmetries in bargaining power between capital and labor may impede this. Making sure that improvements in productivity result in higher wages requires renewed and stronger unions that are committed to the strategy of value creation in their firms and participating fully in public–private alliances. This is another pending challenge facing social democrats and other progressive forces.

In the context of such a development strategy, policies to support small and medium enterprises and respond to their traditional demands for credit, technical assistance, training, information, management, and quality should receive greater attention. These demands cease to be a concern only for social policy but also become a key axis for a productive transformation with greater equality. For example, access to knowledge is a central component required for economic growth and competitiveness. Education and training, digital education, generalized and low-cost access to broadband, and systematic connectivity (access to information and communication technologies as a citizenship right) become pillars of the productive transformation with equality.

Policies that promote productive development in competitive settings with the right incentives, including safeguarding the environment and incorporating technical progress favoring small and medium enterprises, are a fundamental axis of a development strategy that can reduce excessive productivity and growth differentials as well as link economic and social policy. When this focus is accompanied by vigorous, well-financed, well-managed, and ample social policies, then the region will advance toward the globalized social democracy proposed by President Cardoso (more on this concept below). When the goal of enhancing equality is pursued in such a post-neoliberal manner, the notion of a trade-off between growth and equality makes little sense. By growing this way, income inequality lessens and in turn further stimulates growth.[16]

> *The golden convergence of economic and social policy centers on the creation of more and better jobs as a basis to raise productivity and salaries.*

The golden convergence of economic and social policy centers on the creation of more and better jobs as a basis to raise productivity and salaries. From this perspective, access to innovation, technological diffusion, training, business opportunities, and promotion of the entrepreneurial spirit become another axis of development with equality. Another decisive factor is public–private alliances. It is also necessary to work toward a new conception of the firm, where labor relations, besides stimulating competitiveness and strengthening identification with the goals of the firm, will also be concerned with the security and well-being of the employees. Sophisticated competitiveness, anchored in processes of continual improvement, total quality, synergic relations between clients and providers, teamwork, and incremental innovations, is incompatible with firms that privilege hardware technologies, downsizing, spurious externalization, and resistance to union organization.

Contributing to "Globalized Social Democracy"

Making progress toward development requires leadership, quality institutions, and gradualism in the implementation of reforms. According to Cardoso, in addition to the structural factors, institutional, political, and social actors also play an important role in finding the path to development and reducing inequality. Simply put, history sets the conditions but does not define the results.

Of course, there is a power asymmetry between countries. However, what is interesting about the present historical moment is precisely the transition toward new hegemonies that are still not consolidated. This fluidity opens opportunities for developing countries to gain additional negotiating spaces and make progress on important issues of the international economic agenda. The global and regional outlook will also be very different for Latin America if it is able to take seriously its regional integration and transform itself into a more respected actor on the international stage by speaking with one voice about the main issues on the international agenda. Latin America's recent relationship with China, which is still very fluid, opens up a spectacular opportunity to negotiate its economic and trade relations with the main industrialized economies.

> What is interesting about the present historical moment is the transition toward new hegemonies that are still not consolidated.

President Cardoso goes one step further and proposes a globalized social democracy that would include openness to international markets, robust social policies to reduce poverty, and a transparent and accountable state. These are valid objectives, but instead of just openness to international markets, it may be preferable to speak of an active policy geared toward successful participation in international markets. This is because the notion of openness evokes the passive stance of eliminating restrictions on trade and investment but does not highlight the need for an active policy of maximizing opportunities supported by the transformation of the productive structure and strategic stimulation of innovation and competitiveness. The current challenge is to encourage the gradual internationalization of companies, promoting and enhancing their position in global value chains, trying to set them in those knowledge-intensive segments of those chains.

The Chilean experience with the negotiation of free-trade agreements illustrates some of the ideas behind this "proactive globalization." When it regained democracy in 1990, Chile was already a very open economy to trade and investment due to aggressive unilateral liberalization undertaken since the mid-1970s. However, it lacked stable preferential access to its main export markets. Today, 93 percent of Chile's exports enjoy preferential access to their markets, due to a systematic policy of negotiation of free-trade agreements. The agreements reached between 2002 and 2003 with the United States, the European Union and the Republic of Korea represent a milestone in this effort.

For a small country with limited financial and human resources, simultaneously negotiating with three of the world's largest economies represented a huge challenge. Nevertheless, the strategy of multiple negotiations, far from weakening the position of Chile, strengthened it by allowing Chile to exploit the interest of the European Union in concluding an agreement before the United States, the United States' interest in closing a deal with Chile in order to utilize this achievement to bolster its position in the FTAAA negotiations, and South Korea's desire to be the first Asian country with a free-trade agreement with a Latin American nation.

The parallel negotiation with three "mega markets" demanded a great effort of interagency coordination, as well as an active outreach to Congress, the business sector, labor unions, and civil society more generally. The result was a unified national stance and broad political and popular support for the negotiations, which were seen as an integral part of Chile's development strategy. In this way,

Chile was able to make the most of its negotiating position, even when facing much more powerful partners such as the United States.

Historical experience shows that seizing opportunities in the global economy requires a strategy—that is, a national project agreed to by the main actors. This helps define a shared medium-term outlook, which in turn facilitates the design and implementation of long-term policies that induce investments, innovation, and value added to production and exports.[17] Those developing countries most successful at closing their income gaps with the OECD have a long-term strategy of productive transformation, with a vision that transcends the preservation of macroeconomic equilibrium. While this strategy is important, it should be accompanied by policies that promote participation in dynamic sectors of the global economy by favoring innovation and competitiveness. As is evident, the need to agree on long-term policies quickly leads to incorporating the fight against inequality on the agenda. As a result, competitiveness and social cohesion can be mutually stimulated.

Another observation concerns the importance of relying on competitive markets and not merely "free markets."[18] Monopolistic or oligopolistic markets also generate inefficiencies in the distribution of resources. Therefore, a social democratic agenda should emphasize regulation of noncompetitive markets and, in general, the promotion of competition. This means using public resources to support and strengthen consumer organizations and subsidizing their technical and judicial efforts, in order to make them effective developmental watchdogs.

Last but not least, progressivism, or globalized social democracy, should place more emphasis on the productive dimension of the primary distribution of income without weakening its goal of equality. With levels of inequality as high as the ones in Latin America, social policy alone is insufficient to correct the distributive inequalities that originate in the labor market. To improve equality we should focus on productivity and export diversification, job quality, and narrowing productivity gaps—both the external gap with the industrialized economies and the internal gap—between the advanced sectors of the domestic economy and the ones that have been left behind.

From these observations, an integrated focus on growth with equality has four main axes:

- A countercyclical macroeconomic policy that includes the efficient supervision and prudential regulation of finance.
- Social policies of a wide scope, with stable financing and increased links with productive transformation through education and training programs.
- Policies of productive development that privilege accomplishments in innovation, productivity, and competitiveness, seeking to reduce structural heterogeneity and facilitating the incorporation of small and medium firms into export clusters.
- Active policies of international insertion of national firms in global and regional value chains, with emphasis on policies oriented to improve the technological standards of small and medium enterprises, in order to promote their participation in these value chains.

The social democratic stance with regard to markets is not limited to using them as efficient instruments for allocating resources. The challenge lies in creating markets where they do not exist and stimulating those that are just emerging in areas—such as training, technology, environment, and infrastructure—by using the correct social prices, liberating the barriers to competitive markets and regulating those that are not competitive, and strengthening the regulatory framework for competition and supporting consumer organizations.[19]

Accountability and transparency today is a requirement for the state. This should be complemented with a decisive fight against corruption and by promoting practices of performance evaluation, accountability, and decentralization within a framework of long-term policies that allow for the professionalization of the public sector and its gradual autonomy.

In the face of today's accelerated globalization, these complex tasks can be best met through cooperative efforts among countries. Herein lies the relevance to give more important steps on regional integration in Latin America. Large and integrated markets, featuring common disciplines for trade and investment, the rule of law, and room for productive, technological, and commercial alliances, would not only stimulate important synergies for growth but would also facilitate the formation of regional value chains and more effective international alliances.

The Need For Robust Regional Integration

In the context of rapid globalization, regional integration cannot be limited to trade or restricted to partners with ideological affinities. Instead, it should privilege the creation of regional or subregional value chains. Between 2003 and 2008, despite an economic boom and notable political convergence across countries, Latin America did not experience any substantive advances in its regional economic integration process. It is therefore necessary to tackle the conflicts between the countries of the region by defining precise mechanisms for the resolution of differences in order to advance in the promotion of regional value chains. Strengthening the presence of regional firms in regional or global value chains is a challenge of productive internationalization. This process should start with those activities most closely connected to the region's main export products, usually natural resources, and explore their backward and forward linkages. It is possible, for example, to develop competitive advantages in engineering, biotechnology, or business services connected to natural resources. This, in turn, would open new opportunities for export diversification, allowing exporters to participate in the networks of new business and benefit from a learning process that will allow them to make advances at a regional or global level.

Stimulating the convergence between Latin America–based multinational companies ("Translatinas") and regional integration efforts would help address the region's internationalization challenge. This is because Translatinas are precisely the regional companies that have advanced the most in this regard. Studying their development more closely would allow for not only updating of integration schemes but also making these initiatives more pertinent for firms' business decisions and for the design of trade, innovation, and industrial policies. For example, focusing on vocational training and quality certification for small and medium businesses, so that they can meet specific requirements as suppliers to Translatinas, would allow those smaller firms to access value chains as indirect exporters.

However, the current challenge goes beyond trade. Today the region urgently needs an initiative on regional cooperation to make the most of opportunities of the current international context. The Economic Commission for Latin America and the Caribbean has made eight key proposals in two broad areas: first, proposals to stimulate regional cooperation and second, development of regional strengths to face global challenges.[20] The proposals in the first area include fostering interregional trade supported by greater provision of financing and other concerted measures to facilitate commerce, stimulating investment in infrastructure, strengthening the social dimension of integration, and reinforcing the management of asymmetries. The proposals in the second area emphasize increasing regional cooperation in innovation and competitiveness, making the most of the link with Asia-Pacific to deepen cross-regional interaction, promoting reform of the international financial system by using the presence of Argentina, Brazil, and Mexico in the G20, and, lastly, jointly tackling the challenges of climate change. This is certainly an ambitious agenda, but one that is a product of the current favorable winds for developing economies.

Various developing countries are gradually closing the income gaps with the industrialized economies, placing themselves in advanced segments of global value chains and making important technological breakthroughs. Multiplying these achievements depends precisely on the possibility of moving toward larger integrated markets characterized by common regulatory frameworks, the rule of law, and the gradual convergence of policies.[21] If Latin America makes significant advances in this direction, the argument of Cardoso and Faletto from more than 40 years ago will be more relevant than ever in proving how the region generates new possibilities for growth and social justice, supported by ambitious yet realistic social policies.

Notes

1. Fernando Cardoso and Enzo Faletto, *Dependencia y desarrollo en América Latina* (Mexico: Siglo Veintiuno, 1977). This book was published originally in 1968 and on the occasion of the 40th anniversary of publication, the *Brown Journal of World Affairs* published several articles as a follow-up, including one by Cardoso.

2. It was a quasi-recession because, although economies accounting for 80 percent of world GDP contracted in 2009, several medium and large economies besides China and India were able to grow by around four percent or more. These countries include Bangladesh, Egypt, Zambia, Indonesia, Pakistan, the Philippines, Sri Lanka, and Vietnam.

3. OECD, *Perspectives on Global Development: Shifting Wealth* (Paris: Development Centre, 2010).

4. Eduardo Levy Yeyati, "On Emerging Markets Decoupling and Growth Convergence," *Vox*, November 7, 2009, www.voxeu.org/index.php?q=node/4172.

5. OECD, *Perspectives on Global Development: Shifting Wealth* (Paris: Development Centre, 2010).

6. This means that if China grows at a ten-percent annual rate, the growth floor for middle-income economies will be around four percent annually.

7. Christopher Garroway, et al., "Global Imbalances, the Renminbi and Poor Countries," *Development Centre* (Paris: 2010).

8. Andrew Mold and Annalisa Prizzon, "South–South Trade Liberalisation as Way out of the Financial Crisis" (OECD Development Centre, 2010). For developing-country firms, it would be easier to integrate into South–South value chains because their standards, both in products and processes, are lower. Therefore, these chains could be used as learning processes and as a platform for acceding into more demanding value chains. See: Raphael Kaplinsky, et al., "What happens in Global Value Chains when the Markets Shift from the North to the South" (paper prepared for the World Bank project on Global Crisis and Value Chain Governance, 2010).

9. A "commodity super-cycle" is present in cases of accelerated industrialization and urbanization in high-population economies that lead to strong demand for primary goods of various types, including metals, minerals, and energy. The most important cases are the United States from the end of the 1800s to the early 1900s (during the expansion of the internal frontier and incorporation of various Mexican states and lands that belonged to indigenous groups) and the period between 1945 and 1974 (during the reconstruction of Europe and the Japanese miracle). These super-cycles tend to last between 10 and 35 years. See: OECD, *Perspectives on Global Development: Shifting Wealth* (Paris: Development Centre, 2010).

10. ECLAC, "Latin America and the Caribbean in the World Economy 2009–2010: A crisis generated in the centre and a recovery driven by the emerging economies" (LC/G.2467-P), United Nations publication, sales No. E.10.II.G.5 (Santiago: ECLAC, 2010).

11. Osvaldo Rosales, "Globalization and the new international trade environment," *ECLAC Review*, no. 97 (Santiago: 2009).

12. Jeffrey Sachs and Joseph Stiglitz, *Escaping the Resource Curse* (New York: Columbia University, 2007).

13. The distribution of income only underwent a small transformation. When considering the effect of social policies, the relationship between the income received by the richest 10 percent and the poorest 40 percent was reduced from 14 to 7 times.

14. Osvaldo Rosales, "Balance y renovación en el paradigma estructuralista del desarrollo latinoamericano," *Revista de la CEPAL*, no. 34 (Santiago: 1998).

15. Fernando Fajnzylber, "Industrialización en América Latina: de la 'caja negra' al 'casillero vacío,'" *Cuadernos de la CEPAL* 60 (Santiago: 1990).

16. Joseph E. Stiglitz, *The Price of Inequality: How Today's Divided Society Endangers our Future* (W.W. Norton & Company. New York. 2012)

17. Robert Devlin and Graciela Moguillansky, "Public–Private alliances for long-term national development strategies," ECLAC Review 97 (2009).

18. It is one thing to accept the preponderance of the market in the allocation of resources and quite another to deify it. In other words, we must not confuse the "discreet charm of the market" with the "unbearable lightness of neoliberalism." See: Osvaldo Rosales, "Balance y renovación en el paradigma estructuralista del desarrollo latinoamericano," *Revista de la CEPAL*, no. 34 (Santiago: 1998).

19. Ibid.

20. *Espacios de convergencia y de cooperación régional* (Cumbre de Alto Nivel de América Latina y el Caribe, ECLAC, Cancun, Mexico, February 21 to 23, 2010).

21. Ricardo Lagos, comp., *América Latina: ¿Integración o fragmentación?* (Editorial Edhasa, 2008).

DISCUSSION QUESTIONS

1. How would you summarize the main argument of the article in a sentence or two?

2. The author sees the first 20 years of the post-Cold War, roughly since 1993, as a period dominated by a global shift in global economic weight from OECD countries toward emerging markets. Is (was) he correct in this regard? What can you point out as evidence?

3. Considering China and other emerging economies' successes, the author advocates increased South-South trade relations. What are some of the challenges facing the developing countries in the South for increased trade among them?

4. The author believes that a convergence of economic and social policy is achievable where both economic growth and equality can be achieved. What does he mean by that? What are some of the components of such an approach, and how is that different from the "growth now, redistribution later" approach?

5. The author argues for Latin American countries to pursue "proactive globalization" and "robust regional integration" of integrated markets through common regulatory framework, the rule of law, and gradual convergence of policies. What does he mean by "proactive globalization" and "robust regional integration"? How can they be achieved?

6. Why does the author think we need to update and revise the framework for understanding center-periphery relations?

International Trade, WTO and Economic Development

By Siddiqui Kalim

Abstract: This article examines the existing literature on trade liberalisation and its effect on the economies of developing countries. It will also briefly examine the theory of comparative advantage which is seen as justification for global trade liberalisation under the auspices of the World Trade Organization. This process is also associated with greater openness, economic interdependence and deepening economic integration with the world economy. The study is important because once again the international institutions strongly advocate trade and financial liberalisation in developing countries. The proponents of trade liberalisation argue that multilateral trade negotiations would achieve these goals, and poor countries particularly would benefit from it. However, such policies may increase vulnerability and make developing countries further hostages of international finance capital. Adoption of open market policies in agriculture would also mean the abandoning of self-reliance and food sovereignty, which may have wider consequences in terms of food shortages, food prices and rural employment.

Key words: WTO; trade liberalisation; industrialisation; international financial institutions; developing countries

Introduction

The World Trade Organization (WTO) is widely seen as promoting prosperity through trade, especially favouring developing countries. This is presented so as to achieve "fair trade" and economic growth in developing countries (WTO 2013). A new round of global trade negotiations, the Doha Round, has taken place under the WTO. It is said that increased trade and interdependent goods and services and money markets underscore the importance of international cooperation to contain crises and promote growth. The proponents of trade liberalisation argue that multilateral trade negotiations would achieve these goals, and poor countries particularly would benefit from it; while critiques

Kalim Siddiqui, "International Trade, WTO and Economic Development," *World Review of Political Economy*, vol. 7, no. 4, pp. 424-450. Copyright © 2016 by Pluto Journals. Reprinted with permission. Provided by ProQuest LLC. All rights reserved.

say that trade rules under the WTO and international financial institutions will acquire more power, which could restrict the ability of developing countries to pursue an independent economic policy.

Globalisation is described as a process of integration into the world economy. It consists of three key areas, namely trade, investment and finance. This process is also associated with greater openness, economic interdependence and deepening economic integration with the world economy. The aim of this article is to study the issue of "free trade" in the light of past experiences and whether we can draw some lesson from it.

This article aims to examine free trade in a historical perspective in order to understand its implications and future prospects for development. The focus of the study also briefly discusses previous attempts by military force to open up economies in the name of "free trade" in the colonies by the European powers during the late 19th century. Britain adopted "free trade" policies in the 19th century when it had relatively more advanced technologies and industries compared with other European countries. Such policies were extended to the colonies to further its business and trade interests. Since the mid-19th century, Africa and Latin American countries were integrated into the world economy as the supplier of primary commodity, as envisaged by the "comparative advantage" model. However, after the Second World War these countries opted in favour of industrialisation, with different degrees of political commitment and state involvement via "import substitution industrialisation" policies. Despite a number of constraints, their growth rate performance was in fact better than it had been during the period of market liberalisation. However, such policies came to a dead end due to debt crisis and in the changing international environment (Ghose 2004; Siddiqui 2012a).

Under such circumstances (i.e., both domestic and international), there was strong pressure on developing countries to accept trade and financial liberalisation by the International Monetary Fund (IMF), World Bank. But the difficulties of the Doha Round negotiations under the WTO were due, it seems, not only to lack of reaching a consensus on agriculture, but also to loss of national policy manoeuvres felt by the developing countries. The governments displayed an inability to deploy effective policies in situations where their assistance might be needed to spur economic development or fight high levels of underemployment. Their domestic policy space and flexibility was being constrained by the proposals under the WTO negotiations based on comparative advantage, which has major weaknesses on both theoretical and empirical grounds. On theoretical grounds, its weakness stems from not addressing externalities such as market failures, environmental costs and investment in education.

On empirical grounds we have examples of successful economic development in East Asian economies such as Malaysia (Siddiqui 2012b), South Korea, Singapore and Taiwan, and more recently in China. The success of their higher growth rates shows a clear role for governments in smoothing out the difficulties. These countries have successfully taken independent policy measures to spur economic development, which has proved very critical in the early years of their path to industrialisation (Siddiqui 2016). A number of studies have pointed out that the governments in East Asian countries have invested in major outlays on infrastructure, education and skills development, import licensing, quotas, exchange rate controls and wage restraints (Rodrik 2004; Siddiqui 2012a). Enactment of all such policies by the states has resulted in the successful development of the manufacturing sector, with government-subsidised credits from state banks being extended to manufacturing in exchange for concrete results.

It can be argued that all subsidies would encourage "rent seeking" behaviour that would make it difficult for the developing countries to pick winners (Krueger 1996). Government bureaucracy needs to maintain neutrality and should be above from sectional interests of seeking rents. As Amsden finds, public institutions in countries such as South Korea, Taiwan and Singapore disciplined the economic behaviour of companies based on their information and performance assessment.

> Reciprocity disciplined subsidy recipients and thereby minimized government failures. Subsidies were allocated to make manufacturing profitable—to convert moneylenders into financiers and importers into industrialists—but did not become giveaways. Recipients of subsidies were subjected to monitorable performance standards that were redistributive in nature and result oriented. The reciprocal control mechanism thus transformed the inefficiency and venality associated with government intervention into collective goods. (Amsden 2005, 222)

Various studies have shown that state intervention in the national economy has proved to be a crucial policy element in achieving successful economic development (Amsden 2005). There seems to be a need for state management to make the market friendlier towards national economic developmental needs. Many developmental policies that are now criticised by developed countries are the very same policies that were once essential in the early years of their industrialisation process. As Rodrik (2004) emphasises,

> Almost all successful cases of development in the last fifty years have been based on creative and often heterodox policy innovations ... At the time, GATT rules were sparse and permissive, so nations combined their trade policy with unorthodox policies: high levels of tariff and non-tariff barriers, public ownership of large segments of banking and industry and export subsidies, domestic content requirements, import-export linkages, patent and copyright infringements, directed credit and restrictions on capital flows ... In all of these countries, trade liberalisation was a gradual process, drawn out over a period of decades rather than years. (cited in K. P. Gallagher 2005, 8)

Free Trade and Intervention in the Past

The period from 1870 to 1914 was the period known as the age of laissez-faire and government intervention was minimal. This period saw a rapid increase in trade, and it was estimated that during this period growth in world trade was 3.9% annually, which was much faster than growth in world output at an average 2.5% per annum (Nayyar 2006). The share of world trade in world output rose steadily during this period. On average, the developed countries share of exports in GDP rose from 18.2% in 1900 to 21.2% in 1913 (Maddison 2006a; World Bank 2014).

Trade barriers began to come down in Europe with the Anglo-French treaty on trade, seen as a first step towards this direction. However, lowering the barriers to trade was then confined to Europe, while the US practised protection during the period 1870 to 1914, where average tariff levels were around 40%–50% on manufactured goods (Chang 2002).

In Europe, Britain and the Netherlands continued to practice free trade. Moreover, once European countries colonised the rest of the world, especially Asia and Africa, they imposed free trade on their colonies. In 1842, China was forced by Britain to sign a treaty that led to the opening of the Chinese market to European products, with an import tariff as low as just 5%, and also in the 1840s, free trade was imposed on India by Britain. The Netherlands removed tariff barriers on Indonesia. In 1858, Japan was also forced to accept free trade under US navy threats. The Commodore Perry and Shimoda-Harris treaty was signed with the aim of opening up Japanese markets for US products (Chang 2002).

Morocco in 1856 was forced to accept a maximum import duty of 10% by Britain. The Anglo-Turkish commercial convention of 1838 led to the imposition of very low tariffs of only 3% on Ottoman territories. As a result, British merchants were granted free access to trade in all parts of the Ottoman Empire without paying any internal duties (Maddison 2006a). Torrens argues in 1820 that

> For while England's growth rate could be augmented through the further unleashing of productive forces in manufactures and the by-passing of the natural impediments in the primary producing sector, her trading partners would be trailing behind in terms of their rate of accumulation. Upon perceiving this development . . . more aggressively opening markets for English products as well as tapping new or expanded sources of supply to satisfy her needs for raw products. (cited in Ho 1996, 28)

Portugal took the lead in opening trade with Asia by the end of the 17th century. Its trading activities were established by a strong navy and with the help of armed ships to control shipping routes and also to intimidate the local producers in coastal areas. Portuguese traders set up bases around deep harbours in Mozambique, Hormuz in the Persian Gulf, Goa in India, Jaffna in Ceylon, Macau, and Timor in Indonesia. In the beginning, the Portuguese trade in Asia consisted of pepper and spices and their merchants paid in bullions for their purchases as Asian countries had no interest in European products (J. Gallagher and Robinson 1953). The Portuguese soon began to charge fees on Asian ships using their harbours. Such claims remained unchallenged as the Chinese and Japanese slowly withdrew from their participation in international trade. The Portuguese occupied the western coastal part of India, where they hardly faced any challenge; then the Mughal Empire in Delhi and Vijayenagar rulers in South India, where they merely derived their income from land taxes and had no significant financial interest in foreign trade.

However, by the 1650s the Dutch defeated the Portuguese and captured most of their ports in Asia, leading to the Dutch company (VOC) accounting for 45% of the European voyagers in Asia from 1640 to 1800 and being given a monopoly charter. Their ships were armed and the Company had the power to wage war, and establish treaties with Asian rulers. Over the period between 1640 and 1800, the VOC sent nearly one million sailors, soldiers and admin staff to its 30 Asian trading ports (Habib 1995); certainly, buying cheap to sell dear by the monopoly chartered companies engaging in long distance trade, where these companies made huge monopoly profits (Bagchi 2010). The British took over Bengal in 1757, which greatly weakened the Portuguese position in Asia. Until the first quarter of the 19th century, the impact of European colonisation in Asia was modest. In Asia, the level of technology was much more sophisticated and the major Asian countries such as the Ottoman territories, Safavid in Iran, the Mughal in India, and China and Japan were far better equipped to resist occupation than the Aztecs and Incas and North American indigenous tribes (Bagchi 2010).

However, in China the British military attack and political hold failed to break down Chinese economic self-sufficiency. The opium wars of the 1840s and again in the 1850s and the burning of the summer palace in 1860 widened British trade, but they did not succeed in making the Chinese dependent on British products. Despite forcible opening of the Chinese markets by the British and French and bringing the country into semi-colonial relations in the mid-19th century, lasting until the mid-20th century, the European attempt to break the country's self-sufficiency and sell European products into Chinese markets largely failed. China remained self-sufficient and did not become a large market for European products in the 19th century.

British officials in Egypt had relied on Gladstonian policies that assumed that the free market is critical to expand its interests. To achieve this balanced budget, government spending and taxation should be kept low. Egypt was initially occupied by Napoleon, but its market was fully opened by Britain; thus Egypt was forced to accept a "free trade" treaty in the 1841 Khedive's attempt to modernise its economy, through borrowing and also by encouraging European immigration and businesses to invest in Egypt (Owen 2004). The Egyptian government invested heavily especially in the sugar and cotton industries; these finished products were mainly aimed for foreign markets. As a result, the production of sugar and cotton increased rapidly in the 1850s and 1860s. However, due to a slump in export demands and mismanagement in the 1870s, these industries witnessed a deep crisis and exports fell sharply. With the dwindling export markets, Egypt began to increasingly rely on foreign borrowing, especially from Europe. Egypt's foreign debts increased along with corruption and nepotism. Between 1862 and 1880, Egypt's long-term debt rose from UK£ 3 million to UK£ 68 million (Owen 2004). As J. Gallagher and Robinson (1953, 13–14) found:

> Foreign loans and predatory bankers by the 1870s had wrecked Egyptian finances and were tearing holes in the Egyptian political fabric. The Anglo-French dual financial control to safeguard the foreign bondholders and to restore Egypt as a good risk provoked anti-European feeling. With the revolt of Arabi Pasha in 1881, the Khedive's government could serve no longer to secure either the all-important Canal or the foreign investors' pound of flesh.

The British then focused on negotiating a financial settlement to the law of liquidation of the 1880s that would ensure debt repayment through rigorous budgetary control and also guarantee discipline of long-term financial control and stability. In 1882, Brailsford (1998, 101) notes, "Egypt was already a nation emerging from the lethargy and oppression of centuries when it was invaded by Britain at the behest of the owners of its usurious debt." Prior to the occupation in 1882, Lord Cromer was already working as a British Agent-General and the effective ruler of Egypt. Lord Cromer kept expenditure on education miserably low, which soon became the main reason for the stranglehold on any attempt to modernise the economy (Brailsford 1998; Chang 2008).

Britain's trade with India until the mid-18th century consisted mainly of imports of textiles, silk and spices. India remained the largest exporter of cotton textiles in the world until the end of the 18th century. Since Britain had nothing to offer India, Britain had to pay in gold and silver for its imports. The huge amount of gold and silver looted from Latin America was used as payment for its imports (Bagchi 2010; Siddiqui 1990).

With victory in the Battle of Plassey in 1757, Britain began to occupy more territories and with this it raised land revenue in India to meet its war expenses and also to pay for her imports from India. Britain's total imports from India were paid for by Indian revenue and thus constituted a "drain," or the "tribute" paid by India to Britain as a cost of being colonised. This tribute was very critical to Britain's economic developmental process. Irfan Habib (1995) calculated that in 1801, during the period of Britain's industrial development, the "tribute" to Britain from India represented about 9% of the entire GNP of the British occupied territories in India which was equal to nearly 30% of the British domestic savings available for capital formation in Britain.

India's trade consisted of two parts, its trade with Britain and its trade with the rest of the world. India had an export surplus on its merchandise account with the rest of the world, but always had a trade deficit with Britain mainly because of British manufacturing charging higher prices. They also found vast markets in India by compulsorily opening up India's markets (Siddiqui 1990). However, India's surplus with the rest of the world far exceeded the trade deficit with Britain, leaving an overall merchandise export surplus for India, which rose over time. To appropriate India's global foreign exchange earnings and surplus, all Britain did was to administratively impose tribute charges to be paid in pounds sterling; such practice was not seen for any sovereign nation (Bagchi 2010).

Once the industries in Britain began to expand and industrialisation took firmer roots, its interest in the colonies changed. Rather than simply buying and selling, investment in mining and production of raw materials for British industries became more crucial tasks and later on demanded greater access to markets in the colonies. As a result, in India, for example, the absolute decline of the manufacturing sector took place, which is known as de-industrialisation. The reallocation of labour and the urban population from manufacturing activities to primary production led to overcrowding of the agriculture sector (Habib 1995; Siddiqui 1990). For example, India was prevented from developing their long-term comparative advantage in manufacturing, as local manufactures and handicrafts had no social or political influence or connections with the colonial governments, meaning their interests were ignored against the pressures and interests of the foreign manufacturers. The colonial government during the Great Depression of the 1930s in India consistently pursued deflationary policies despite falling output and exports. In the colonies, there was no political or organised opposition against policies to transform the colonies into specialisers in supplying raw materials in the name of David Ricardo's theory of comparative advantage (Siddiqui 2015c); at the same time the developed countries, in order to continue their control over the colonies, necessitated the monopolisation of high technologies and offensive military technologies, thus also creating disunity among the colonies (Brown 1993).

Even at the end of the 18th century, India's share of the world's manufacturing output was as high as 19.7%, but had fallen to 8.6% by 1860. As J. Gallagher and Robinson (1953, 4) note,

> In India it was possible, throughout most of the period of the British Raj, to use the governing power to extort in the form of taxes and monopolies such valuable primary products as opium and salt. Furthermore, the characteristics of so-called imperialist expansion at the end of 19th century developed in India long before the date 1880 ... Direct governmental promotion of products required by British industry, government manipulation of tariffs to help British exports, railway construction at high and guaranteed rates of interest to open the continental interior—all these techniques of direct political control were employed in ways which seem alien to the so-called age of *laissez faire*.

Despite the adoption of free trade policy during the colonial period, the growth rate of per capita income in India was almost stagnant between 1820 and 1913, while independent countries such as Europe, the US and Japan witnessed a rapid increase in growth rates and successfully built their industrial sector.

Angus Maddison (2006a) estimated the world's GDP between 1500 and 2001. As Table 4.1 indicates, after colonisation, the Western Europe share began to rise, while Asia's share began to fall. The process rose sharply as large parts of Asia were colonised and by 1913 the Asian global GDP share was merely two-thirds that of Western Europe. Together China and India produced nearly half of the world's total GDP share in the 18th century. At the beginning of the 19th century, India was the largest economy in the world with nearly one quarter of the world's output, which was then greater than that of the entire Western Europe region and more than eight times that of Britain. However, at the end of the two centuries of colonial rule, India's share had fallen to a mere 4.2% and even less than two-thirds of Britain's GDP in the 1950s (Maddison 2006a).

Table 4.1 Share of the World's GDP (% of World Total)

Year	1500	1700	1820	1870	1913	1950	1973	2001
Britain	1.1	2.9	5.2	9.0	8.2	6.5	4.2	3.2
Western Europe	17.8	21.9	23.0	33.0	33.0	26.2	25.6	20.3
US	0.3	0.1	1.8	8.8	18.9	27.3	22.1	21.4
China	24.9	22.3	32.9	17.1	8.8	4.5	4.6	12.3
India	24.4	24.4	16.0	12.1	7.5	4.2	3.1	5.4
Asia (excluding Japan)	61.9	57.7	56.4	36.1	22.3	15.4	16.4	30.9

Source: Maddison (2006b, Table 8b).

Free Trade, Openness and Industrialisation

In the mid-19th century, the UK became the promoter of free trade policies, which were then not suitable for Germany or the US. Friedrich List demonstrated this by likening Britain's promotion of free trade to "kicking away the ladder" by which it had risen to deprive others of the means of climbing up (Chang 2008). As Friedrich List (1966, 368) commented,

> It is a very clever common device that when anyone has attained the summit of greatness, he kicks away the ladder by which he has climbed up, in order to deprive others of the means of climbing up after him ... Any nation which by means of protective duties and restrictions on navigation to such a degree of development that no other nation can sustain free competition with her, can do

nothing wiser than to throw away this ladder of her greatness, to preach other nations the benefits of free trade ...

On the question of laying the foundations of industry in a country that is behind and needs to catch up in the industrialisation process, the country must take steps in clear policy measures to protect and build industries. As List suggests, catching up with a country such as Germany, first it has to lay grounds for industrial development. "In order to allow freedom of trade to operate naturally, the less advanced nation must first be raised by artificial measures to that stage of cultivation to which the English nation has been artificially elevated" (List 1966, 131).

The industrial revolution in Britain had shown other countries the path to industrialisation and how to learn from its experience and move forward. But copying and industrialisation could lead to increased competition to procure inputs and markets for their finished products. However, the first countries to follow Britain were independent nations who had full control over their resources and economic policies. For example, in the US, British businesses turned cotton production to their advantage and wanted to repeat this in the mid-west region of the US as well. But the political leadership of the US then stood firmly against it, which resulted in the industrial lobby successfully campaigning to raise tariffs, despite the strong opposition from those sections that relied on and profited from the British connections (Chang 2008).

The interests of manufacturing capital in the developed countries prioritised securing access to markets and lower prices for their imported raw materials, while their businesses had an interest in keeping higher prices for their manufactured goods. Often in their colonies European businesses had a better chance of earning monopoly profits. Pursuing the trade objectives dominated by their manufacturing and financial interests required the creating of conditions whereby the economies of the colonial countries were transformed to complement the industrial interests of the European countries; while at the same time manufacturing or any sort of potential competition must disappear to make way for the greater demands of the manufactured goods from the colonial powers.

Figure 4.1 shows that the US economy was far less open prior to the two World Wars and the Great Depression and we find that in the post-war period its economy has opened remarkably. Following the Second World War, the US and other developed countries negotiated under the Uruguay Round to reduce trade barriers which contributed to rising world trade (Wade 2003; World Bank 2014).

Recent multilateral trade deals, besides liberalising trade in goods and services, have strengthened monopolies in the pre-production phase through control over knowledge in the form of intellectual property rights such as patents and industrial design and in the post-production phase, as well as by increased enforcement of branding and marketing. As a result, the value added of such trade seems to be concentrated in the developed countries while the developing countries compete over the spoils of the low-value segments.

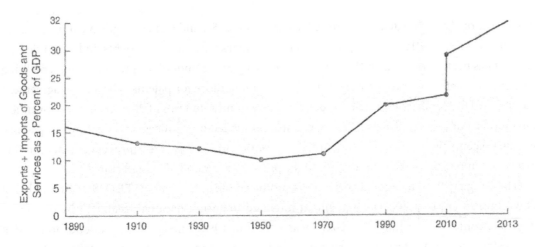

FIGURE 4.1 Openness of the US Economy from the Period of 1890 to 2013

Source: US Census Bureau, US Trade in Goods and Services, at http://www.census.gov/foreign-trade/.

The WTO was established in 1995, taking over from GATT (General Agreement of Trade and Tariffs). Trade liberalisation negotiations have taken place since 1947 in a series of lengthy "Rounds" negotiations. These rounds of talks were meant to enable countries to reach agreement over access to each other's markets and also trade relationships between developed and developing countries. They also accepted that "special differential treatment" would apply in which developing countries were supposed to have preferential access to markets in the developed countries, as well as some sort of providing time to build industries in their own countries. However, with the establishment of the WTO, earlier proposed policies were altered and special and differential treatment was redefined with merely allowing developing countries longer adjustment periods in which to implement neoliberal policies and make the adjustment period shorter (Sen 2005).

The WTO is being presented as the only "development" model available for developing countries. It is also aimed at the enlargement of the markets for global monopolies in the areas of manufacturing, agriculture and services through the Uruguay Rounds of negotiations where it is being referred to as expansion of trade for the development and well-being of everyone, that is, a win–win game for all participants. "Building supply-side capacity" is the key towards higher exports and ultimately higher incomes and employment for the developing countries. However, such policies ignore the economic and political space for self-determination and development based on local realities and needs. Here, it appears that the focus is largely on GDP growth based on Western models (Siddiqui 2015b).

In the WTO meeting in Hong Kong, and later on in Bali, the developing countries were offered a so-called developmental package that would enable them to build supply-side capacity including infrastructure to promote trade-related activities. The emphasis was also on promoting the cultivation of cash crops in developing countries for export. Of the three major areas of agreement under the WTO negotiations—Agreement on Trade-Related Aspects of Intellectual Property Rights (TRIPS),

Agreement on Trade-Related Investment Measures (TRIMS), and General Agreement on Trade in Services (GATS)—TRIPS covers protection of trademarks, patents, copyrights, industrial design, etc, and has been in force since 1995 and it imposes a global standard for protecting and enforcing all forms of intellectual property rights (IPR), including those for patents. The TRIPS agreement requires WTO Members to provide protection for a minimum term of 20 years for any invention for a product or process. Prior to TRIPS, countries provided only process and not product patents. Product patents provide for absolute protection of the product, whereas process patents provide protection in respect of the technology and the process or method of manufacture.

The Uruguay Round negotiations in 1994 produced the agreement on TRIMS. It aims to bring down investment barriers. The agreement intended to ensure national treatment by removing domestic content provisions. The GATS was signed in 1994. The agreement intends to remove any restrictions and internal government regulations in the areas of service delivery that are considered to "barriers to trade." The strategy, for instance, is to transform education into a tradable commodity. GATS educational agenda has the potential to further privatization to a higher level in education and also opening the door for international competition. The developing countries will be adversely affected in terms of their sovereignty on cultural policy and the quality and accessibility of their public education systems in general (Stiglitz and Charlton 2006; Wade 2003). At present, as far as the question of knowledge and technology, the developed countries are net producers and the developing countries are net consumers. TRIPS will increase the price of patentable knowledge to consumers and as a consequence, the flow of rents from the developing countries to developed countries will increase. These changes in policy measures will limit the authority of the developing countries to have any say in the choices of companies operating in their countries. It appears that with the current agenda of universal trade liberalisation, not only will development space shrink but self-determination and economic sovereignty will also be undermined (Siddiqui 2012a).

For example, more than half of the world's service exports are accounted for by West European countries, while on the other hand, for the largest exporter of services, i.e., China, services accounts for less than 3% of its total trade. As Table 4.2 shows, services, including patent fillings, are very important for developed countries.

GATS (The General Agreement on Trade in Services), TRIPS and TRIMS are committed to promoting neoliberal policies. GATS is also designed to further open up markets for services with penalty clauses and sections against governments found breaching GATS regulations. For GATS, the central point of the agreement is to achieve market liberalisation in services. However, trade liberalisation also includes finance, insurance, transport, education and health. It is also said that de-regulation in financial markets and implementation would most likely increase speculation-led activities dominated by the financial sector and short-term rather than long-term investment. Foreign direct investment (FDI) from developed countries is currently more than five times that originating

Table 4.2 Patent Fillings by Selected Countries in 2013

Country	Number of Patent Fillings
US	51,625
Japan	43,660
Germany	18,617
France	7,851
Switzerland	4,190
Netherlands	4,071
South Korea	11,848
China	18,617

Source: World Intellectual Property Organisation, The International Patent System: Monthly Statistics Report, 2013, at http://www.wipo.int/export/sites/www/ipstats/en/ statistics/pct/pdf/monthly_report.pdf.

from developing countries. FDI inflows into developing countries encourage Mergers and Acqui-sitions (M&A) which will further add to the concentration of economic and market powers and towards building of monopolies and oligopolies rather than competitive markets, as envisaged by the neo-classical theorists (Siddiqui 2015b).

Earlier, the treaties under the GATT negotiations recognised Special and Differential Treatment for developing countries. However, later on in 1994 the Uruguay Round treaty changed this to a single-tier system of rights and obligations, meaning that developing countries have to implement in full all the rules, seen as quid pro quo, for market access in the textile and agriculture sectors, which are highly protected in developed countries. Any autonomous developments will eventually require wider policy choice, which is being limited to developing countries (Stiglitz 2005). TRIMS does not permit practices such as local product linkages between foreign and local investors or foreign exchange earning requirements. TRIPS will further encourage privatisation and monopoly ownership of knowledge and will severely limit and reverse the initiatives achieved by the public sector in manufacturing and medicine in developing countries.

As a consequence of the implementation of WTO-backed trade and services, liberalisation would certainly mean that the developmental option and economic diversification would be shrinking for most developing countries. Even the policies of the recent past to upgrade technologies and structural

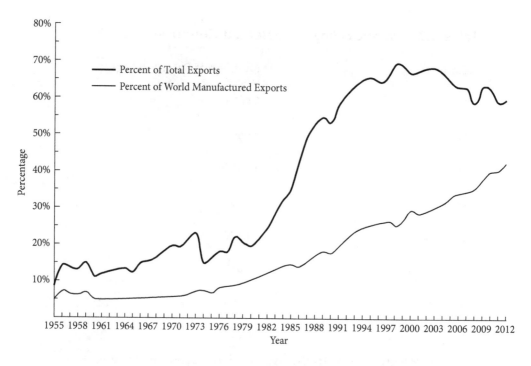

FIGURE 4.2 Share of Developing Countries in World Exports of Manufactured Goods

Source: UNCTAD Statistical Handbook, http://unctadstat.unctad.org.

changes with state active assistance will no longer be available to most developing countries. The options of sovereign decision making and promoting a policy suitable to their specific conditions will be seen as a hostile move by the WTO and international financial institutions. Their key priority is "opening-up markets" and for that they have key international agreements—TRIPS, TRIMS and GATS (Wade 2003).

Figures 4.2 and 4.3 show that the share of developing countries in the world's export of manufacturing has steadily increased since 1955 and also that these countries have been importing high tech and manufactured goods from the developed countries. However, East Asian countries have done considerably better than other developing countries. In this region, a mixture of both state and market were used to promote economic development and industrialisation. A recent example of Chinese government intervention to facilitate and promote businesses and exports could not be ignored. Public investment in infrastructures and education sectors played a key role in attracting inflows of foreign capital. Moreover, China controlled inflows of foreign capital and the government managed large parts of trade and owned heavy manufacturing industries. On the other hand, most sub-Saharan African countries are largely dependent on primary commodities exports. For instance, for the 18 African countries, exports of primary commodities consisted of 70% of their export earnings in 2000 (Stiglitz 2005).

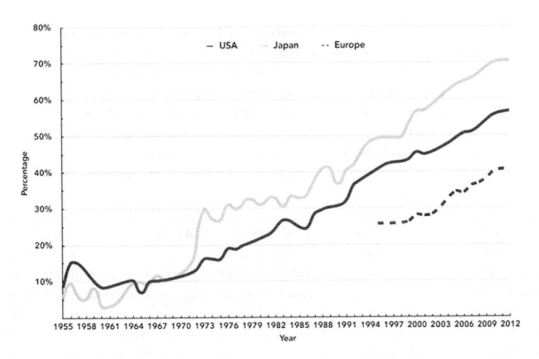

FIGURE 4.3 Share of Developing Countries in Manufactured Goods Imports of Developed Nations

Source: UNCTAD Statistical Handbook, http://unctadstat.unctad.org.

State and Trade Policies

Past experience has shown that the state played an important role in economic development, and developmental state policies were necessary in order to successfully accomplish industrialisation in developing countries.

Early development of industries benefited from proactive state measures and protective support. Ha-Joon Chang identifies at least four distinct phases of British trade policies, where the state played a crucial role. Henry VII and his successors started laying clear policy measures in the 16th century in support of building and protecting the development of domestic industries, the modern version of which is infant industries promotion. Later on in 1721, the British Prime Minister further undertook protectionist and regulatory measures to promote industries, especially the woollen industry. Such policies were promoted throughout the industrial revolution period in the late 18th and early 19th century until Britain attained a technological lead and industrial supremacy, and finally, the Corn Laws were repealed and free trade was promoted. It was intended to halt the move to industrialisation of other European countries (Brown 1993; Chang 2008).

As Engels argued, Britain, in order to achieve industrial supremacy, adopted a policy combination of mercantilism and imperialism. He wrote comments for a preface to Marx's speech on free trade.

It was under the fostering wing of protection that the system of modern industry … was hatched and developed in England during the last third of the 18th century. And, as if tariff protection was not sufficient, the wars against French Revolution helped to secure England the monopoly of the new industrial methods. For more than 20 years, English men of war [fighting ships] cut off the industrial rivals of England from their respective colonial markets, while they forcibly opened their markets for English commerce … the progressive subjugation of India turned the people of all these immense territories into customers of English goods. (Engels 1990, 522)

Moreover, Britain and other European countries in the past exported their large number of unemployed and social discontent section of the population overseas. This was made possible by the invasion and seizure of vast territories from indigenous inhabitants in the Americas, South Africa and Australia. Certainly, such massive land grabs and looting of resources and outmigration did provide huge assistance in facilitating the process of industrialisation in European countries, especially Britain. For example, between 1812 and 1914 about 20 million people migrated from Britain and nearly two-thirds went outside the Empire. Furthermore, from 1870 to 1914, migration particularly to new territories was enormous and more than 50 million people migrated from Europe to Canada, the US, South America, South Africa, Australia and New Zealand. This huge emigration from Europe amounted to one-eighth of the European population during that period. Moreover, outmigration countries such as Britain, Italy, Portugal and Spain amounted to between 20% and 40% of their total population (Stalker 1994). Without taking all aspects into account, especially the occupation of new territories and the outmigration from Europe, would mean not looking at the entire matter in totality.

In contrast to West European countries, Japan in the East Asian colonies invested heavily in infrastructure, education and modern technologies, which played a crucial role in raising productivity and economic diversification. This reversal in colonial policies in the past had quite different outcomes. For example, during the colonial period Taiwan's agriculture became highly efficient and productive. Japan was also in a hurry to set up heavy industries in its colonies. It was envisaged that in the case of war such policies would prove to be beneficial and strategically important. Since importing labour was almost a closed option, this meant transferring Japanese industries to the colonies such as Taiwan and Korea with the availability of cheap raw materials and labour costs (Amsden 2005; Siddiqui 2013).

Globalisation in the 19th century coincided with the rapid changes in technology, particularly in transportation costs and time, both of which were reduced drastically. This period also witnessed the invention of steamships, the telegraph and railways and all these led to further reduction in the costs of freight by two-thirds and, furthermore, the opening up of the Suez Canal in 1869 halved the distance from Bombay to London. These technological developments had even more dramatic impact on reducing geographical barriers in 1914; the long-term FDI in the world economy was distributed in an uneven manner, e.g., more than half of FDI (i.e., 55%) went to developed countries, i.e., 30% to Europe and 25% to the US, while 45% went to poor countries and to European colonies, i.e., 20% to Latin America and 20% to Asia and Africa. In 1913, the primary sector accounted for 55% of long-term total global foreign investment, while investment in transport, etc., accounted for another 30% and the manufacturing sector only 10%, which was mainly concentrated in Europe and the US (Bagchi 2010).

Comparative Advantage

The theory of comparative advantage is provided as support for worldwide trade liberalisation. The theory claims that free trade is beneficial for all countries. It is further said that free trade will automatically lead to the realisation of various other benefits. For example, once the poor countries open up their markets and join free trade, living conditions will improve. The WTO argues that economic welfare can be maximised through free trade. However, comparative theory rests on assumptions that there are no trade imbalances between countries (Bhagwati and Krueger 2001; WTO 2013).

The theoretical support for free trade rests on David Ricardo's theory of comparative advantage. In his 19th-century proposition, he argued England and Portugal could engage in mutually beneficial exchange of cloth and wine, regardless of respective productivities and prices. However, in the 20th century Heckscher-Ohlin-Samuelson (H-O-S), while primarily basing his view on Ricardo's theory, said that countries must export products based on inputs they have in abundance and import products based on inputs that are scarce. However, the trade pattern does not confirm such a claim, as most trade occurs among countries that possess similar endowments. To explain this, Paul Krugman (1987) put forward a new trade theory that justified policy intervention such as tariffs and subsidies. In fact, the difference between the economies of developed and developing countries does have an impact on trade.

For instance, suppose the developing countries specialise in sectors for which they have abundant supply, as recommended by the H-O-S module. This would mean developing countries would focus on primary products that have little added value. Moreover, prices of primary products tend to decrease compared with manufactured products, and manufacturing plays a very important role not only in expanding areas for employment, and also in raising overall productivity in the economy, including the agriculture sector. Earlier, the World Bank study predicted welfare gains in 2015 of US$96 billion (one-fifth of 1% of the world's GDP). Developed countries stand to gain US$80 billion (82%), compared with US$16 billion (18%) for the developing countries. However, a major proportion of the developing countries' share would go to countries such as China, India and Brazil, US$1 billion each, whereas African countries would be net losers of US$3 billion (Anderson and Martin 2005). While Polaski (2006) found that global gains from further trade liberalisation would be 0.2% of the world's GDP, even if the Western market were more opened, most gains would go to China, India and Brazil.

Paul Krugman argues that trade patterns could be explained by increasing the returns to scale and imperfect competition. On trade theories, he complains that "Since mainstream trade theory derived its power and unity from being stated in formal general equilibrium terms, alternative views were relegated to the footnotes" (Krugman 1987, 133). Trade theory places much emphasis on relative prices and costs in explaining international trade. However, recent experiences of the developing countries show that this is not the case. In fact, a number of studies have shown that price levels have accounted for very little in explaining international trade. And as such Ricardo's comparative advantage theory seems to be inadequate due to a number of assumptions such as perfect competition, full employment, homogeneous goods and empirical irrelevance (Barker 1977).

The comparative advantage model presents a picture of the past trade openness and the rise of Europe in a very mechanical way. For instance, such explanation ignores the divergent forms and trajectories of geopolitical accumulation, which played a very important role in the industrialisation of Europe and making the transition to capitalism (particularly in Netherlands, Britain and France). During the 1800–1900 century, the geosocial conditions and rules of reproduction in Europe and in Asia were in turn required varied types of military capabilities. Meanwhile, both regions had different types of external threat environments and challenges, which led to the development of different priorities and pressures for developing certain military technology over others (Anievas and Nisancioglu 2015). Under those circumstances, both internal and external factors interacted, certain European countries were able to acquire what became a decisive comparative advantage. This explains the full picture of Europe ascendancy to global prominence in the 19th century. Such explanation "help[s] us to explain how the Europeans extended their control over the total land area of the globe from 35% in 1800 to 84% in 1914, it cannot explain how they managed to acquire that initial 35%" (Anievas and Nisancioglu 2015, 230). To answer this important question, Philip Hoffman concluded that

> one area in which Western Europe possessed undeniable comparative advantage well before 1800 seems to have been overlooked—namely, violence. The states of Western Europe were simply better at making and using artillery, firearms, fortifications, and armed ships than other advanced parts of the world and they had developed the fiscal and organisational system that armies and navies equipped with this technology required. The Europeans had this advantage long before 1800. By then they had conquered some 35% of the globe, and they controlled lucrative trade routes as far away as Asia. (cited in Anievas and Nisancioglu 2015, 230)

According to neo-classical theory, productivity growth in one country leads to an appreciation of its currency and trade to, "the happy result that all countries will be able successfully to participate in international trade in the sense that they will benefit from such trade and be able to generate export revenues equal to the value of imports" (Milberg 2004, 56–57). The country's higher productivity is balanced by disadvantageous movements of the exchange rate. Furthermore, its factor price equalisation model even postulates that the difference in real wages would be reduced and ultimately eliminated. The neo-classical theorists argue that countries would conform to the wage level of rich countries and free trade policies are seen as a great equaliser among countries. It is argued that free trade alone has "the potential for development and convergence between rich and poor countries" (Kiely 2007, 15). Contrary to such claims, Kaldor suggests such effect "is nothing else than the inhibiting effect of superior competitive power of industrially more efficient and dynamic countries, as compared to others" (1981, 597). According to him, some countries benefit more from free trade while others benefit less or might even suffer losses depending on their level of development. Kaldor observes that "under more realistic assumptions unrestricted trade is likely to lead to a loss of welfare to particular regions or countries" (1981, 593).

Empirical studies also do not support the expected associations between trade liberalisation and increase in income levels. Rodrik (2001, 11) finds "that there is no convincing evidence that trade liberalisation is predictably associated with subsequent economic growth." It is also true that countries that export mainly agricultural and primary commodities have witnessed declining terms of trade and have also seen an uninterrupted sharp rise in their trade deficits. The imbalances are not only far from balanced out as the theory suggested but rather have led to further accumulation of debts and debt crises.

The Heckscher-Ohlin-Samuelson model was validated with experiences in Europe and North America, where in fact the evidence suggests a commodity-price convergence took place. The price gap between exporting and importing countries which was substantial in 1870 diminished rapidly up to 1914. This convergence in commodity prices extended to North America and Europe and improved the terms of trade for all the major European countries and North America.

The neo-classical assumptions could be rejected on theoretical, logical and empirical grounds. Therefore, comparative trade theory cannot determine international trade patterns (Maneschi 1992). The issue of a possible causal link between trade liberalisation and reduction in income inequality is unclear. Neo-classical theorists predict that the growth of world trade would lead to a reduction in income disparities across countries. However, these claims are based on a number of assumptions whose validity is being questioned by various empirical researches and are also far from the past experiences of the developed countries.

Another Crucial Assumption

Neo-classical growth theory, the Solow (1956) model emphasises that when a poor country starts out with lower levels of initial capital, returns to investment will be higher due to the high marginal productivity of workers. Therefore, the rich countries will invest in poor countries, leading to a rise in capital generation. In short, the Solow model predicts that with the adoption of trade liberalisation, the poor countries will catch up on growth with the rich countries (Siwach 2016). It is said that trade liberalisation will lead to income convergence between countries. However, Garima Siwach's (2016) analysed the effect of liberalisation on per capita income of 19 developing countries, after their economies were opened in the 1980s and 1990s. The study compared the trade effects on convergence rates by looking at the patterns of pre- and post-liberalisation. Such study of growth and convergence has a significant impact on long-term growth policies of an economy and also provides us implications for poverty, which is the most important policy for the poor countries seeking to address. Siwach (2016, 118) concludes that

> there is no significant change in convergence that can be attributed to trade liberalisation. Through a first difference analysis that estimates convergence rates between trade groups before and after liberalisation, we find no significant change in convergence for developing countries towards their major partners of trade. The results are robust when large country biases are taken care of as well.

Moreover, it is widely recognised that, for example, the gap in average per capita between the richest and the poorest countries has increased substantially in recent decades (Ghose 2004). Since the adoption of neoliberal economic policies in the 1980s and with the abandonment of Keynesianism, meant to limit government fiscal policy measures to stimulate the economy, there has been a rapid increase in income and wealth inequalities in most developing countries (Cornia 1999).

The neo-classical theory assumes the existence of full employment, and therefore, a rise in trade that can affect growth only through factor allocation and the increase of levels of competition and technology in the economy. As a result, not only will economic growth increase but also efficiency and productivity as well. It is further assumed that if the developing countries relax on foreign capital inflow regulation then inflows of capital will increase into the developing countries (Krueger 1996).

At present, trade policies suggested by neo-classical economists for developing countries have exclusively focused on the Pareto-Optimality conditions in multiple markets which are achievable under free trade. It is further said that any deviations from competitive equilibrium are treated as "distortions" in terms of the favoured Pareto-Optimal model (Bhagwati and Krueger 2001). However, little attention is paid to deteriorating living conditions and incomes and overall aggregate demands in the country (Sen 2005). Theoretically, untested free trade theory is still referred and propagated by international institutions and Western countries, pushing for reduction in tariffs and opening of the markets in developing countries (Sen 2005).

It seems useful to briefly discuss development of modern businesses in India, especially in the 20th century. Indian businesses are embodiments of pre-industrial forms of capital accumulation through money lending and trading. During the two World Wars and the Great Depression they had more freedom in the sense of setting up industries and had capital accumulation including black marketing and swindling in government contracts. British interests were more diverted towards railways, engineering, jute and tea plantations (Tyabji 2015). Levkovsky (1966) also argues that development of businesses in India under British rule was very different from that in West European countries. Unlike in Western Europe, in India, the emergence of industries did not follow a transition from independent artisans to manually operated manufacturers to modern power-driven factories. In India, manufacturers were closely linked with the merchants' and usurers' capital. For a relatively long period, Levkovsky finds, manufacturers continued to engage in money lending and trading along with industrial operations (Levkovsky 1966; Siddiqui 2015a).

In fact, the merchant and usury capital and industrial capital are distinct forms of capital that employ different methods of accumulation (Siddiqui 2014b). Merchant capital generates profits through buying and selling commodities, usury capital makes profits through the interest on loans advanced by moneylenders, while industrial capital on the other hand makes profits by buying raw materials and employing workers and producing manufactured products and innovations of new products. As Dobb examined, in Western European countries, with the expansion of industries the importance of industrial capital increased over time, while the merchant capital operation declined relatively. The usury role also declined over time with the decline of peasant-based agriculture. As Tyabji (2015, 102) observes,

> The existence of a class of businessmen does not automatically mean the existence of a group of industrially oriented entrepreneurs, because the development of industries is not necessarily the only money-making activity available to these businessmen ... In the Indian case, colonialism and "arrested development" formed the context within which emerged the group of businessmen responsible for managing industrial ventures after independence. They were part of an imperfectly formed group of industrialists possessing characteristics that reflected their background of engagement in non-industrial activities; activities in which they continued to be involved, even as they acquired control over industrial companies.

Global economic integration without taking into consideration the different levels of developing and the specific economic situation of the country would be a futile and meaningless attempt at such integration. Sachs and Warner (1995) argue that the globalisation process and global market integration, as measured by the international flow of goods and services, will promote growth and convergence in income levels between developed and developing countries. According to them, economic integration began in the 1980s, supported by the IMF, World Bank and WTO, which also meant to increase not only market-based trade and financial flows, but also institutional harmonisation with regards to trade policy, legal codes, tax systems, ownership patterns and other regulatory arrangements (Sachs and Warner 1995, 2).

Ha-Joon Chang (2008) examined the earlier industrial and trade policies of the developed countries such as Britain, Germany, France, the US and Japan and found that when these countries were in the process of building their industries they used protectionist policy measures to develop their "infant industries." He says the current international rules imposed via the IMF/World Bank and WTO would not facilitate the development of an industrial sector in these countries. Chang notes, "Neo-liberal globalisation has failed to deliver on all fronts of economic life—growth, equality and stability. Despite this we are constantly told how neo-liberal globalisation has brought unprecedented benefits" (Chang 2008, 28).

It is difficult to explain why, despite higher levels of economic integration between countries within the last three decades, the outcomes have been "negative externalities" such as a rise in income inequality and persistence of poverty in sub-Saharan Africa, Latin America and South Asia (Siddiqui 1998).

Present globalisation involves further integration of countries into the globalised markets, which is supported by fast communication channels and high technology. Globalisation could be identified according to the following characteristics: Capital has more freedom both in terms of investment opportunities and selling of products in global markets; increased integration of national markets with the global market; and dominance of finance (Perrotta and Sunna 2013). However, all these are undermining and making it difficult to make and implement sovereign economic policies suitable for local conditions.

The neo-classical theory uncritically accepts the role of the markets and argues that if markets are given freedom, then economic growth could be attained with efficiency and ultimately will be able to achieve higher output, consumption and distribution, which is defined as Pareto Optimum (Krueger 1996). This theory under the pretext of harmony ignores what Karl Polanyi's book *Great Transformation* terms "double movement" during the rise of capitalism, i.e., expansion of market relations, with legislation made to protect society from its consequences, which is far from self-regulating. In effect, expansion of markets proceeded with dispossessions and displacements of people from their habitations (Siddiqui 2014c).

The current wave of globalisation began in the 1980s in spheres of production and finance and is a bit different from the previous one. During this wave of globalisation, we find that foreign capital and multinational corporations and international portfolios flow are far more important players than in the earlier period (Siddiqui 2014a). This has led to the acceleration of capital investment in the manufacturing sectors in the former colonies, which was in the earlier globalisation phase largely limited to mining and railways. De-industrialisation via trade and transfer of surplus from colonies remains a very crucial element in the analysis of the past economic history of the developing countries. Foreign investment is tied to intra-firm trade and has been increasing at a faster rate than world output, especially since the 1980s. For instance, FDI inward stock rose from 7% of world GDP in 1980 to 30% in 2010. This seems to be due to global companies expecting to receive very high profits and establishing strategic control over their supply lines. As a result, there has been a massive increase in the export-oriented industries, especially in the East Asian region including China. Moreover, in 2010, for the first time more than 50% of FDI went to developing countries and foreign capital is now the biggest source of external funding for these countries (Perrotta and Sunna 2013; Siddiqui 2009).

During the past quarter century, we have witnessed the signing of a number of treaties and agreements, whereby international capital imposes further rules and regulations on governments, which limits the autonomy of the sovereign countries and in turn forces them to ask for assistance from international capital and governments of the developed countries; this will ultimately restrict their adoption of independent policies and undermine any possibilities of the poor countries building autonomous development.

Unlike GATT, the WTO includes mechanisms for dispute settlement and most likely would favour the interests of big corporations that can afford high legal costs and lobby to pursue their own interests. Moreover, the TRIPS agreement provides multinational corporations greater powers than currently held. Furthermore, agricultural trade liberalisation is undermining food security in most developing countries and many of them will become food importers. At the same time, trade liberalisation in the agriculture sector would benefit agricultural exporting developed countries that have experience, technology and capital to take advantage of the new situation (Reinert 2007).

Conclusion

The study finds that globalisation and policies of "free trade" in the past decades did not lead to rapid growth and economic convergence in most developing countries. The theory of comparative advantage is presented in support for worldwide trade liberalisation. The theory claims that free trade is beneficial for all countries. It further assumes that free trade will automatically lead to the realisation of various other benefits. The contribution of this article is that a number of empirical evidence from the majority of developing countries proves such claims are a fallacy.

Trade and services liberalisation also includes TRIPS, which covers protection of trademarks, patents, industrial design and copyrights. At present, as far as the question of knowledge and technology is concerned, the developed countries are net producers and the developing countries are net consumers. TRIPS will increase the price of patentable knowledge to consumers and as a consequence, the flow of rents from the developing countries to developed countries will increase. It appears that new regulations such as GATS and TRIMS are designed to benefit the large companies of the developed countries to make it easier for them to enter and exit markets with fewer restrictions and obligations and to protect their appropriation of technological ownership rents.

The developing countries need to adopt trade and economic policies that are more suitable to their stages of development, which they face, so as to enable them to achieve higher rates of growth. The economic development should be put as centre stage in WTO negotiations which may require a drastic change in the culture and conduct of such negotiations. At present, it appears to be steeped in narrow mercantilism rather than any long-term vision of a trading system that benefits most of the developing countries.

The study concludes that state intervention in the national economy has proved to be a crucial policy element in achieving successful economic development. The recent experiences, not only in East Asian countries, but also in developed countries since the Second World War, show the role of the state to be important for achieving economic development. There seems to be a need, both on theoretical and empirical grounds, for state management to make the market friendlier towards national economic developmental needs. Therefore, developing countries need to change their course of economic strategy away from global financial instability and dependence on foreign markets to, instead, relying on domestic investment, wage and employment-led growth.

References

Amsden, A. 2005. "Promoting Industry under WTO Law." In *Putting Development First: The Importance of Policy Space in the WTO and IFIs*, edited by K. P. Gallagher, 216–32. London: Zed Books.

Anderson, K., and W. Martin, eds. 2005. *Agriculture Trade Reform and the Doha Development Agenda*. Washington, DC: World Bank.

Anievas, A., and K. Nisancioglu. 2015. *How the West Came to Rule: The Geopolitical Origins of Capitalism*. London: Pluto Press.

Bagchi, A. K. 2010. *Colonialism and the Indian Economy*. Delhi: Oxford University Press.

Barker, T. 1977. "International Trade and Economic Growth: An Alternative to Neo-classical Approach." *Cambridge Journal of Economics* 1: 153–72.

Bhagwati, J., and A. Krueger. 2001. *The Dangerous Drift to the Preferential Trade Agreements*. Washington, DC: AEI Press.

Brailsford, H. N. 1998. *The War of Steel and Gold*. Bristol: Thoemmes Press.

Brown, M. B. 1993. *Fair Trade*. London: Zed Books.

Chang, H.-J. 2002. *Kicking Away the Ladder: Development Strategy in Historical Perspective*. London: Anthem Press.

Chang, H.-J. 2008. *Bad Samaritans: The Myth of Free Trade and Secret History of Capitalism*. New York: Bloomsbury Press.

Cornia, G. A. 1999. "Liberalisation, Globalisation and Income Distribution." Working paper, no. 157, Helsinki: UNU-WIDER.

Engels, F. 1990. "Protection and Free Trade." In *Marx/Engels Collected Works*, vol. 26, by K. Marx and F. Engels, 521–36. New York: International Publishers.

Gallagher, J., and R. Robinson. 1953. "The Imperialism of Free Trade." *The Economic History Review* (Second Series) 5 (1): 1–15.

Gallagher, K. P., ed. 2005. *Putting Development First*. London: Zed Books.

Ghose, A. K. 2004. "Global Inequality and International Trade." *Cambridge Journal of Economics* 28: 229–52.

Habib, I. 1995. "Colonisation of the Indian Economy." In *Essay in Indian History: Towards a Marxist Perception*, edited by I. Habib, 304–46. New Delhi: Tulika.

Ho, P. S. 1996. "Reappraising Torrens Contribution to the Analysis of Trade, Growth and Colonisation." *Contribution to Political Economy* 15: 1–31.

Kaldor, N. 1981. "The Role of Increasing Returns, Technical Progress and Cumulative Causation in the Theory of International Trade and Economic Growth." *Economic Applique* 34 (4): 593–617.

Kiely, R. 2007. *The New Political Economy of Development: Globalisation, Imperialism and Hegemony*. Basingstoke: Palgrave Macmillan.

Krueger, A. 1996. *The Political Economy of Trade Protection*. Boston: National Bureau of Economic Research.

Krugman, P. 1987. "Is Free Trade Passé?" *Journal of Economics Perspective* 1 (2): 131–44.

Levkovsky, A. I. 1966. *Capitalism in India: Basic Trends in Its Development*. Delhi: Peoples Publishing House.

List, F. 1966. *The National System of Political Economy*. New York: Augustus Kelley.

Maddison, A. 2006a. "Asia in the World Economy 1500–2030 AD." *Asian Pacific Economic Literature* 20 (2): 1–37.

Maddison, A. 2006b. *The World Economy*, vol. 1. Paris: Organisation for Economic Co-operation and Development.

Maneschi, A. 1992. "Ricardo's International Trade Theory: Beyond the Comparative Cost Example." *Cambridge Journal of Economics* 16: 421–37.

Milberg, W. 2004. "The Changing Structure of Trade Linked to Global Production Systems: What Are the Policy Implications?" *International Labour Review* 143 (1–2): 45–90.

Nayyar, D. 2006. "Globalisation, History and Development: A Tale of Two Centuries." *Cambridge Journal of Economics* 30: 137–59.

Owen, R. I. 2004. *Lord Cromer: Victorian Imperialist*. Oxford: Oxford University Press.

Perrotta, C., and C. Sunna, eds. 2013. *Globalization and Economic Crisis*. Rome: Universita del Salento.

Polaski, S. 2006. *Winners and Losers: Impact of the Doha Round on the Developing Countries*. Washington, DC: Carnegie Endowment for International Peace.

Reinert, E. 2007. *How Rich Country Got Rich and Why Poor Countries Stay Poor*. London: Constable & Robinson.

Rodrik, D. 2001. *The Global Governance of Trade: As if Development Really Mattered*. New York: United Nations Development Programme.

Rodrik, D. 2004. *How to Make the Trade Regime Work for Development*. Cambridge, MA: Harvard University Press.

Sachs, J., and A. Warner. 1995. Economic Reform and the Process of Global Economic Integration. *Brooking Papers on Economic Activity*, no. 1: 1–118.

Sen, S. 2005. "International Trade Theory and Policy: What Is Left of the Free Trade Paradigm?" *Development and Change* 36 (6): 1011–29.

Siddiqui, K. 1990. "Historical Roots of Mass Poverty in India." In *Trends and Strains*, edited by C. A. Thayer, J. Camilleri, and K. Siddiqui, 59–76. Delhi: Peoples Publishing House.

Siddiqui, K. 1998. "The Export of Agricultural Commodities, Poverty and Ecological Crisis: A Case Study of Central American Countries." *Economic and Political Weekly* 33 (39): A128–A137.

Siddiqui, K. 2009. "The Political Economy of Growth in China and India." *Journal of Asian Public Policy* 1 (2): 17–35.

Siddiqui, K. 2012a. "Developing Countries' Experience with Neoliberalism and Globalisation." *Research in Applied Economics* 4 (4): 12–37. doi:10.5296/rae.v4i4.2878.

Siddiqui, K. 2012b. "Malaysia's Socio-Economic Transformation in Historical Perspective." *International Journal of Business and General Management* 1 (2): 21–50.

Siddiqui, K. 2013. "Experiences of Developmental State in India and Taiwan." *Think India Quarterly* 16 (4): 91–121.

Siddiqui, K. 2014a. "Flows of Foreign Capital into Developing Countries: A Critical Review." *Journal of International Business & Economics* 2 (1): 29–46.

Siddiqui, K. 2014b. "Growth and Crisis in India's Political Economy from 1991 to 2013." *International Journal of Social and Economic Research* 4 (2): 84–99. doi:10.5958/2249-6270.2014.00487.5.

Siddiqui, K. 2014c. "Modernisation and Displacement of Rural Communities in India." *Journal of Social Business* 4 (2–3): 3–27.

Siddiqui, K. 2015a. "Challenges for Industrialisation in India: State versus Market Policies." *Research in World Economy* 6 (2): 85–98. doi:10.5430/rwe.v6n2p85.

Siddiqui, K. 2015b. "Foreign Capital Investment into Developing Countries: Some Economic Policy Issues." *Research in World Economy* 6 (2): 14–29. doi:10.5430/rwe.v6n2p14.

Siddiqui, K. 2015c. "Trade Liberalisation and Economic Development: A Critical Review." *International Journal of Political Economy* 44 (3): 228–47. doi:10.1080/08911916.2015.1095050.

Siddiqui, K. 2016. "A Study of Singapore as a Developmental State." In *Chinese Global Production Networks in ASEAN*, edited by Y.-C. Kim, 157–88. London: Springer.

Siwach, G. 2016. "Trade Liberalisation and Income Convergence: Evidence from Developing Countries." *Economic and Political Weekly* 51 (22): 115–20.

Solow, R. 1956. "A Contribution to the Theory of Economic Growth." *Quarterly Journal of Economics* 70 (1): 65–94.

Stalker, P. 1994. *The Work of Stranger: A Survey of International Labour Migration*. Geneva: International Labour Organization.

Stiglitz, J. 2005. "Development Policies in a World of Globalisation." In *Putting Development First*, edited by K. P. Gallagher, 15–32. London: Zed Books.

Stiglitz, J., and A. Charlton. 2006. *Fair Trade for All*. Oxford: Oxford University Press.

Tyabji, N. 2015. "The Politics of Industry in Nehru's India." *Economic and Political Weekly* 50 (35): 97–103.

Wade, R. 2003. "What Strategies Are Viable for Developing Countries Today? The World Trade Organization and the Shrinking of 'Development Space.'" *Review of International Political Economy* 10 (4): 621–44.

World Bank. 2014. *The Development Report.* Washington, DC: World Bank.

WTO (World Trade Organization). 2013. *The Case for Open Trade.* https://www.wto.org/english/thewto_e/whatis_e/tif_e/fact3_e.htm.

DISCUSSION QUESTIONS

1. How would you summarize the main argument of the article in a sentence or two?

2. According to the article, what were the effects of colonization of the rest of the world by the European powers, especially for India and China?

3. According to the article, why did the Great Britain become a promoter of free trade by the mid-1800s?

4. What are TRIPS, TRIMS, and GATS? How do they fit in to the author's discussion of liberal world economy and its impact on the welfare of developing countries?

5. What is the role of the state in explaining the early developers' successes in economic growth and conquest of the rest of the world? What does the neoliberal economic theory say about the role of the state in the economy and economic development?

6. Why does the author suggest that developing countries need to change their economic strategy away from global financial instability and dependence on foreign markets to relying on domestic investment, wage, and employment growth?

Global Warming: Where the World is Moving

By Subhankar Dutta

Case Study

"The warnings about global warming have been extremely clear for a long time. We are facing a global climate crisis. It is deepening. We are entering a period of consequences."[1]

—Albert Arnold "Al" Gore, Jr., American Politician and Environmentalist

"Global warming is too serious for the world any longer to ignore its danger or split into opposing factions on it."[2]

—Anthony Charles Lynton Blair (Tony Blair), British Labour Party Politician

The global warming was recognised as a natural phenomenon that actually raised the temperatures of the atmosphere, seas and surface levels. According to the observations made by experts and environmentalists, the environmental sustainability of the planet had come to at stake mainly due to the hazardous effects of global warming, particularly starting from 19th century onwards. Historically, in 1896, the severe impact of the global warming on earth was first time noticed by the scientists. Permafrost, forest fires, water vapour, sunspots, etc. and different anthropogenic incidents, namely, burning of fossil fuels, deforestation, unethical landfills, overpopulation, mining activities, using of injurious fertilisers in agricultural fields, industrialisation process, etc. were some of the major reasons behind the happenings of global warming in reality.

Due to the occurrences of global warming, the earth was affected by various natural calamities including the rise in average temperatures, melting of ice, extreme weather conditions, increasing of sea levels, acidifying the seas and oceans, heinous effects on plants and animals, social effects, to name a few. On this issue, the UK Met Office had estimated that the international temperature might alarmingly rise, mainly due to the effects of global warming and climate change during 2015-16.

While observing the harmful effects of global warming and climate change on earth, the international community had unanimously agreed to form an agreement, especially to control the carbon emissions into the environment. As a result of that, over 190 countries had taken part in the Paris Climate Summit from November 30th to December 11th 2015, particularly to discuss about

Subhankar Dutta, "Global Warming: Where the World Is Moving?" pp. 1-11. Copyright © 2016 by The Case Centre. Reprinted with permission.

introducing a new global agreement on climate change. By initiating such event, almost all countries had agreed to minimise the international greenhouse gas emissions in future. Besides that, experts opined for more protective approaches like planting trees, lessening in thermal power generating stations, minimising the usages of paper, to name a few, mainly for combating the global warming crisis in the coming days. In spite of adopting all such counteractive steps, would the negative effects of global warming and climate change on earth be significantly cut off in the coming days?

Global Warming: An Overview

Global warming was considered as a major environment-related phenomenon, which gradually increased the average temperature of earth's surface, oceans and atmosphere. As per the observation made by the Environmental Protection Agency (EPA), the earth's average temperature had soared up by 1.4 degrees Fahrenheit (0.8 degrees Celsius) over the previous centuries. Moreover, the temperature was predicted to inflate approximately 2-11.5 degrees Fahrenheit (1.133 to 6.42 degrees C) over the coming 100 years (2015-24). In this connection, Keith Peterman, Professor of Chemistry at York College of Pennsylvania, and Gregory Foy, Associate Professor of Chemistry at York College of Pennsylvania, asserted, "We know through high-accuracy instrumental measurements that there is an unprecedented increase in CO_2 in the atmosphere. We know that CO_2 absorbs infrared radiation [heat] and the global mean temperature is increasing."[3] On this issue, experts highlighted that the global temperature had recorded a negative trend, during 1880-1935. However, it had gradually started heating up from 1980 onwards[4] (Figure 4.4). NASA had also stated that the levels of Arctic ice and land ice had begun significantly decreasing over decades, mainly due to the global warming[5] (Figure 4.5).

Historically, in 1896, Svante Arrhenius (Arrhenius), Swedish Scientist, first time claimed that the combustion of fossil fuel had ultimately caused the occurrences of global warming in nature.[6] On this issue, Josef Werne (Werne), Associate Professor in the Department of Geology and Planetary Science at the University of Pittsburgh, stated, "The basic physics of the greenhouse effect were figured out more than a hundred years ago by a smart guy using only pencil and paper (Svante Arrhenius in 1896)."[7] (Figure 4.6). After examining the reasons behind occurrences of global warming in reality, Arrhenius postulated that there existed a direct relationship between temperature and carbon dioxide (CO_2) concentrations in the atmosphere. He further observed that the average surface temperature of the earth had remained approximately 15°C, mainly due to the infrared absorption capacity of water vapour and CO_2. Furthermore, such phenomenon was universally recognised as the natural greenhouse effect in the environment.[8] Likewise, experts noticed that a small rise in atmospheric levels of CO_2 might cause a considerable level of increase in earth's temperature.[9] Besides that, the invisibility of CO_2 was considered the prime factor behind the occurrences of the global warming[10] (Figure 4.7).

While observing the potential reasons behind the outbreaks of the global warming in environment, experts found that both natural as well as anthropogenic factors had caused the overall damage. In this context, they pointed out several natural incidents such as forest fires, permafrost, sunspots, water vapour, etc. that had caused the global warming in actuality. In addition to that, different anthropogenic issues like man-induced deforestation activities, burning of fossil fuels, unethical landfills, rising overpopulation, mining initiatives, usage of harmful fertilisers in agricultural fields, etc. had further aggravated the global warming menace in nature.[11] While speaking about the anthropogenic factor behind the occurrences of human-made natural disaster, Barack Hussein Obama II, President of the United States, commented, "All across the world, in every kind of environment and region known to man, increasingly dangerous weather patterns and devastating storms are abruptly putting an end to the long-running debate over whether or not climate change is real. Not only is it real, it's here, and its effects are giving rise to a frighteningly new global phenomenon: the man-made natural disaster."[12]

Consequently, the global warming had possessed a number of long-lasting and devastating effects on the earth such as increasing in average temperatures, extreme weather conditions, melting of ice, rising of sea levels, acidifying the sea levels and oceans, harmful effects on plants and animals, social effects, etc.[13] (Figure 4.8). Talking on the effects of rising global warming, Michel Jarraud, Secretary General of the World Meteorological Organisation (WMO), stated, "It means hotter global temperatures, more extreme weather events like heatwaves and floods, melting ice, rising sea levels and increased acidity of the oceans. This is happening now and we are moving into unchartered territory at a frightening speed."[14] Werne, further emphasised, "We can observe this happening in real time in many places. Ice is melting in both polar ice caps and mountain glaciers. Lakes around the world, including Lake Superior, are warming rapidly –in some cases faster than the surrounding environment. Animals are changing migration patterns and plants are changing the dates of activity (e.g., leaf-flush in spring to fall in autumn is longer)."[15]

As per the report published by the Scientific American, some cities in the US had recorded the warmest summers in 2014, mainly due to the global warming. In addition to that, the WMO had published one environmental report on July 3rd 2014, specifying that the deaths occurred due to the rising heat had inflated by over 2000% over the past decade.[16]

Besides, experts observed that the hurricanes might become more intense in nature, specifically because of the climate change phenomenon. In this connection, experts explained that hurricanes formed their energy from the temperature difference between the cold upper atmosphere and the warm tropical ocean. Such disparity in temperatures was mainly intensified by the global warming effects. Sobel, Columbia University professor in the departments of Earth and Environmental Sciences, and Applied Physics and Applied Mathematics, therefore, asserted, "Since the most damage by far comes from the most intense hurricanes –such as typhoon Haiyan in the Philippines in 2013 –this means that hurricanes could become overall more destructive."[17]

Furthermore, because of the melting of two major ice blocks in Greenland and Antarctica, many countries could experience the rising sea levels in future. As a result of the increasing sea levels, millions of people residing in these affected nations might displace from their native lands to other countries for safety.[18]

Commercially, the global warming could drastically affect the economic growth of any country. In this connection, Stern Review had stated that the negative effects of climate change might severely hit the fundamental requirements of life, i.e., accessing to water, food production, health benefits and the sustainable environment for people worldwide. Moreover, the global warming could lead to desertification, hampering the overall agricultural production growth. Besides that, the rising sea levels, mainly caused by the effect of global warming, might incur substantial land area losses and further, it could damage the structural development of any country.[19]

Also, as of 2014, the Copenhagen Consensus Center had reported that the rising global warming might worsen the economic growth in the coming days.[20] In addition to that, some other researchers estimated that the cost of both climate change and air pollution would increase to approximately 3.2% of the global GDP within 2030. On this occasion, experts further predicted that the economies of least developed countries might experience commercial losses up to 11% of their respective GDPs. While speaking about the possible impact of global warming on the Bangladesh economy, Sheikh Hasina, Prime Minister of Bangladesh, commented, "A 1C rise in temperature [temperatures have already risen by 0.7C globally since the end of the 19th century] is associated with 10% productivity loss in farming. For us, it means losing about 4m tonnes of food grain, amounting to about $2.5bn. That is about 2% of our GDP. Adding up the damages to property and other losses, we are faced with a total loss of about 3-4% of GDP. Without these losses, we could have easily secured much higher growth." Furthermore, Michael Zammit Cutajar, Former Executive Secretary of the UN Framework Convention on Climate Change, stated, "Climate change is not just a distant threat but a present danger –its economic impact is already with us."[21]

During 2015-16, as per the observation made by the UK Met Office, the global temperature could drastically increase due to global warming and climate change. Highlighting on this major issue, Professor Adam Scaife, Analyst at the UK Met Office, therefore, stated, "We will look back on this period as an important turning point. That is why we are emphasising it, because there are so many big changes happening at once. This year and next year are likely to be at, or near, record levels of warming."[22] Michel Jarraud (Jarraud), Secretary General of the WMO, further noted, "The state of the global climate in 2015 will make history for a number of reasons. Levels of greenhouse gases in the atmosphere reached new highs and in the Northern hemisphere spring 2015 the three-month global average concentration of CO_2 crossed the 400 parts per million barrier for the first time. 2015 is likely to be the hottest year on record, with ocean surface temperatures at the highest level since measurements began. It is probable that the 1°C Celsius threshold will be crossed."[23]

Menace of Climate Change: Is Environmental Sustainability a Myth?

On December 4th 2012, during the opening ceremony of the United Nations Framework Convention on Climate Change (UNFCCC) in Doha, Ban Ki-Moon (Moon), UN Secretary General, declared that the climate change had especially caused due to the industrialisation process taken up by the developed countries in yester years. In this connection, Moon declared, "The climate change phenomenon has been caused by the industrialization of the developed world. It's only fair and reasonable that the developed world should bear most of the responsibility." Supporting Moon's comment, China and other developing nations had further highlighted that the capitalist countries had possessed the historical responsibility behind the occurrence of global warming. On this issue, they pointed out that during the industrialisation era, the factories of these rich nations had emitted dangerous amount of carbon into the environment, polluting the ecological balance of nature.[24] In this context, experts further noted that the UK was mostly responsible for changing the climate especially by producing more carbon emissions into the atmosphere from the era of industrial revolution onwards.[25] Furthermore, in the journal Climatic Change, the European researchers claimed, "In the past, developed countries used high-emission technologies because no better technologies were available –for example, the UK has a long history of high emissions due to the use of inefficient steam engines."[26] Moreover, policymakers highlighted that the impact of cut in carbon emissions varied across different countries, mainly due to the dependency on the carbon intensity of their overall production volume.[27]

Apart from that, Julia Pongratz (Pongratz), Research Scientist at the Washington-based Carnegie Institution for Science, revealed an important fact that the carbon emission from the pre-industrial period had still possessed an impact on the climate, as the carbon dioxide concentration had remained present in the atmosphere for several centuries. "The relatively small amounts of carbon dioxide emitted many centuries ago continue to affect atmospheric carbon dioxide concentrations and our climate today, though only to a relatively small extent," stated Pongratz. She further added, "Looking into the past illustrates that the relatively large amount of carbon dioxide that we are emitting today will continue to have relatively large impacts on the atmosphere and climate for many centuries into the future."[28]

On the other hand, the European researchers further asserted that both the developed and developing nations were equally responsible for damaging the environmental sustainability, which actually in turn contributed towards the negative climate change.[29]

Apart from that, in 2013, both the developed as well as the developing nations had involved in a dilemma about how to raise capital fund for helping the emerging countries to cope up with the devastating impacts of the global warming. On this occasion, Bolivia and other developing nations had blamed the failing willingness of the capitalist countries to discuss about the financial aid and compensation, particularly required for combating the losses due to global warming. Moreover, the outbreak of devastating Typhoon Haiyan in the Philippines in 2013 had raised the urgency of monetary compensation for several affected poor countries in the world. Jayanthi Natarajan, Former Environment Minister of India, therefore, commented, "The compensation that those countries require is something that is absolutely fundamental and crucial." In response, Connie Hedegaard, European Union's Climate Commissioner, asserted, "We cannot have a system where there will be automatic compensation whenever severe weather events are happening at one place or other around the planet."[30]

In an attempt to conserve the environmental sustainability in future, in June 2015, the leaders of G7 countries, i.e., the US, Britain, Canada, Germany, France, Italy and Japan supported the Intergovernmental Panel on Climate Change recommended target of reducing the greenhouse gas emission rate about 40-70% below 2010 levels within 2050. Moreover, they committed to the globally agreed goal of lessening the warming condition to less than 2°C over the pre-industrial levels. Besides that, they acknowledged that the "deep cuts in global greenhouse gas emissions are required with a decarbonisation of the global economy over the course of this century."[31]

In addition to that, more than 190 countries had participated in the Paris Climate Summit held from November 30th to December 11th 2015, aiming to discuss about a probable new international agreement on climate change. The main objective of the summit was to lessen the global greenhouse gas emissions in order to combat the growing threat of harmful climate change.[32] As a result of that, on December 12th 2015, the parties to the UNFCCC had unanimously committed to follow an agreement and subsequently, it had adopted major decisions[33] (Figure 4.9). On this issue, Moon declared, "All countries have agreed to hold global temperature rise to well below 2 degrees Celsius. And recognizing the risk of grave consequences, you have further agreed to pursue efforts to limit temperature increase to 1.5 degrees. Governments have agreed to binding, robust, transparent rules of the road to ensure that all countries do what they have agreed across a range of issues." Christiana Figueres, Executive Secretary of UNFCCC, told, "We did it in Paris. We have made history together. It is an agreement of conviction. It is an agreement of solidarity with the most vulnerable. It is an agreement of long-term vision, for we have to turn this agreement into an engine of safe growth." Mogens Lykketoft, President of the UN General Assembly, too supported the commencement of the Paris climate agreement by stating that, "Today's agreement signals nothing less than a renaissance for humankind as we collectively embrace the global challenge of climate change and endeavor to transition to a more sustainable way of living that respects the needs of people and our planet."[34]

After the adoption of the new Paris agreement for climate change in 2015, Moon further commented, "The Paris Agreement is a monumental triumph for people and our planet." Moreover, he seemed very optimistic about achieving the probable success of this climate change agreement, when he emphasised, "It sets the stage for progress in ending poverty, strengthening peace and ensuring a life of dignity and opportunity for all. You have worked collaboratively to achieve something that no one nation could achieve alone. This is a resounding success for multilateralism."[35] Furthermore, while talking about attaining the diplomatic success of the Paris climate change agreement in reality, Kumi Naidoo, Executive Director of Greenpeace International, stated, "It sometimes seems that the countries of the UN can unite on nothing, but nearly 200 countries have come together and agreed a deal. Today, the human race has joined in a common cause. The Paris agreement is only one step on a long road and there are parts of it that frustrate, that disappoint me, but it is progress. The deal alone won't dig us out of the hole that we're in, but it makes the sides less steep."[36]

Subsequently, in an attempt to control the greenhouse gas emissions in the environment in the coming days, Jarraud requested the governments of almost all nations in the world for adopting necessary protective measures. In this connection, he mentioned, "Greenhouse gas emissions, which are causing climate change, can be controlled. We have the knowledge and the tools to act. We have a choice. Future generations will not."[37] Besides that, experts advocated implementing several possible control steps such as reducing the thermal power generating plants, lessening the usages of paper, planting trees, etc. to control the greenhouse gas emissions, thereby counteracting the global warming menace.[38]

Moreover, on March 18 2015, during a lecture to the students at Georgetown University in Washington, D.C., Jim Yong Kim (Kim), World Bank Group President, mentioned five major policy related strategies and growth choices mainly to control the drivers of the climate change. According to him, by putting a price on carbon emissions, abolishing of fossil fuel subsidies, building of low-carbon and resilient cities, developing energy efficiency and using of renewable energy, and finally, executing of climate-smart agriculture and nurturing forest landscapes could largely benefit minimising the drivers of climate change. In this connection, Kim asserted, "We have to keep the economy growing –there is no turning back on growth. What we have to do is decouple growth from carbon emissions."[39]

Besides that, while stating about the importance of implementing carbon pricing systems, Kim emphasised, "A price on carbon is the single most important thing we have to get out of a Paris agreement. It will unleash market forces." Also, he ruled out the fact that the fossil fuel subsidies had a positive impact to financially benefit the poor people. In this connection, Kim commented, "The evidence shows that fossil fuel subsidies are not at all about protecting the poor."[40]

Apart from that, being one of the chief capital providers of finance, the World Bank Group had usually invested in disaster preparedness services, renewable energy resources, energy efficiency conditions, city planning and development initiatives, etc. In addition to that, it helped the decision-makers by offering appropriate tools and data for making them suitable to adopt right decisions in order to combat the climate change menace. Above all, the World Bank Group had tracked the commercial commitments for climate mitigation adaptation co-benefits, monitoring for disaster and climate risks, using greenhouse gas accounting cost and pricing on carbon emissions. On this issue, Kim stated, "What we really want to do is see how we can attack this problem in just about everything we do."[41] Under such viewpoint, would these mitigation strategies be enabled to minimise the global warming as well as climate change effects in long run?

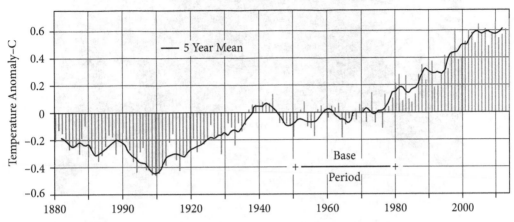

Global Temperature, 1880–2014
Land - Ocean Index: 1951–1980 Base

Source: Goddard Institute for Space Studies (GISS) and Climate Research
Unit (CRU), prepared by ProcessTrends.com, updated by globalissues.org

FIGURE 4.4 Global Temperature Index During 1880-2014

Sources: GISS Surface Temperature Analysis, NASA, accessed January 25, 2015; Global temperature, 1800-2006, ProcessTrends.com, accessed October 27, 2009 (link no longer available)

Source: Shah Anup, "Climate Change and Global Warming Introduction",
http://www.globalissues.org/article/233/climate-change-and-global-warming-introduction, February 1st 2015

According to NASA
- Carbon dioxide levels are at 399.2 ppm as of November 2014
- The global temperature has risen 14 F (7.8 C) since 1880
- The global Arctic ice minimum (the extent of sea ice in warm months) is decreasing by 13.3 percent each decade
- Land ice is decreasing by 258 billion tons (234 million kilotons) each year
- Due to melting ice, the sea level has risen by 0.12 inches (3.17 millimeters) per year

FIGURE 4.5 General Facts about Global Warming

Source: Bradford Alina, "What Is Global Warming?", http://www.livescience.com/37003-global-warming.html, December 15th 2014

FIGURE 4.6 The Greenhouse Effect

Source: Strickland Jonathan and Grabianowski Ed, "How Global Warming Works", http://science.howstuffworks.com/environmental/green-science/global-warming2.htm

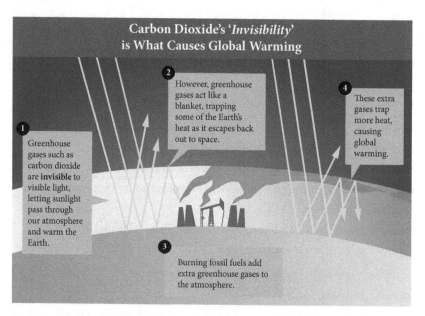

FIGURE 4.7 Invisibility of Carbon Dioxide Causing Global Warming

Source: "Invisible carbon dioxide", http://www.skepticalscience.com/graphics.php?g=87

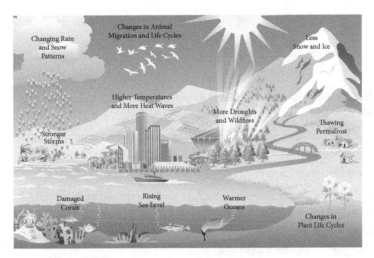

FIGURE 4.8 Impact of Global Warming

Source: Dechert Sandy, "Global Warming Or Climate Change? What's The Difference?", http://planetsave.com/2015/06/02/global-warming-or-climate-change-whats-the-difference/, June 2nd 2015

- Reaffirm the goal of limiting global temperature increase well below 2 degrees Celsius, while urging efforts to limit the increase to 1.5 degrees;
- Establish binding commitments by all parties to make "nationally determined contributions" (NDCs), and to pursue domestic measures aimed at achieving them;
- Commit all countries to report regularly on their emissions and "progress made in implementing and achieving" their NDCs, and to undergo international review;
- Commit all countries to submit new NDCs every five years, with the clear expectation that they will "represent a progression" beyond previous ones;
- Reaffirm the binding obligations of developed countries under the UNFCCC to support the efforts of developing countries, while for the first time encouraging voluntary contributions by developing countries too;
- Extend the current goal of mobilizing $100 billion a year in support by 2020 through 2025, with a new, higher goal to be set for the period after 2025;
- Extend a mechanism to address "loss and damage" resulting from climate change, which explicitly will not "involve or provide a basis for any liability or compensation;"
- Require parties engaging in international emissions trading to avoid "double counting;" and
- Call for a new mechanism, similar to the Clean Development Mechanism under the Kyoto Protocol, enabling emission reductions in one country to be counted toward another country's NDC.

FIGURE 4.9 Major Outcomes of the UNFCCC Conference at Paris in 2015

Source: "Outcomes of the UN Climate Change Conference in Paris", http://www.c2es.org/international/negotiations/cop21-paris/summary

Notes

1. "Quotes on Global Warming", http://www.notable-quotes.com/g/global_warming_quotes.html

2. ibid.

3. Bradford Alina, "What Is Global Warming?", http://www.livescience.com/37003-global-warming.html, December 15th 2014

4. Shah Anup, "Climate Change and Global Warming Introduction", http://www.globalissues.org/article/233/climate-change-and-global-warming-introduction, February 1st 2015

5. "What Is Global Warming?", op.cit.

6. Enzler S.M., "History of the greenhouse effect and global warming", http://www.lenntech.com/greenhouse-effect/global-warming-history.htm

7. "What Is Global Warming?", op.cit.

8. "History of the greenhouse effect and global warming", op.cit.

9. "Global Warming FAQ", http://www.nmsea.org/Curriculum/Primer/Global_Warming/fossil_fuels_and_global_warming.htm

10. "Invisible carbon dioxide", http://www.skepticalscience.com/graphics.php?g=87

11. "Causes of Global Warming", http://www.conserve-energy-future.com/GlobalWarmingCauses.php

12. "Quotes on Global Warming", op.cit.

13. Bradford Alina, "Effects of Global Warming", http://www.livescience.com/37057-global-warming-effects.html, December 17th 2014

14. Connor Steve, "Global warming: World already halfway towards threshold that could result in dangerous climate change, say scientists", http://timesofindia.indiatimes.com/home/environment/global-warming/Global-warming-World-already-halfway-towards-threshold-that-could-result-in-dangerous-climate-change-say-scientists/articleshow/49734570.cms, November 10th 2015

15. "Effects of Global Warming", op.cit.

16. "Effects of Global Warming", op.cit.

17. ibid.

18. Markham Derek, "Global Warming Effects and Causes: A Top 10 List", http://planetsave.com/2009/06/07/global-warming-effects-and-causes-a-top-10-list/, June 7th 2009

19. "Global Warming and its effect on the economy", http://student.purduecal.edu/~ktownsel/2500%20word%20final%20webtext.htm

20. Nuccitelli Dana, "More global warming will be worse for the economy, says the Copenhagen Consensus Center", http://www.theguardian.com/environment/climate-consensus-97-per-cent/2014/jan/24/more-global-warming-worse-economy, January 24th 2014

21. Harvey Fiona, "Climate change is already damaging global economy, report finds", http://www.theguardian.com/environment/2012/sep/26/climate-change-damaging-global-economy, September 26th 2012

22. Carrington Damian, "2015 and 2016 set to break global heat records, says Met Office", http://www.theguardian.com/environment/2015/sep/14/2015-and-2016-set-to-break-global-heat-records-says-met-office, September 14th 2015

23. Steafel Eleanor, "Global warming to make 2015 hottest on record", http://www.telegraph.co.uk/news/earth/environment/climatechange/12017510/Global-warming-to-make-2015-hottest-on-record.html, November 25th 2015

24. Ritz Erica, "U.N. Chief Blames 'Industrialization' for Global Warming Crisis, Says Rich Countries Need to Pay Up", http://www.theblaze.com/stories/2012/12/05/u-n-chief-blames-industrialization-for-global-warming-crisis-says-rich-countries-need-to-pay-up/, December 5th 2012

25. Gray Louise, "Developing world caused more climate change before Industrial Revolution", http://www.telegraph.co.uk/news/earth/earthnews/9373195/Developing-world-caused-more-climate-change-before-Industrial-Revolution.html, July 3rd 2012

26. Kirby Alex, "Are developing nations equally to blame for climate change?", http://www.climatechangenews.com/2013/09/17/developing-nations-equally-to-blame-for-climate-change-report/, September 18th 2013

27. Mattoo Aaditya, et al., "Can Global De-Carbonization Inhibit Developing Country Industrialization?", https://openknowledge.worldbank.org/bitstream/handle/10986/4317/WPS5121.pdf?sequence=1&isAllowed=y, November 2009

28. "Developing world caused more climate change before Industrial Revolution", op.cit.

29. "Are developing nations equally to blame for climate change?", op.cit.

30. Chestney Nina, "Rich vs. poor: Divide deepens over who should pay for climate change", http://www.nbcnews.com/business/rich-vs-poor-divide-deepens-over-who-should-pay-climate-2D11624117, November 20th 2013

31. "Industrialized countries at G7 summit acknowledge need to decarbonize the global economy", http://climateobserver.org/industrialized-countries-at-g7-summit-acknowledge-need-to-decarbonize-the-global-economy/, June 10th 2015

32. Gosden Emily, "Paris climate change conference: Everything you need to know about the UN summit", http://www.telegraph.co.uk/news/earth/paris-climate-change-conference/11991964/Paris-climate-change-conference-Everything-you-need-to-know-about-the-UN-summit.html, November 30th 2015

33. "Outcomes of the U.N. Climate Change Conference in Paris", http://www.c2es.org/international/negotiations/cop21-paris/summary

34. "COP21: UN chief hails new climate change agreement as 'monumental triumph'", http://www.un.org/apps/news/story.asp?NewsID=52802#.Vsbh4EDRo_4, December 12th 2015

35. ibid.

36. Harvey Fiona, "Paris climate change agreement: the world's greatest diplomatic success", http://www.theguardian.com/environment/2015/dec/13/paris-climate-deal-cop-diplomacy-developing-united-nations, December 14th 2015

37. "Global warming to make 2015 hottest on record", op.cit.

38. Kakkar Rahul, "Essay on Global Warming: Causes, Effects, Impact and Prevention of Global Warming", http://www.importantindia.com/11701/essay-on-global-warming/, August 7th 2015

39. Arki Benjamin, "5 Ways to Reduce the Drivers of Climate Change", http://www.worldbank.org/en/news/feature/2015/03/18/5-ways-reduce-drivers-climate-change, March 18th 2015

40. ibid.

41. ibid.

DISCUSSION QUESTIONS

1. How would you summarize the main argument of the article in a sentence or two?

2. What are some of the natural and anthropogenic factors contributing to global warming?

3. What is global warming, and why is it considered a threat to both the developed and the developing countries?

4. Can you discuss some of effects of rising sea levels?

5. Who is responsible for global warming, the developed or the developing countries? Why the finger pointing? How can we "decouple" economic growth from carbon emissions?

6. What is the 2015 Paris Climate Change Agreement? Why is it called a triumph for multilateralism? What is the position of the United States on the Paris Agreement?

Democracy and Governance

By Ali R. Abootalebi

I n its annual survey of freedom in the world,[1] Freedom House reports that 2017 marked the 12th consecutive year in which democracy has declined around the world; 71 countries suffered net declines in political rights and civil liberties, with only 35 registering gains. Those countries experiencing setbacks in political rights and civil liberties far outnumbered those showing improvements. Over the period since the 12-year global slide began in 2006, 113 countries have seen a net decline, and only 62 have experienced a net improvement. Countries as diverse as Venezuela, Turkey, Thailand, Mexico, South Africa, Poland, and Hungry, among others, have experienced democratic degradation due to corruption, increased role of the military in politics, authoritarian executive tendencies, and/or weakening rule of law. In other cases, civil wars, ethnic rivalry, and conflict, or simply bad governance has caused tremendous hardship for millions of peoples across the Arab World, Afghanistan, and Myanmar. In Europe, Right-wing populists gained votes and parliamentary seats in France, the Netherlands, Germany, and Austria during 2017. The United States under President Donald Trump has also abandoned its role as the world's leading state championing democracy.

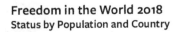

Freedom in the World 2018
Status by Population and Country

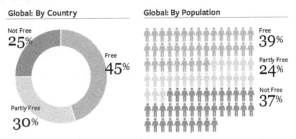

FIGURE 4.10
Source: https://freedomhouse.org/report/freedom-world/freedom-world-2018.

Popular support for democracy remains strong, as the populace everywhere continues expecting governments to deliver on core democratic values like open elections, press freedom, official accountability, and equality before the law. Most of the countries that embraced democracy during the past century remain democratic today. Polling consistently shows strong global support for democracy, especially where greater wealth exists, meaning that economic prosperity and support for democracy go hand in hand.[2] The question remains, How vulnerable are democracies to a breakdown, and is the current democratic turndown a temporary setback or a reversal in democracy, instigated by a perfect storm of severe economic and financial slowdown, wars and refugees, and uncertainties associated with globalization?

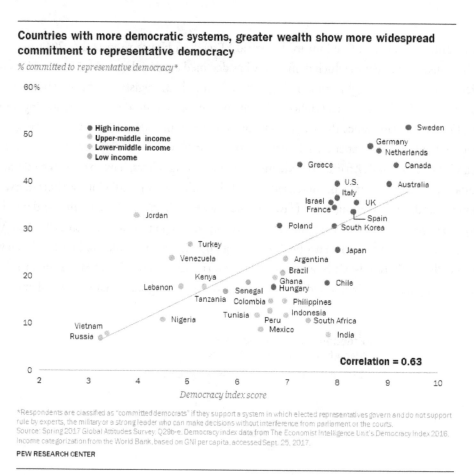

Countries with more democratic systems, greater wealth show more widespread commitment to representative democracy

% committed to representative democracy*

*Respondents are classified as "committed democrats" if they support a system in which elected representatives govern and do not support rule by experts, the military or a strong leader who can make decisions without interference from parliament or the courts.
Source: Spring 2017 Global Attitudes Survey. Q29b-e. Democracy index data from The Economist Intelligence Unit's Democracy Index 2016. Income categorization from the World Bank, based on GNI per capita, accessed Sept. 25, 2017.

PEW RESEARCH CENTER

FIGURE 4.11
The scatterplot also reveals another pattern: Countries that are classified as more fully democratic and that have a higher percentage of the public committed to representative democracy also tend to be wealthier.
Source: http://www.pewglobal.org/2017/10/16/globally-broad-support-for-representative-and-direct-democracy.

The state rests at the heart of any discussion of democracy, its prerequisites, inauguration and consolidation, the expansion of democratic politics, and the propagation of democratic norms and values. The state remains indispensable in the realization of popular aspirations for prosperity and freedom while ensuring sovereignty and national security. Yet, the tendency of the state elite to monopolize and abuse state power and national resources is a real and persistent threat to legitimate rule and good governance. This is true, especially where the authoritarian state uses a variety of methods to perpetuate the dominant position of the political elites and their institutional power, including Patrimonialism and Rentierism, military dominance and rule, executive dominance through rigged elections and corruption. The democratic states are also vulnerable, to varying degrees, to political decay and democratic reversal, as the cases of Turkey under President Erdogan or Jacob Zuma's South Africa, or President Victor Orban's Hungry testifies. Authoritarian trends and tendencies can also be the result of an erosion in the democratic norms and behavior, as in the United States under President Donald Trump. Norms are unspoken rules and conventions that hold democracy together, including "mutual toleration" and "institutional forbearance."[3] A recent study reminds us by of the historical example of a "profound miscalculation" and gradual slide into authoritarianism in Germany in the 1930s. In the U.S case, a significant number of the congressional Republicans have provided protection to Donald Trump, in support of a government that has "imported the spirit of thuggery, crookedness, and dictatorship into the very core of the American state."[4]

The state of democracy in the world today may be troubling, while the long-term prognosis for democratic survival and blossoming rests with not the state alone but with the effect of globalization on the existing *parameters* of the state-society relations. Democracy cannot thrive in the long run without active societal engagement in matters of governance. Peoples' participation in democratic politics and expectations for civil and civic engagement in the realization and the expansion of their rights and freedom is perpetual. In discussing governance, however, Mark Bevir and colleagues, professor of political science at the University of California, Berkeley, argues that since the 1980s the hierarchical Westphalian state structure, organization, function, and policy has been challenged by forces of market, deregulation and privatization, and a plethora of transnational corporations, nongovernmental organizations, clubs and associations, and citizens groups. Governments are no longer the central actors in governance.

The globalization of trade and finance, communication and information technology, and the proliferation of social media have empowered, and challenged, both the state and the society, albeit with different degrees and intensity. The state everywhere is under pressure to deregulate and to privatize while maintaining peace and security and social harmony in an increasingly competitive world where corporations and financial institutions can overshadow the power of the state. Globalization also is gravely vulnerable to cyclic destabilization, epitomized in the 2008 American financial implosion, the hazards of altered geopolitical landscapes, deepening resource restraints, and climate change. This makes a cosmopolitan sensibility an even more urgent survival requirement.[5]

In the United States, the age of globalization and technological revolution has dashed the earlier hopes of the millennial generation for a secured and free future in the face of irresponsible politics, much of it in a span of only a few years since the end of the cold war in 1989. The deregulation of the 1980s and the globalization of finance and market capitalism since the 1990s have sharpened the labor-business divide over the distribution of economic and social resources and the extent of government intervention in the market and society. The promise of a trickledown effect to create viable, long-term full-time and competitive jobs remains highly dubious. The intention to drastically increase the defense expenditures, cut back on Wall Street regulations, and reduce corporate taxes by hundreds of billions of dollars only guarantee large corporate gains. The evidence shows a shrinking American middle class and an extraordinary wealth gap between the top 1 percent of the Americans and the rest of the populace, as well as racial, ethnic, and income disparities.[6] The members of the European Union have cut back on their commitment to social-welfarism in the post-cold war era, and especially since the 2008 economic and financial crisis. The French popular reaction to the state reversal to its historical commitment to social welfare is manifested in the Yellow-vest demonstrations that have engulfed Paris and other cities in the past, as of this writing, 14 weeks. As one observer notes, "[T]he yellow vests served as an impromptu uniform, which gave the movement not only a name but also a symbolic resonance: the vests are intended for use in emergencies, and protesters used them to convey the message that they were living in such dire straits that even a small tax increase, insignificant to the bureaucrats in Paris, could drive them to rebellion."[7]

The reemergence of nationalism and identity politics in Europe and the West in general since 2008 reflects the "excesses" of neoliberalism exuberance in the 1990s in the promotion of globalization and a "borderless" world while neglecting the maldistribution of the benefits of globalization within and across countries. The Islamic movements of the late 20th century and the advent of the Arab Spring movement since 2011 intensified militarization of U.S. foreign policy since 2001, and the rise of more nationalistic China and India and other emerging developing countries partly reflects the impact of the gap between the promise and the actual realization of globalization benefits. Ultimately, the state ability to respond to the challenges of globalization and to successfully govern determines its ranking in the global environment.

It is only natural to think of national governments and power once the question of governance arises, but governance is broader than just the government; Merriam-Webster defines governance as the way that a city, company, and so on is controlled by the people who run it. The World Bank refers to good governance as the way "power is exercised through a country's economic, political, and social institutions"[8] The United Nations' Development Program sees it as "[t]he exercise of economic, political, and administrative authority to manage a country's affairs at all levels. It comprises mechanisms, processes, and institutions through which citizens and groups articulate their interests, exercise their legal rights, meet their obligations, and mediate their differences."[9] Democracy is an essential element of good governance; its presence may not be a guarantee of peace, but its absence and attempts to suppress it are significant risk factors for war.[10]

At its most basic level, good governance is also about local neighborhoods and communities organizing themselves into more effective units in dealing with local issues, whether in cooperation with agencies of the national and local governments or with private individuals and agencies of civil society or a combination of such forces. It is increasingly apparent that network governance and shared public-private management of resources at national level (relegation of state responsibilities to local governments and private sector agents and associations) and at global level (e.g., sustainable development) is encroaching on governments' traditional role to govern. For example, the transformation of social inclusion responsibility from the state to a third sector (e.g., voluntary associations, public-private partnership) is taking hold in some welfare states. Global governance, similarly, demands appropriate resource management policy to avoid the "tragedy of the commons" phenomenon.[11]

The successful state-society relationship in the age of high technology, globalization, and transnationalism, demands good governance. Good governance encompasses democracy and democratic principles. As the UNDP notes, Good governance is, among other things, participatory, transparent, and accountable. It is also effective and equitable. And it promotes the rule of law. Good governance ensures that political, social and economic priorities are based on broad consensus in society and that the voices of the poorest and the most vulnerable are heard in decision making over the allocation of development resources. The World Development Report[12] delineates that mechanisms for assuring good governance have three key elements: internal rules and restraints (for example, internal accounting and auditing systems, independence of the judiciary and the central bank, civil service and budgeting rules); voice and partnership (for example, public-private deliberation councils and service delivery surveys to solicit client feedback); and competition (for example, competitive social service delivery, private participation in infrastructure, alternative dispute resolution mechanisms, and outright privatization of certain market-driven activities).

Corruption is antithetical to good governance.; it saps a government's right to rule and is detrimental to legitimate governance. Consequently, prospects for a healthy economy and economic growth diminishes drastically, where corruption leaves the market uncertain, about rules and mechanisms governing it, and erode social trust. As Cortright, et al. suggest, economic growth is dependent on policies that protect and support free markets, but markets flourish best in governance systems that promote equality of access, provide social safety nets, enhance human capital, respond effectively to market failures, and guard against exploitation and abuse.[13]

The rise of militant religious movements and groups since the 1980s and political right in major Western democracies since 2008 are of concern. The established older democracies like the Europeans or the United States have survived serious upheavals in their democratic experiences, with some like Germany, Italy, and Japan falling into the abyss of military rule and fascism. The struggle in defense of democracy also took its toll in the United States at different periods in time through years of slavery and civil war, economic depression and suppression of labor and minority rights, and the overall widespread deprivation of mass numbers of people. The culmination of decades of popular pressure and civil society advocacy for wider civil rights only succeeded in the American political elite bowing to the Civil Rights Act of 1964. The ongoing economic and refugee "crises" in Europe have given pause to some critics of neoliberal policies of Western democracies, but the popular support for the fundamentals of democratic rule and human rights remain strong. The struggle in the mature Western democracies is over the preservation of hard-earned principles and practiced good governance that have virtually guaranteed, for several decades, prosperous societies and high citizenry.

In its simplest formulation, democracy is understood as "demos" and "kratos," meaning "people power." Demokratia, in turn, represented the Greek notion of direct democracy as opposed to modern representative democracy. Centuries later, we still debate what constitutes people power and how best to implement it. The technological revolution of the late 20th century has facilitated the realization of easier and more deliberate people's participation in all aspects human interactive activities. The forces of market capitalism and globalization and information technology have facilitated the dramatic expansion of public space by reconfiguring and redefining people's sociopolitical and economic participation through individual, group, and social interactions. The Internet and the proliferation of "blogosphere" and social media seems to have also crumbled all borders, separating people of different identifications based on creed, religion, ethnic, racial, and linguistic characterizations. As such, democracy today is more than a question of political system type or what constitutes broadly and vaguely as people power; its realization is a necessary step forward toward what constitutes good governance. Democratic deficit is noticeably evident in the MENA region, and particularly in the Persian Gulf Arab States, hindering good governance.

Political democracy, if understood as a means to an end, offers the best chance for social organization and governance at local or national levels. At its core, political democracy would require the presence of free, fair, and frequent elections to gauge the health of the relationship between the governed and the governors. Political democracy also is about a continuous process of push and pull between the state and society, as structural and cultural changes always require political adjustments to meet the ever-changing societal needs and demands. The presence of viable political institutions such as political parties and independent legislative and judiciary branches of the government help solidify the legitimacy of the political system, resulting in better governance.

The establishment of political democracy requires certain socioeconomic and political requisites in place; otherwise, newly inaugurated democracies can experience a breakdown in democracy. In other words, the maintenance of political democracy, in the long run, depends on the conditions under which political democracy is inaugurated in the first place. Countries suffering from economic underdevelopment, high rates of illiteracy, low levels of institutionalization, elite fragmentation and rivalry, and social fragmentation along ethnic, religious, linguistic, or other divisions face greater challenges in establishing and maintaining political democracy. Transition to democracy from authoritarian rule rests mainly on whether domestic forces are present and instrumental in such transition.[14]

Democracy is not about culture, ethnicity, or religion per se but the management of political power and the competition over socioeconomic resources within agreed-upon normative principles and values and institutional arrangements, whereby individual citizens through elections and other forms of political participation determine their own choices through elected representatives. In other words, political democracy is (can be) an instrumental method in the resolution of identity conflicts over cultural and nationalistic issues by providing legal and institutional venues for resolution of differences and conflicts to groups in competition over socioeconomic resources and political power. The competition among cultural groups in a given society is not so much about the superiority or inferiority of certain value systems or way of life *per se* but how the competition translates into control over local, regional, and national resources while realizing the ambitions and aspirations of all cultural groups. This is especially true, where legal and institutional venues for dispute settlement and conflict resolution and power sharing among competing cultural groups are weak or are seriously lacking. In such cases, it becomes natural for a dominant culture to try imposing its ethos and belief systems, through cooperation or coercion, on minority groups, monopolizing control over socioeconomic resources and political power. The prevailing historical and cultural characteristics and forces present in any given community can help the cause of local organizing (e.g., tribal order and affiliation or community mosques as places of both worship and mobilization and networking in the support of, or in opposition to, democratic rule).[15]

Secularism and liberalism may have proven instrumental in the evolution of political democracy and civil liberties in the Western tradition, but they should not be considered as preconditions for the inauguration and the evolution of democracy elsewhere. Recall also that the appearance and the evolution of political democracy in Europe took centuries and remains and will persist as an ongoing process. Every society must formulate its own strategy and travel toward political democracy and determining the levels and degrees of civil liberties within its defined cultural and socioeconomic milieu. As Bruce Rutherford elaborates on Islamic democracy, the interaction between liberal constitutionalism and Islamic constitutionalism is likely to produce a *distinctive form of democracy* that resembles Western democracy in institutional terms but differs about the purpose of the state, the role of the individual in politics and society, and the character and function of law. That is, the place and duties of the Islamic State remains controversial since it is the state that must ensure the presence of Islam in society, sanctioning rules and laws that can violate the individual rights of the citizen (e.g., hijab, minority rights, women rights, inheritance, family planning, testimonials, and role of judges, etc.)[16]

In a similar argument, it is proposed that Islam or other religions be interpreted as systems of sacred beliefs and practices wherein some elements may be compatible with contemporary world realities and others may not; it is not true that religion encompasses either all aspects of our lives or all aspects of Muslim societies.[17] Thus, the parameters of democracy in a Muslim country may differ from those of Western societies. If so, the gates of experimentations with Islamic governance and popular participation (e.g., an Islamic Republic) are wide open.[18] This is precisely why political democracy can assist the cause of the realization of Islamic Republicanism. This is also what happened in the case of the Jewish nationalism, beginning in the late 1800s.

As the experimentation with Jewish democracy has been arduous and controversial and with obvious limitations, so would be the notion of Islamic democracy. The presence of democratic political institutions, despite the traditional modern dichotomy in the Jewish personal and national experiences, helped the earlier Zionist leadership with visioning a modern state based on a democratic foundation but that is Jewish in its core. (The successes and failures of this experimentation is clearly a matter of debate and not discussed here for the sake of space.) As Asma Afsaruddin[19] demonstrates, "Islam's fit for the modern man and women who still concede a role to religion in their private and public lives." The liberal West commitment to socioeconomic and political justice at a global level, instead of narrow nationalist concerns and narrow political agendas, is needed to help with the transformation of Muslim-majority societies.[20] The rise of civil society and democracy necessitates a certain level of socioeconomic development but, more important, it requires a balanced development. Balanced development in turn depends on the state's role and policies vis-a-vis the society. Indeed, it is quite possible for societal preconditions for democracy to exist and yet authoritarian rule to persist where the state refuses to give in to pressures from society for popular participation. The dominant position of the state in the Arab World, for example, has meant the rule of politics by powerful families, elites, and military and bureaucratic sub-classes. The emergence and growth of independent groups and associations, in contrast, has been slow. Primary agents of civil society, like independent political parties and labor unions, remain either nonexistent or are repressed or coopted by the state. Elites in charge of the state, which might be willing to open the system to popular participation, usually face a weak, divided society, making political reform a dangerous enterprise. In other words, the inauguration, and stability, of democracy is possible not only when its social requisites are present, but also when the state-society relationship is one of balanced power.[21]

A recent book "seeks to trace the interaction between domestic actors and international actors in bringing about transitional opportunities. Authors evaluate 15 cases of successful (Russia, Poland, Serbia, Ukraine, South Africa, and Chile), incremental (Ghana, Mexico, Turkey), and near but failed transition (Algeria, Iran, China, and Azerbaijan) cases. They find domestic factors like mass mobilization, indigenous civil society organizations, and independent media and communications technology as important factors explaining transition than in earlier literature. External factors— democracy advocate actors like NGOs and transnationals, democratic ideas and scripts, and foreign media—boosted the work of indigenous organizations in cases that succeeded but were little involved in cases that failed. In the end, however, "domestic actors really make (or break) a transition to democracy."[22] In the end, a balance distribution of socioeconomic resources and political power, where no one group can monopolize power is best suited for transition to democracy in developing countries. External forces often impact the distribution socioeconomic resources and political power through overt and covert interactions with power elites, including, among others, economic, financial, investment, and trade exchanges, military, security, and political interactions, and diplomatic and propagandist engagements.[23]

The failure of politics and political leaders in Arab Muslim countries in securing legitimate, popular participation in national and local governance has galvanized radical thinking and the emergence of militant groups in the name of Islam. This is nothing but a crisis of governance. At a more fundamental level, a crisis of governance has gripped, for example, the Islamic Middle East and Northern African (MENA) region because of the failure of the Westphalian State model to emerge. Militant Muslim movements have once again emerged as voices for justice at the time of political turbulence, dating as far back to the *Kharijite* movement[24] in the early Islamic history in 657 AD. Modern militant movements like the Wahhabi movement[25] since the 18th and 19th centuries in tribal Arabia, the Muslim Brotherhood beginning in the 1920s, and the Islamic movements inspired by the Iranian Revolution in the 1980s have offered different visions for an Islamic governance. The Taliban, the al-Qaeda. ... since 1980s, and the Daesh (ISIL or ISIS), and a plethora of other militant movements in the past few decades have utilized violence to counter Western domination and authoritarian rule at home and to restore Islamic governance.

The inadequacies of the state and its institutions and bureaucracy and the presence of weak and divided society have been a prominent problem in the Arab MENA region. The state authoritarian rule and traditional value systems and institutions still pose serious challenges before Arab societies striving for democratic rule and social justice. The opposition in Arab countries also has failed to mobilize the populace around a common ideology to challenge the state.

Most Arab regimes lack legitimacy to rule and are marred with insecurity. The Arab governments in the past one hundred years have done a poor job in their attempts at building viable nation-states, the shortfall rests with 'political underdevelopment' that is destined to catch up with the ruling elites sooner or later. Arab regimes have relied on different strategies to dominate political power and to endure their authoritarian rule, relying on: foreign security and financial assistance, as in Egypt and Jordan; neo-Patrimonialism, Rentierism and foreign immigrant workers, as in Saudi Arabia and the Persian Gulf states; state largesse and sheer brutality, as in Iraq under Saddam Hussein, Qaddafi's Libya, and Syria under the Assad family; corruption, nepotism, and Patrimonialism as in Yemen under Ali Abdullah Saleh, Tunisia under Ben Ali, and Morocco's King Hassan, or a combination of these.[26] Arab politics' experimentation with Ba'athism, Pan-Arabism, secular nationalism, and monarchism have all failed, paving the way for Islamic movements, mostly colored with radical solutions, to empower society and to thwart foreign influence.[27]

The absence of political democracy, corruption, absence of transparency and accountability in the political arena, and the presence of a weak civil society impede active citizen participation in governance. This situation has resulted in the humiliation of Arab peoples dignity, *al-hogra or ihtiqaar,*[28] and culminated in the still-unresolved Arab Spring movements since 2011. Some Arab societies like Tunisia and Egypt have embarked upon a desperate journey for political freedom, economic opportunity, and human dignity. This has happened while Islamic movements, e.g., Muslim Brotherhood, have been unable to fill the political/ideological void in gaining the trust of popular support in national movements for freedom, prosperity and dignity. Western military interventions have not brought security and democracy and have failed to resolve the deficit of good governance in places like, among others, Libya, Syria, Yemen, Afghanistan, Iraq, and Somalia.

Conclusion

Democratic governance is really about the ability of the political system to continuously respond and adjust to the parameters of authority as the society becomes wealthier, healthier, more educated, more sophisticated, and better organized. Authoritarian rule by definition and nature is antithetical to long-term good governance and is more prone to corruption and abuses of power. Good governance signals the ability of governing institutions to deliver the key public goods needed to maintain order and stability. Governance is "good" and also more likely to advance peace when "it is inclusive, participatory and accountable; when it is characterized by fair procedures and performs well in delivering necessary public goods."[29] Decision making rests at the heart of governing and governance, particularly given the complexities of globalization and the changing dynamics of state-society relations. Guy Peters and John Pierre outline a set of models that present different accounts of the governance roles performed by government, networks, the market, or societal actors in concert with the state. They see decision making as the fundamental activity in governing, in which the state plays a central role in some instances but not in others. Governance can fail if the sociopolitical system fails to conduct efficient decision making, goal selection, resource mobilization, implementation, and evaluation and feedback.[30]

The failure of the Arab Spring movements since 2011 is a testimony to the engrained power of Arab political elites and their foreign supporters. The declared war on terrorism and rise of seemingly sectarian warfare only maintain the political status quo in the Arab world. Gilbert Achcar correctly refutes explanations of the Arab upheaval based on such variables as culture, age, religion, if not conspiracy theories.[31] The U.S. policy response to militant movements and terrorism threat cannot succeed without considerations for the contextual factors in any given Muslim country. The widespread popular dissatisfaction with the sociopolitical and economic status quo across the Arab MENA region cannot be ignored. As authors of *Islam, Democracy, and Cosmopolitanism* point out, the current challenge in Muslim societies is the crisis of the modern state. This, to a large extent, results from "failures of the modern secular state to achieve a democratic and prosperous society—indeed they failed precisely for these reasons."[32] The advantage of an Islamic democracy is the embrace of Islamic culture and not its rejection for the sake of secularism and Western liberalism. Therefore, an Islamic democracy can be instrumental in legitimately confronting militant Muslim groups and tendencies and resolving identity conflicts over cultural and nationalistic issues by providing legal, institutional, and, ideally, non-partisan, normative values to groups in competition over socioeconomic resources and political power.

Lacking historical experience with the mechanics of building a modern nation-state, identity politics substitutes for effective (and democratic) governance to ensure peaceful competition over the distribution of national resources. A recent study on governance and peace,[33] for example, "examines the faces of power that are reflected in different approaches to governance and consider how more decentralized and horizontal forms of new governance create additional possibilities for participation and accountability and how "new social actors and means of discourse are entering the public arena, for good or ill, transforming the nature of public authority and governance"[34] As such, the empowerment of women is seen as an essential. ... element of governance quality, perhaps the most important manifestation of inclusion and participation."[35]

Notes

1. Michael J. Abramowitz, "Freedom in the World 2018: Democracy in Crisis," *Freedom House*, https://freedomhouse.org/report/freedom-world/freedom-world-2018

2. Richard, Wike, Kate Simmons, Bruce Stokes, and Janell Fetterolf, "Globally, Broad Support for Representative and Direct Democracy, *PEW Research Center*, October 16, 2017, http://www.pewglobal.org/2017/10/16/globally-broad-support-for-representative-and-direct-democracy/

3. Steven Levitsky and Daniel Ziblatt, *How Democracies Die* (New York: Crown, 2018).

4. David Frum, *Trumpocracy: The Corruption of the American Republic* (New York: HarperCollins, 2018).

5. Ali Mirsepassi and Tadd Graham Fernee, *Islam, Democracy, and Cosmopolitanism at Home and in the World* (Cambridge: 2014), 17.

6. Signe-Mary Mckernan, Carloine Ratcliffe and C. Egugene Steuerle, "Nine Charts about Wealth Inequality in America," Nonprofit Quarterly, March 27, 2015, https://nonprofitquarterly.org/2015/03/27/nine-charts-about-wealth-inequality-in-america/?gclid=CjwKEAiA3aW2BRCD_cOo5oCFuUMSJA-DiIMILdtCnkpYA3v9wzRJYHIvnpf8yzHMIcFnpxeVPHP7J6BoC4Hvw_wcB

7. Arthur Goldhammer, "How the Gilets Jaunes Brought the French President Low," *Foreign Affairs*, December 12, 2018, https://www.foreignaffairs.com/articles/france/2018-12-12/yellow-vest-protests-and-tragedy-emmanuel-macron

8. The World Bank, Poverty Reduction Strategy Report (PRSP) Handbook.

9. International Center for Parliamentary Studies. http://www.parlicentre.org/Governance.php

10. David Cortright, Conor Seyle, and Kristen Wall, *Governance for Peace: How Inclusive, Participatory and Accountable Institutions Promote Peace and Prosperity* (New York: Cambridge University Press, 2017).

11. Ibid., 176.

12. Mark Bevir, Ed., *The Sage Handbook of Governance* (Thousand Oaks, CA: SAGE, 2011).

13. *World Bank, World Development Report 1997: The State in a Changing World* (New York: Oxford University Press, 1997), https://openknowledge.worldbank.org/handle/10986/5980

14. Cortright, Seyle, and Wall, 130.

15. The literature on democracy and its requisites is rich. For a brief discussion of qualitative and quantitative approaches to democracy and its requisites, see Dietrich Rueschemeyer, Evelyne Huber Stephens, and John D. Stephens, *Capitalist Development and Democracy* (Chicago: University of Chicago Press, 1992). See, also, Ali R. Abootalebi, "Democratization in Developing Countries: 1980–1989," *Journal of Developing Areas 29* (July 1995): 507-30. A more comprehensive list includes Martin Lipset Seymour, *Political Man* (Baltimore, MD: Johns Hopkins University Press, 1981); Robert Dahl, *Who Governs?* (New Haven: Yale University Press, 1961); Arend Lijphart, *The Politics of Accommodation: Pluralism and Democracy in the Netherlands* (Berkeley: University of California Press, 1968); Dankwart A. Rustow, "Transitions to Democracy: Toward A Dynamic Model," *Comparative Politics 2* (April 1970): 337-63; Robert Dahl, *Polyarchy: Participation and Opposition* (New Haven, CT: Yale University Press, 1971); Robert Dahl, *Modern Political Analysis*, 3rd edition (Englewood Cliffs, NJ: Prentice Hall, 1976). On Democracy and dependency, see Edward N. Muller, "Dependent Economic Development, Aid Dependence on the United States, and Democratic Breakdown in the Third World," International Studies Quarterly 29 (1985): 445-69; Guillermo A. O'Donnell, *Modernization and Bureaucratic-Authoritarianism: Studies in South American Politics* (Berkeley: University of California, 1973); Andre Gunder Frank, *Capitalism and Underdevelopment in Latin America: Historical Studies of Chile and Brazil* (New York: Monthly Review Press, 1967); Fernando H. Cardoso and Enzo Faletto, *Dependency and Development in Latin America* (Berkeley: University of California Press, 1979); Immanuel Wallerstein, *The Modern World System* (New York: Academic Press, 1974); Immanuel Wallerstein, *The World Capitalist System* (Cambridge: Cambridge University Press, 1980). On Culture and Democracy, see Joseph Schumpeter, *Capitalism and Democracy* (New York: Harper and Row, 1942); Daniel Lerner, *The Passing of Traditional Society: Modernizing the Middle East* (New York: Free Press, 1958); Gabriel A. Almond and Sidney Verba, *The Civic Culture: Political Attitudes and Democracy in Five Nations* (Princeton, NJ: Princeton University Press, 1963); Gerhard Lenski and Jean Lenski, *Human Societies* (New York: McGraw Hill, 1974); Sidney Verba, Norman H. Nie, and Jae On Kim, *Participation and Political Equality: A Seven Nation Comparison* (London: Cambridge University Press,1978); Samuel H. Barnes, *Political Action: Mass Participation in Five Western Democracies* (Thousand Oaks, CA: SAGE, 1979); Gabriel A. Almond and Sidney Verba Eds., *The Civic Culture Revisited* (Boston, MA: Little, Brown, and Company, 1980); Kenneth A. Bollen and Robert W. Jackman, "Political Democracy and the Size Distribution of Income," *American Sociological Review* 50 (August 1985): 438-57; Ronald Inglehart, *Culture Shift in Advanced Industrial Society* (Princeton, NJ: Princeton University Press, 1990); Edward N. Muller and Mitchell A. Seligson, "Civic Culture and Democracy: The Question of Causal Relationships," *American Political Science Review* 88 (September 1994): 635-52. Democratic breakdown in developing countries are caused by a number of sources, including foreign intervention, dependency, and military intervention in politics. See, for example, Edward Ned Muller, "Dependent Economic Development, Aid Dependence on the United States, and Democratic Breakdown in the Third World," *International Studies Quarterly* 29 (1985): 445-69.

16. Ali R. Abootalebi *Islam and Democracy: State-Society Relations in Developing Countries, 1980-1994* (Comparative Studies in Democratization), NY: New York, Taylor and Francis Group, 2000.

17. Bruce K. Rutherford, "What Do Egypt's Islamists Want? Moderate Islam and the Rise of Islamic Constitutionalism," *Middle East Journal* 60, no. 4 (Autumn, 2006), 707-731.

18. Ali Mirsepassi and Tadd Graham Fernee, *Islam, Democracy, and Cosmopolitanism at home and in the World* (Cambridge, 2014), 160.

19. Ali R. Abootalebi, "Iran's Tenth Presidential Elections: Candidates, Issues, and Implications," *Rubin Center Research in International Affairs*, September 1, 2009, http://www.rubincenter.org/2009/09/abootalebi-2009-09-01

20. Asma Afsaruddin, *Contemporary Issues in Islam* (Edinburgh University Press, 2015).

21. Ibid., 206.

22. Abootalebi, Ali, "Civil Society, Democracy, and the Middle East," *Rubin Center Research in International Affairs,* September 8, 1998.

23. Kathryn Stoner and Michael McFaul, Eds. *Transitions to Democracy: A Comparative Perspective* (Baltimore, Johns Hopkins, 2013), 16-22.

24. Ali R. Abootalebi, *Islam and Democracy.*

25. "Kharijite, the Islamic Sect, Encyclopedia Brittanica, https://www.britannica.com/topic/Kharijite

26. "Islamic Radicalism: Its Wahhabi Roots and Current Representation," The Islamic Supreme Council of America, http://www.islamicsupremecouncil.org/understanding-islam/anti-extremism/7-islamic-radicalism-its-wahhabi-roots-and-current-representation.html

27. Ali R. Abootalebi "40 Years on, is Iran a Status Quo Power or a Threat to ME Regional Security?" *Informed Comment*, 01/31/2019 https://www.juancole.com/2019/01/threat-regional-security.html

28. Rashid Khalidi, Lisa Anderson, Muhammad Muslih, and Reeva S. Simon, Eds. *The Origins of Arab Nationalism* (Columbia University Press, 1991); Bassam Tibi, *Arab Nationalism: A Critical Enquiry*, 2nd edition (Houndmills, Basingstoke, Hampshire: Macmillan, 1990); Michael Hudson, *Arab Politics: The Search for Legitimacy* (Newe Haven, CT: Yale University Press, 1979).

29. Hsain Ilahiane, "Why do Protests Keep Happening in North Africa? It's "al-Hogra," *Informed Comment*, 1/22/2019 https://www.juancole.com/2019/01/protests-happening-africa.html

30. Cortright, Seyle, and Wall, *Governance for Peace*, 47.

31. B. Guy Peters and Jon Pierre, *Comparative Governance: Rediscovering the Functional Dimension of Governing* (New York: Cambridge university Press, 2016).

32. Achcar, *The People Want.*

33. Ali Mirsepassi and Tadd Graham Fernee, *Islam, Democracy, and Cosmopolitanism at home and in the World* (New York: Cambridge, 2014), 160.

34. Cortright, Seyle, and Wall, *Governance for Peace,*

35. ibid, pp. 16–17.

36. Ibid, p. 19

DISCUSSION QUESTIONS

1. How would you summarize the main argument of the article in a sentence or two?

2. Why does the author claim that democracy is not about culture, ethnicity, or religion? If not, what is democracy about?

3. How is democracy related to good governance?

4. How does the author distinguish among democracy, governance, and good governance?

5. What does the author mean by a "balanced development"? How is that relevant to the rise of civil society and democracy?

6. The author claims that violence and wars in the MENA region are a consequence of the crisis of the state and the failure of governance in the Arab countries that also facilitates foreign interventions in the region. How convincing is his argument?